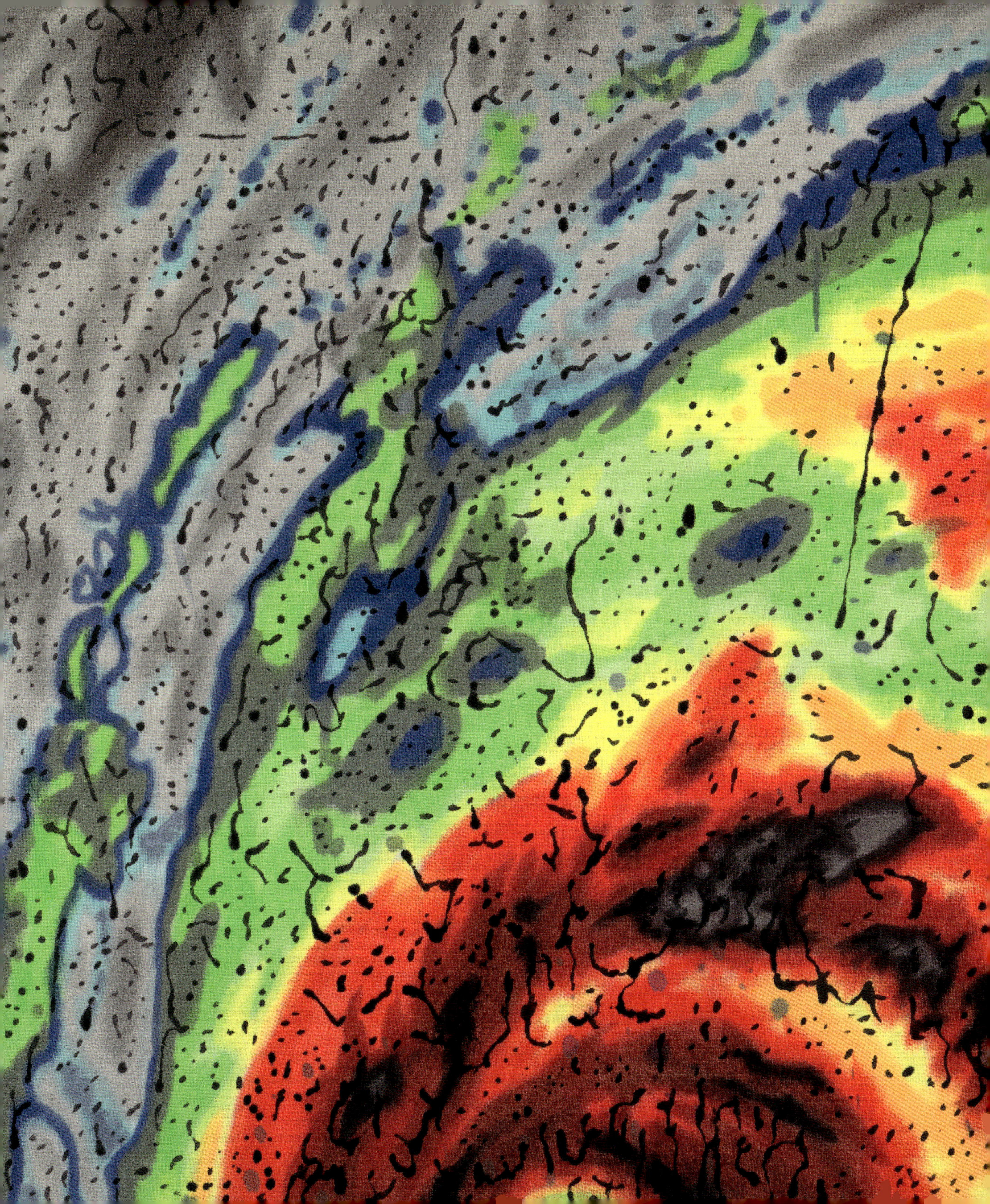

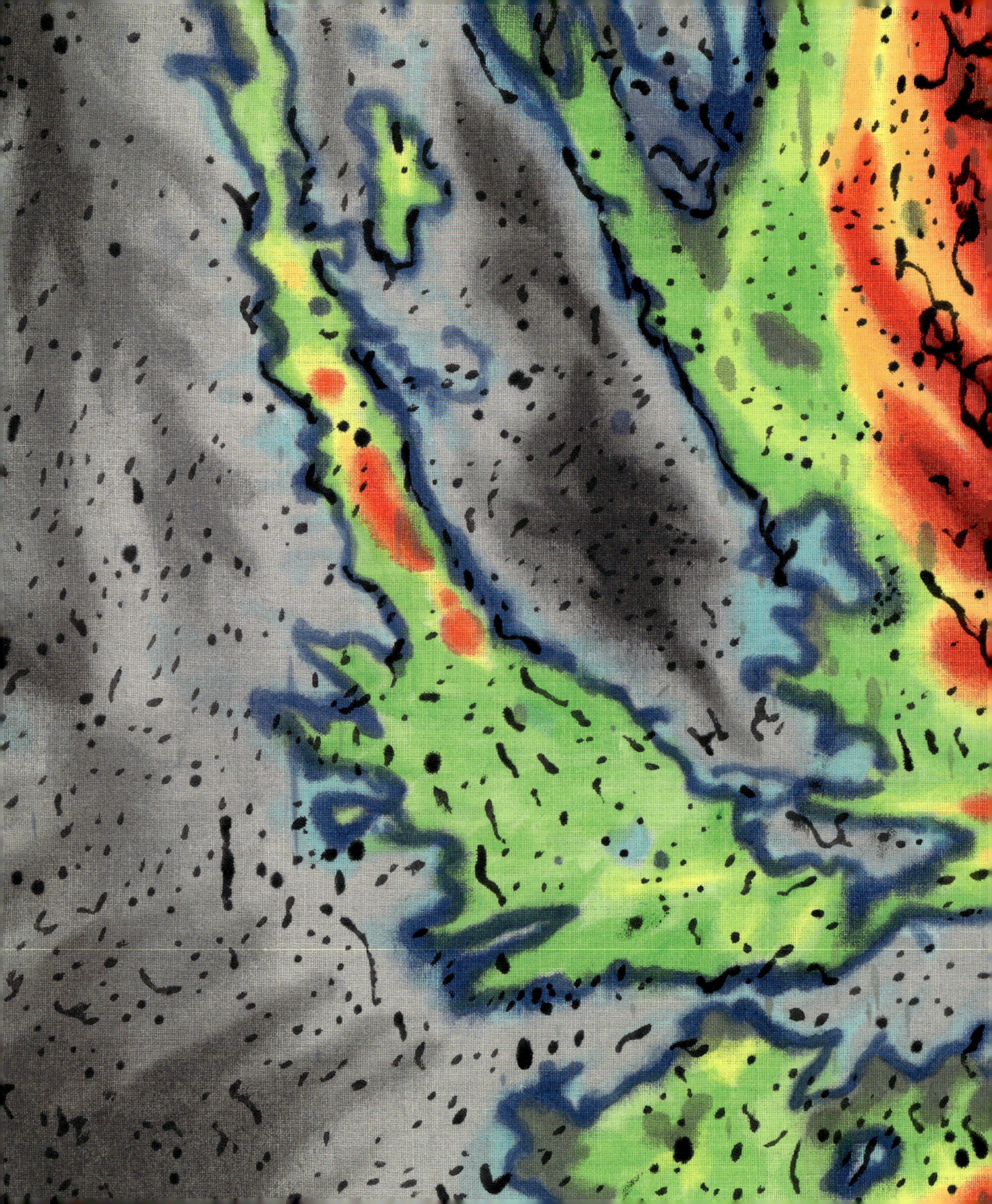

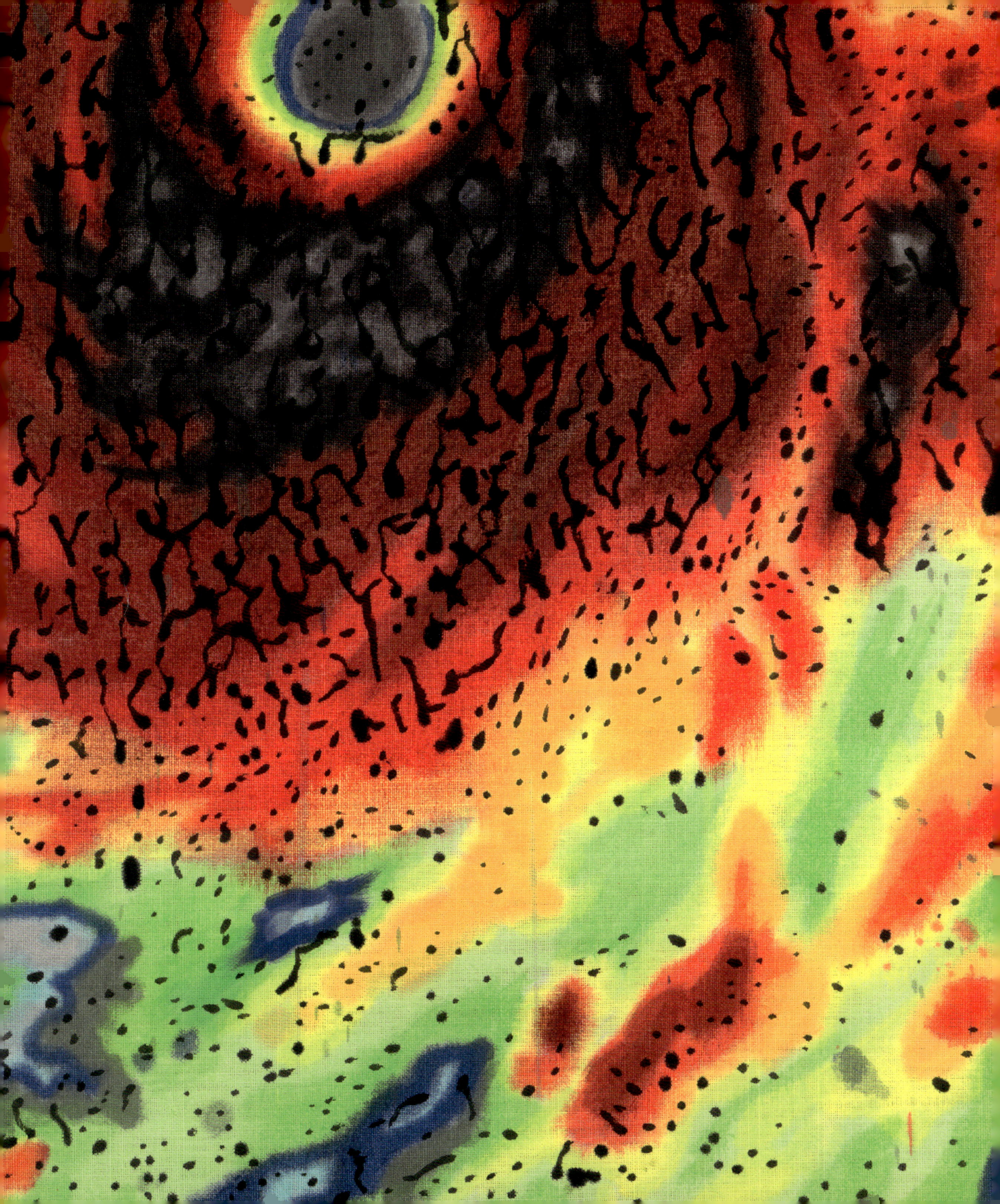

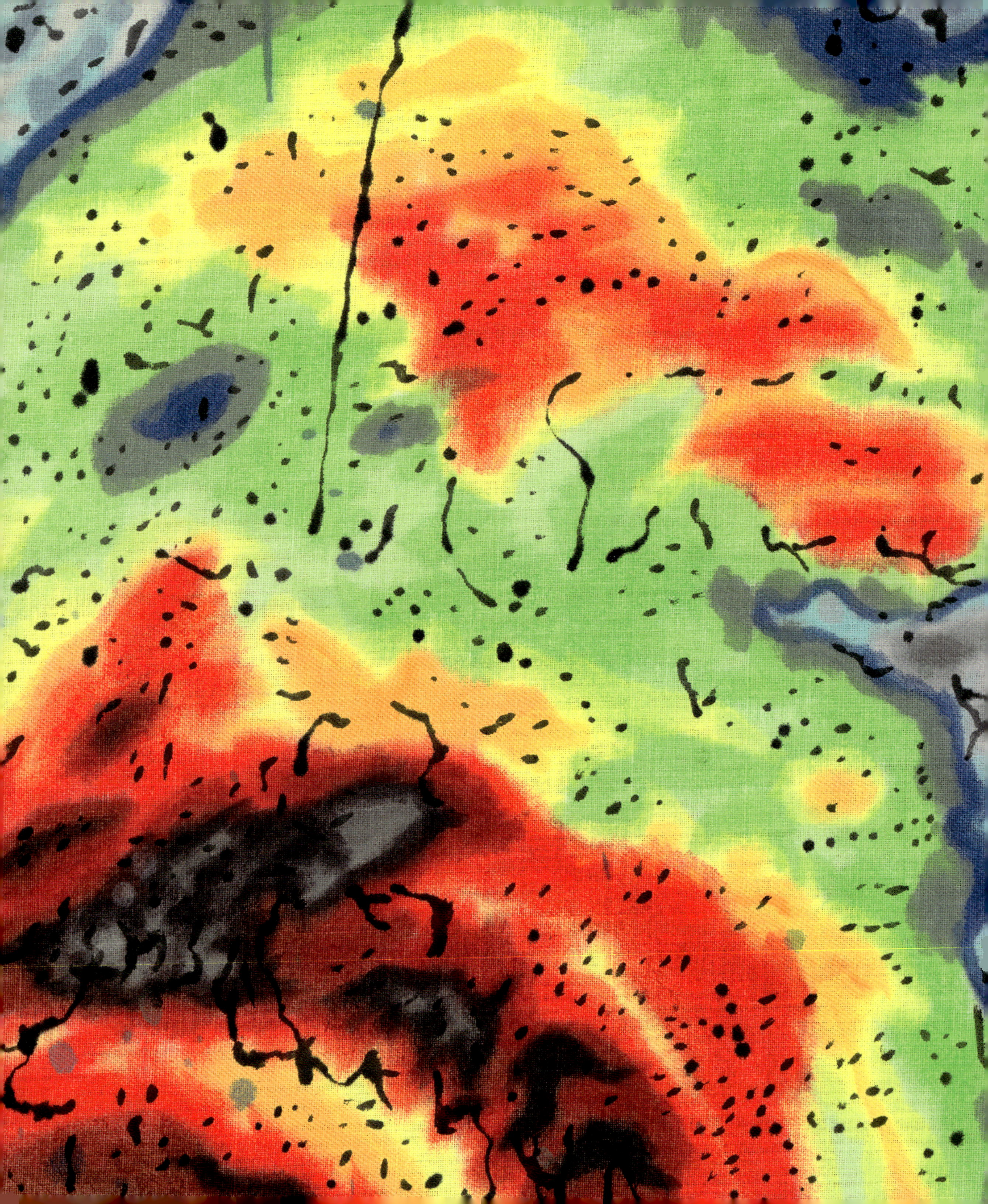

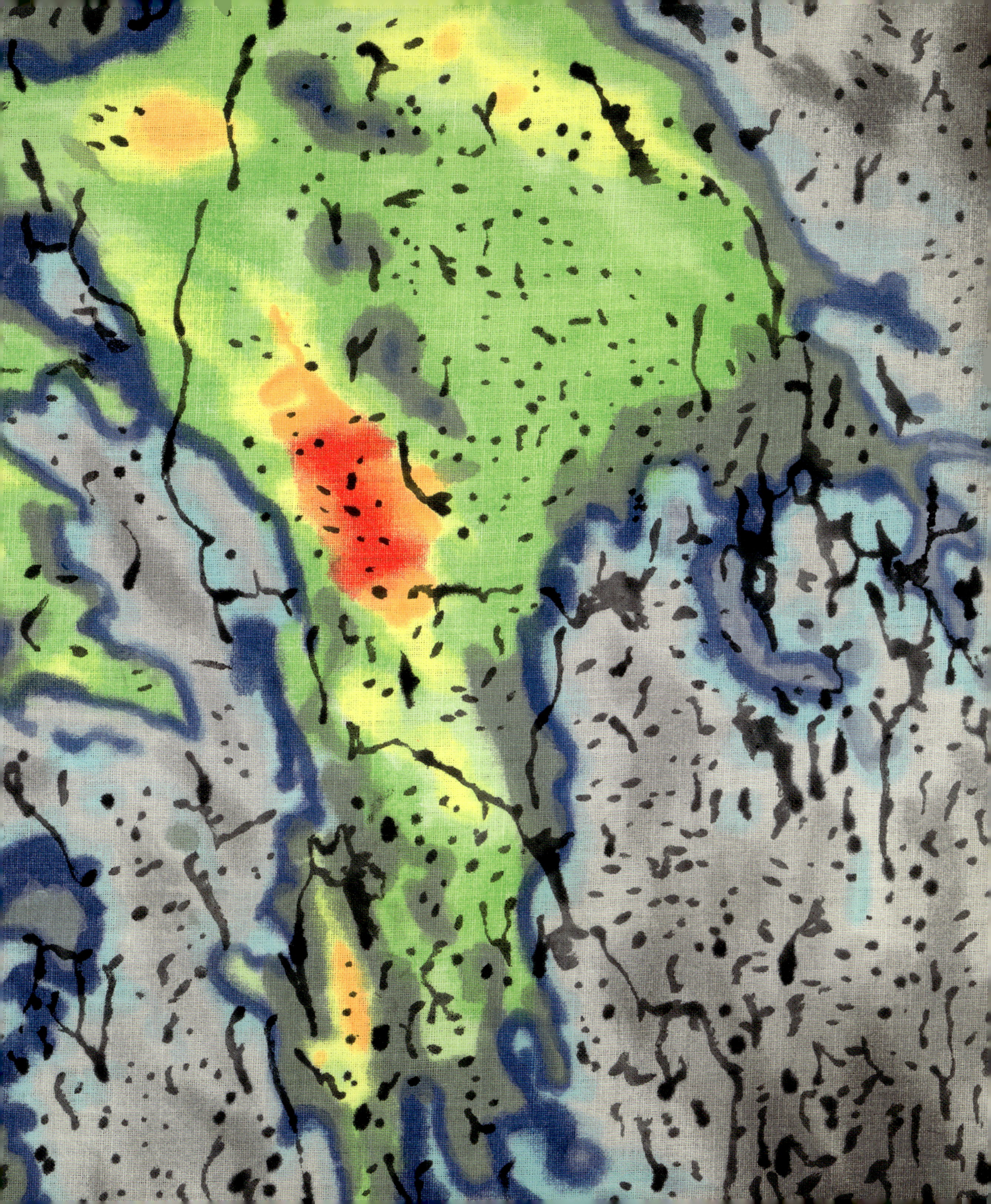

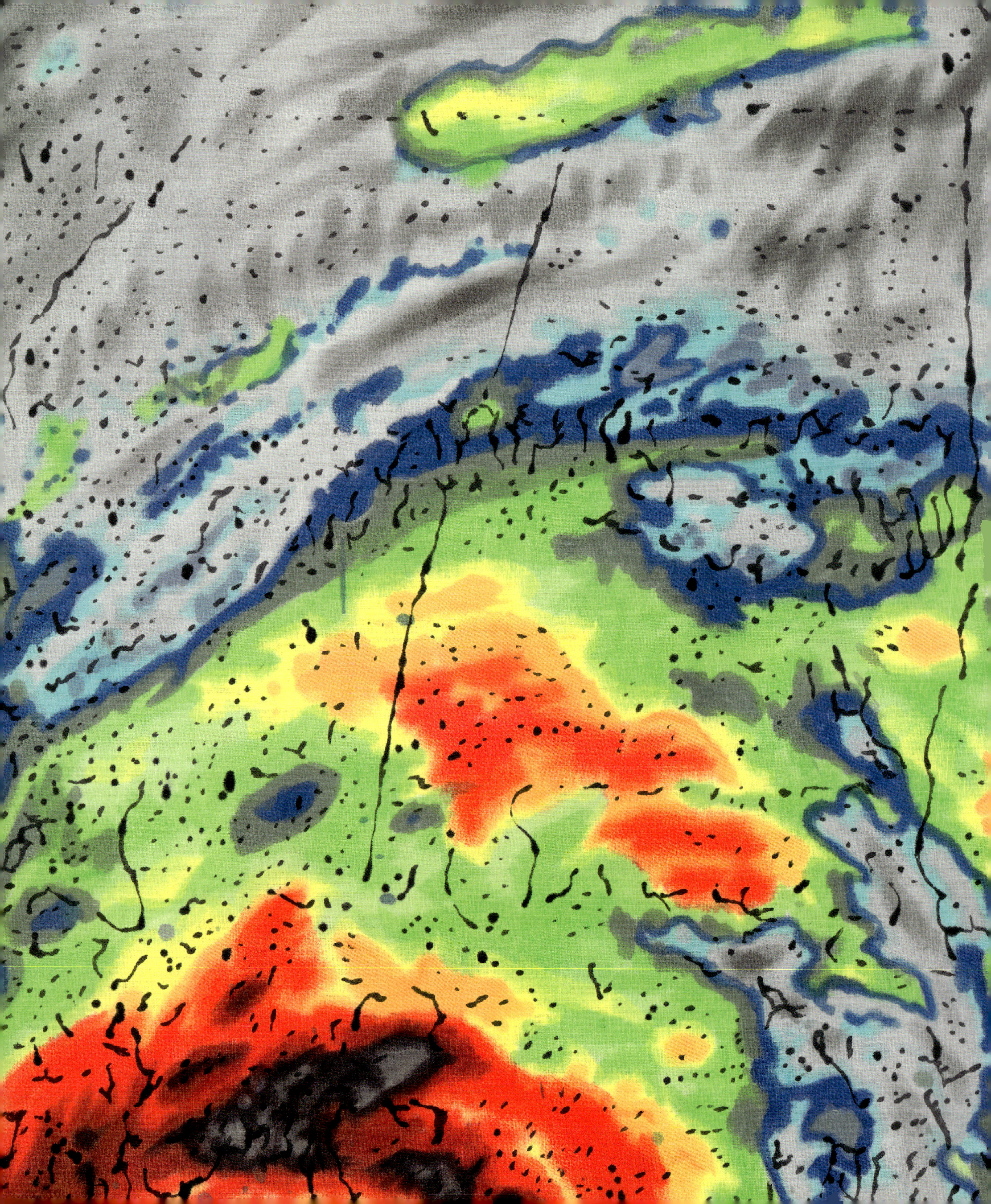

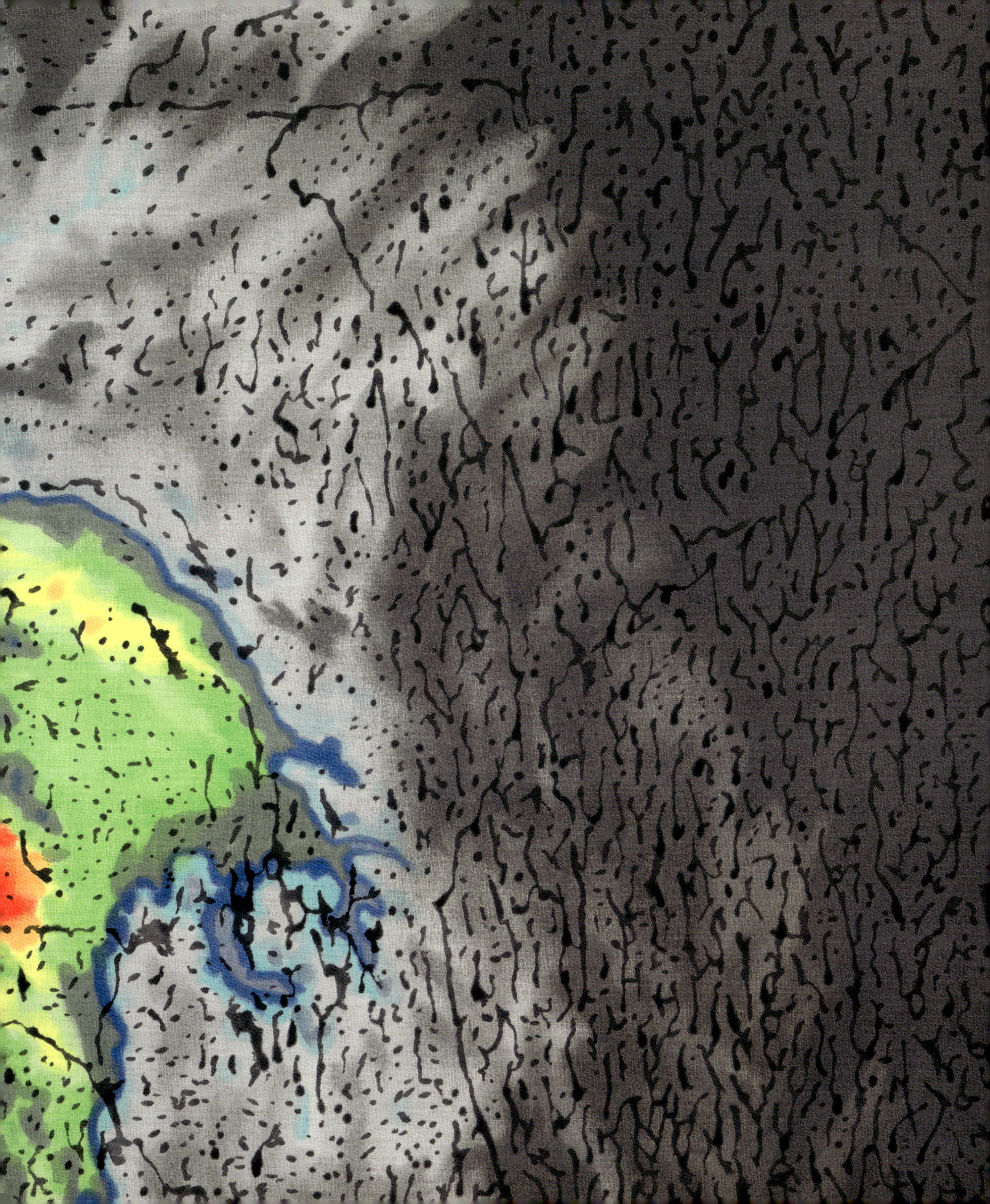

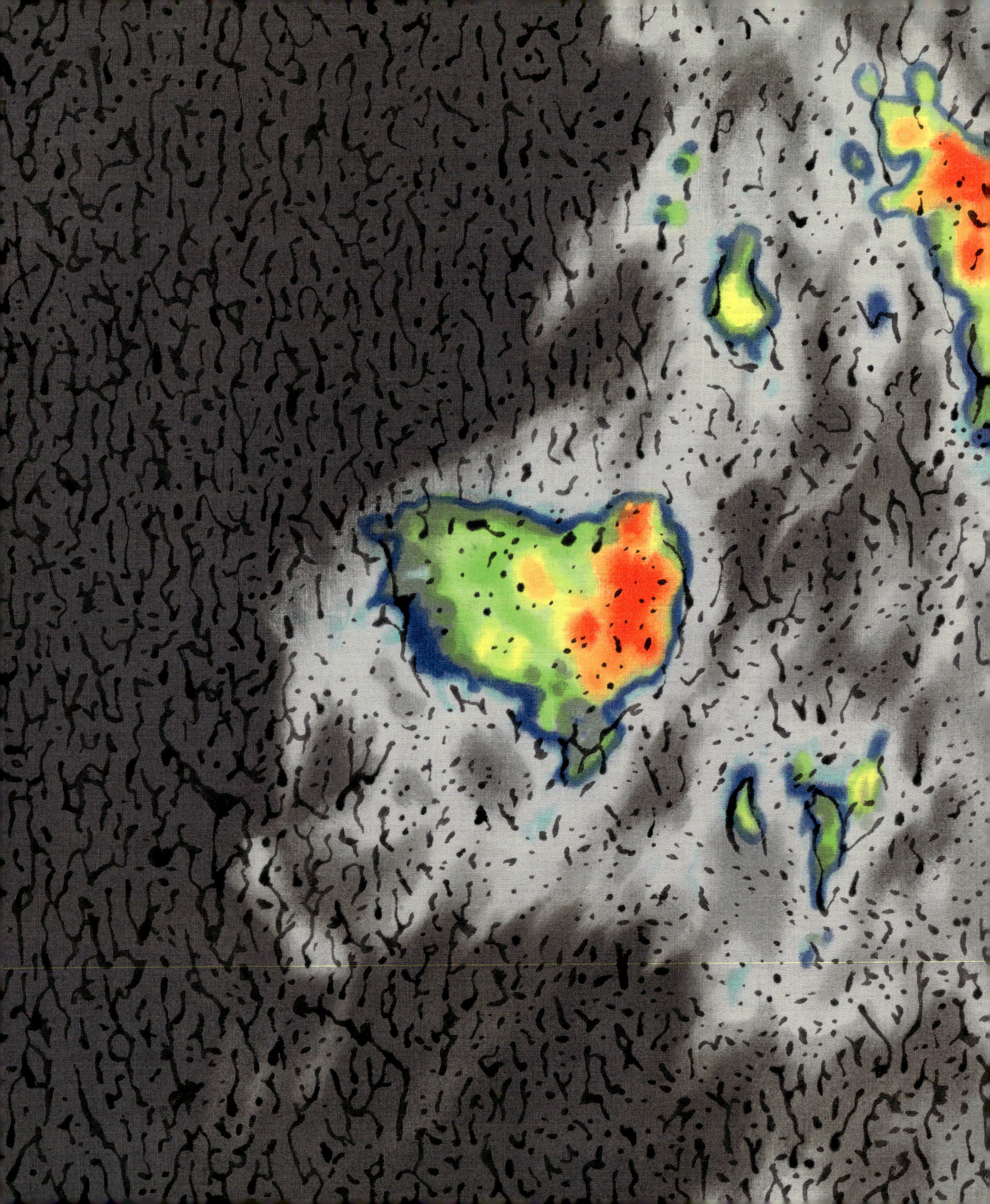

Nate Lowman

David Zwirner Books

Contents

October 1, 2017

 ***Picture 2*, 2019** Oil and alkyd on linen, 66 ⅛ × 96 inches | 168 × 243.8 cm

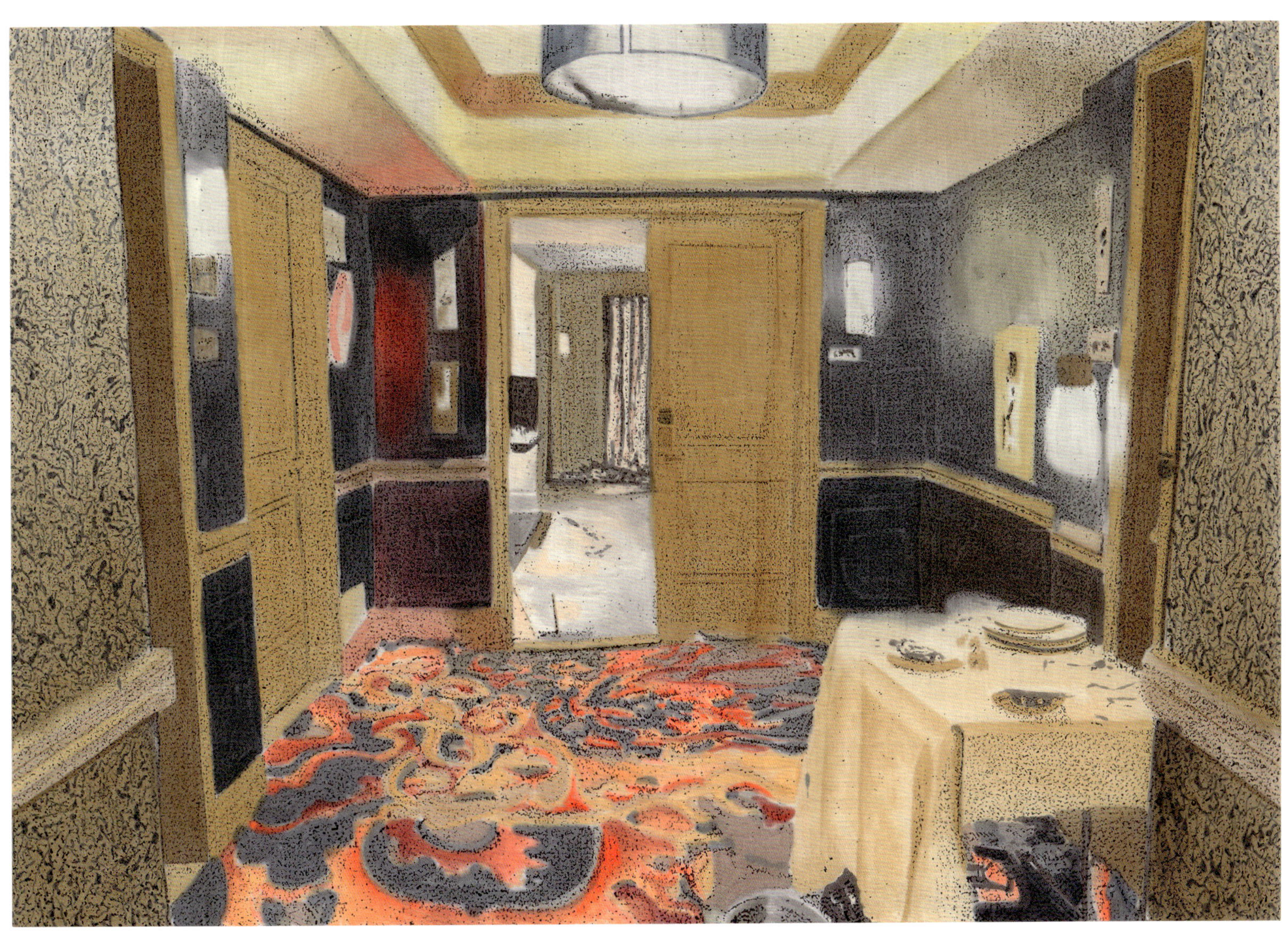

***Picture 4*, 2018** Oil and alkyd on linen, 87 × 60 inches | 221 × 152.4 cm

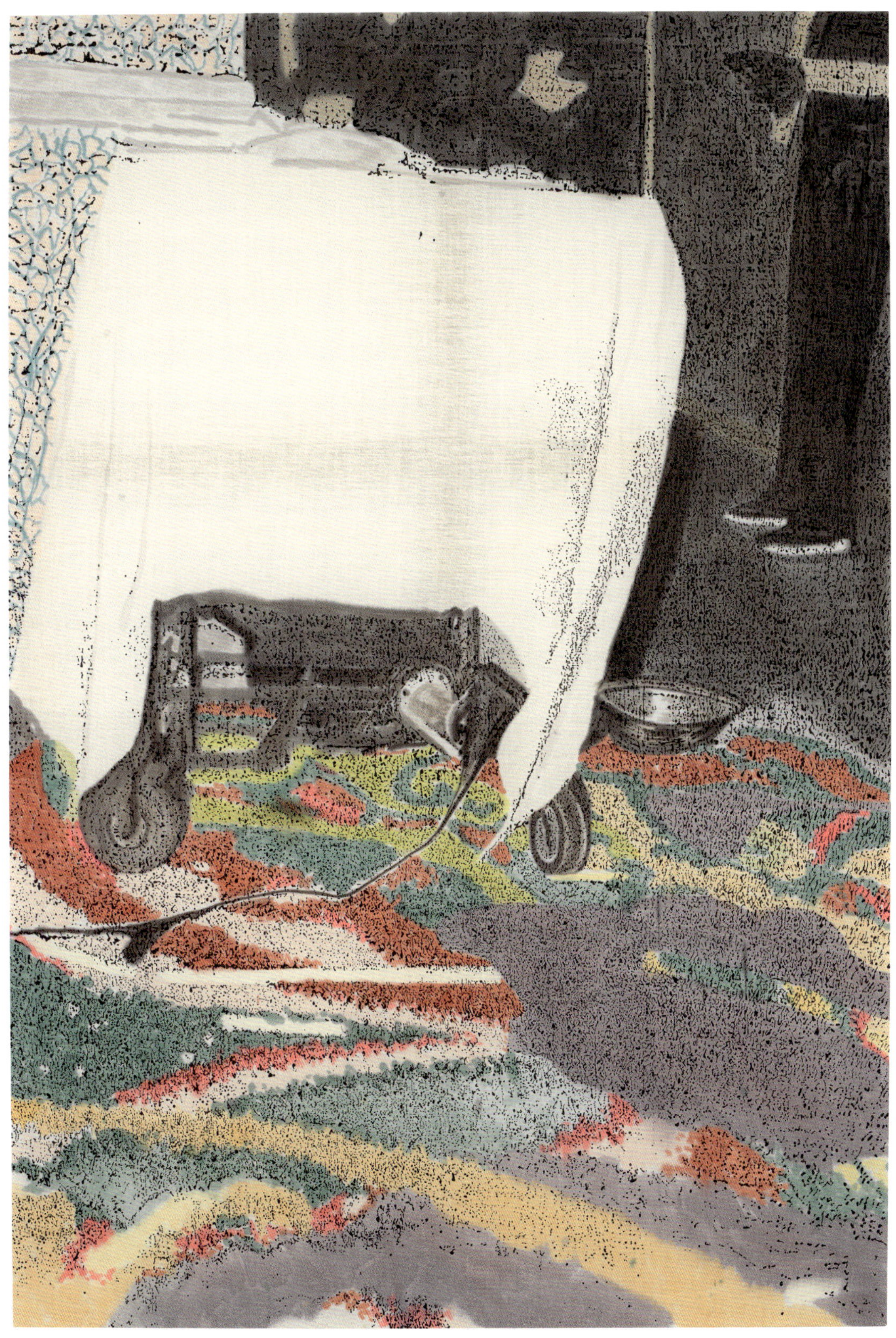

 ***Picture 1*, 2019** Oil and alkyd on linen, 85 ⅛ × 64 inches | 216.2 × 162.6 cm

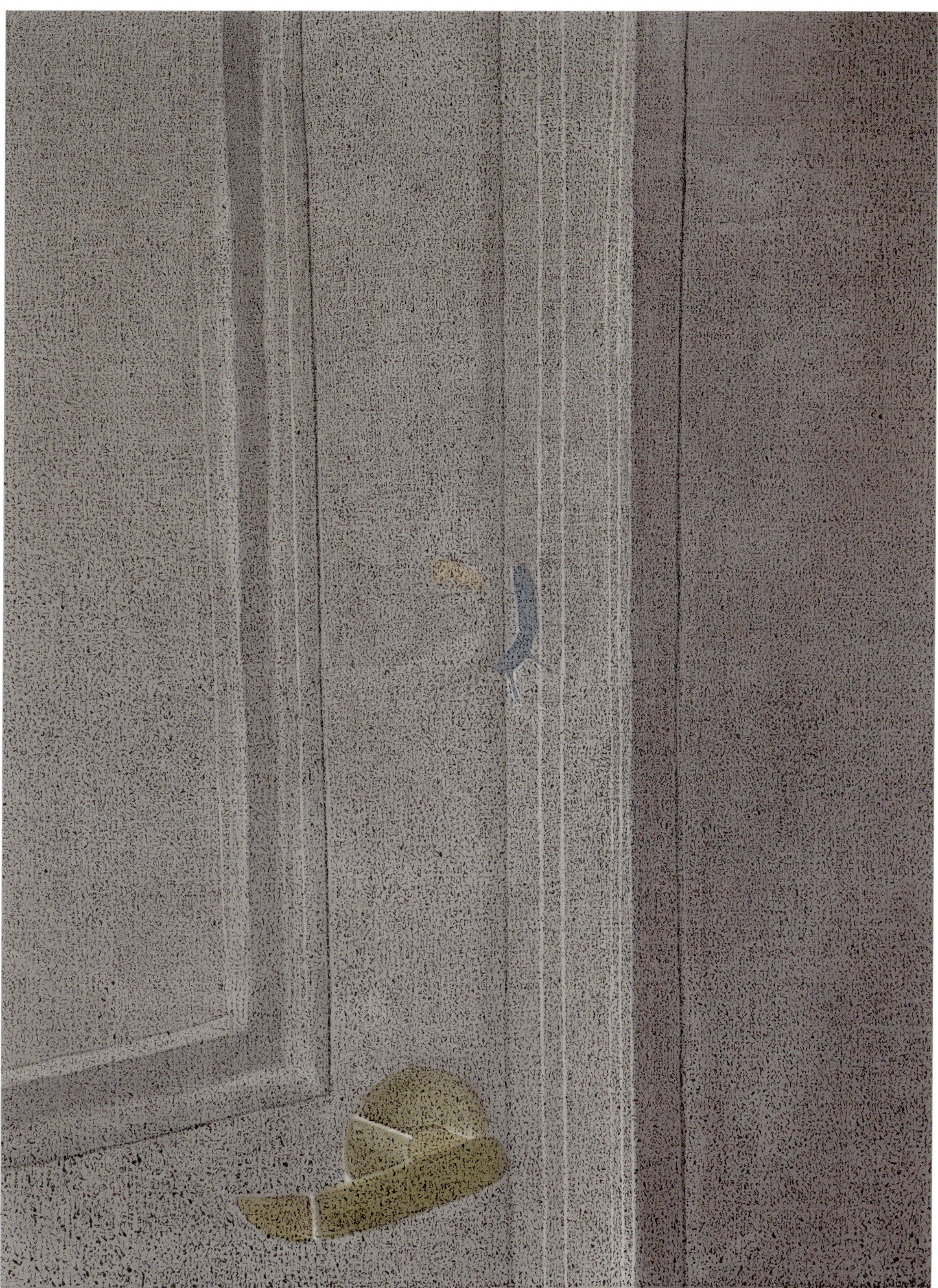

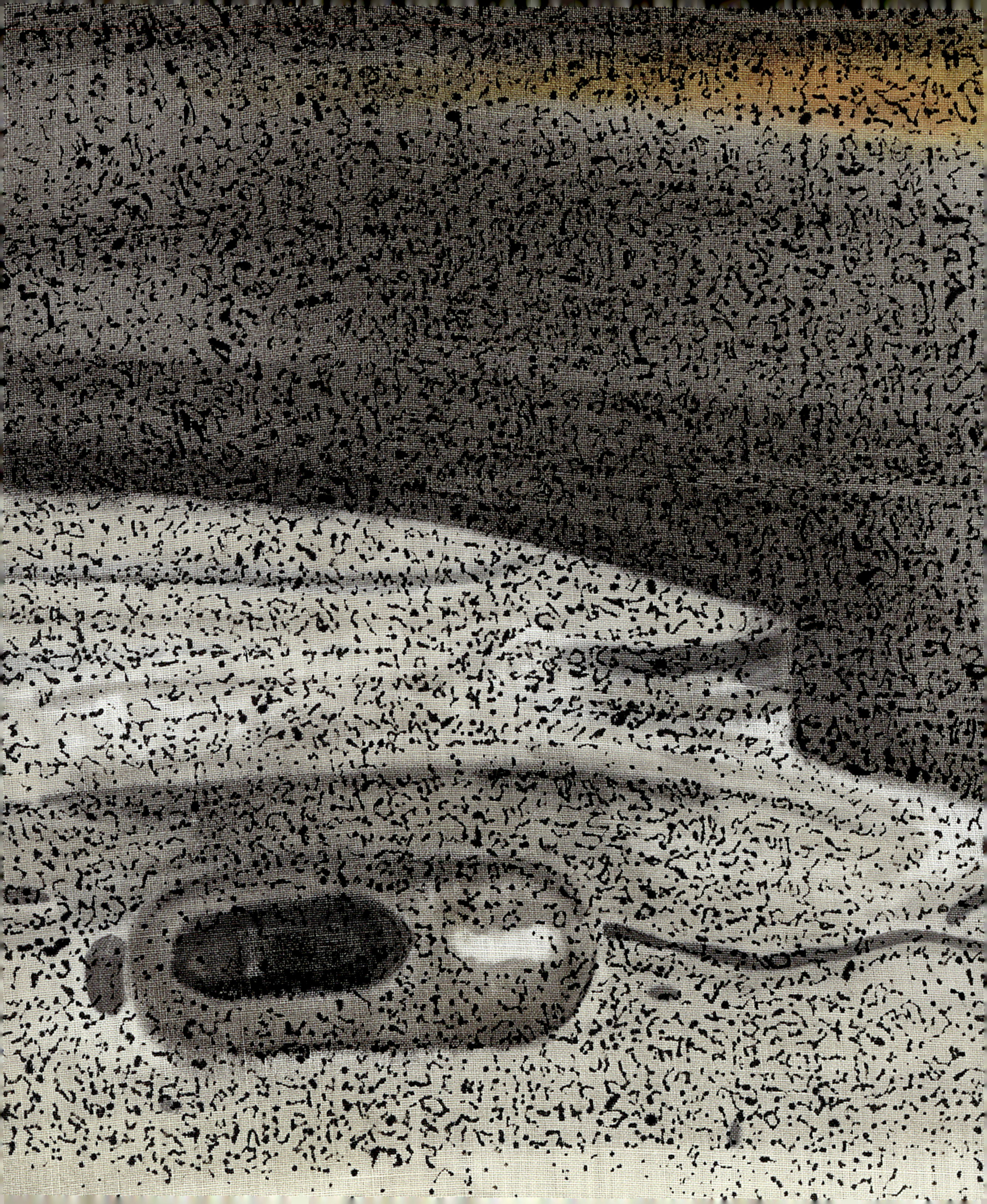

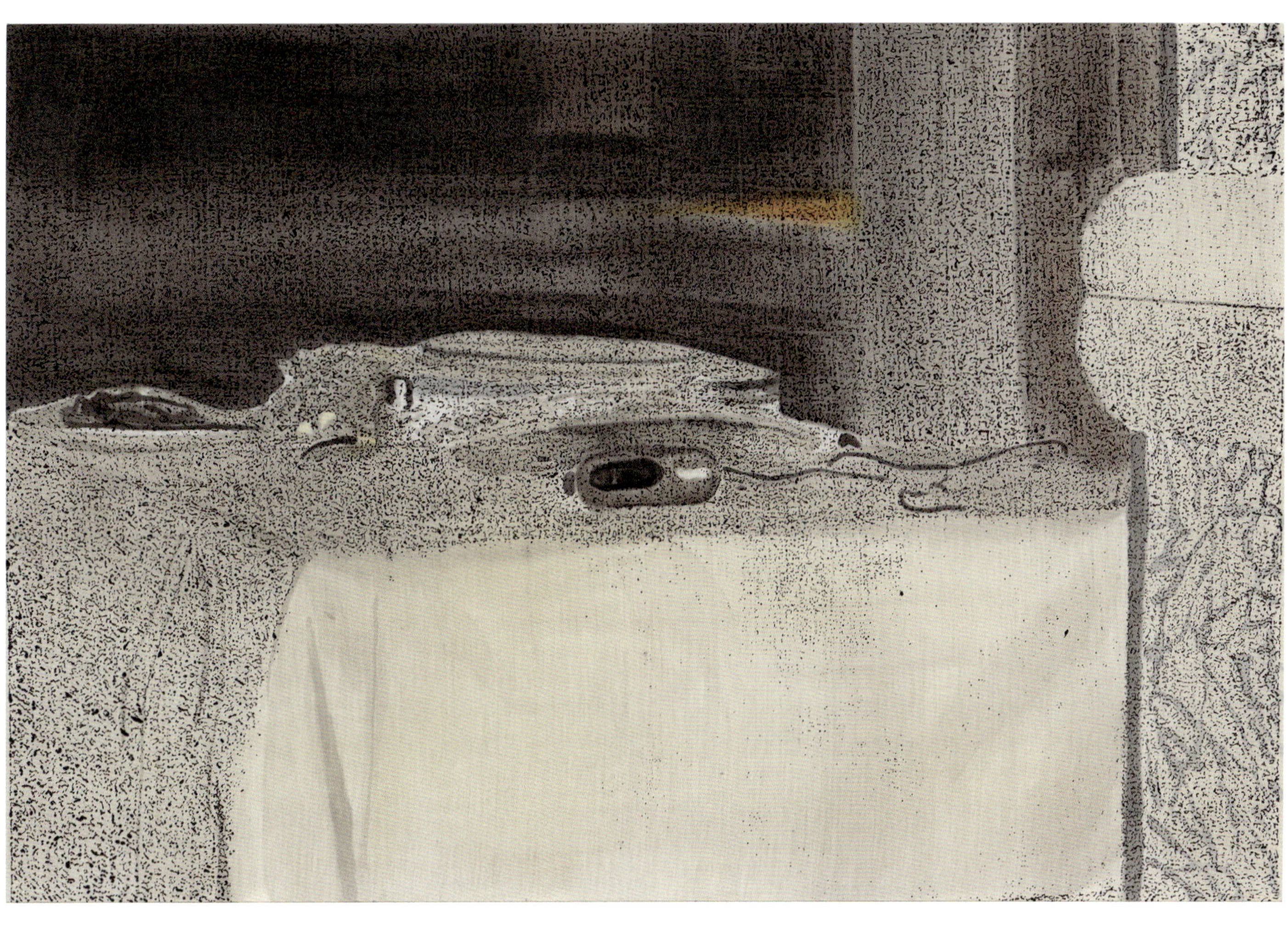

***Picture 3*, 2019** Oil and alkyd on linen, 43¼ × 64½ inches | 109.9 × 163.8 cm

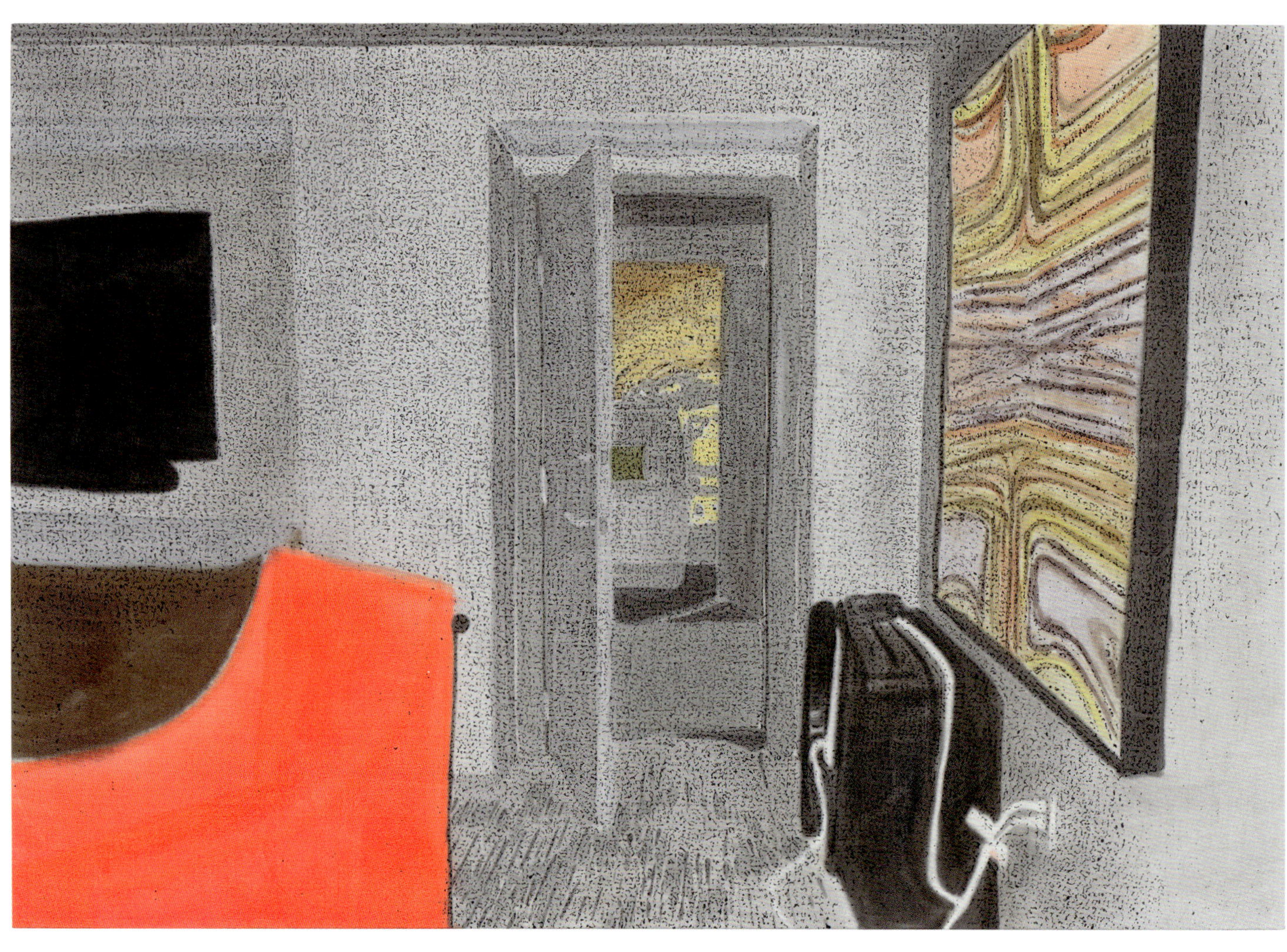

 ***Picture 11*, 2019** Oil and alkyd on linen, 43 × 62⅝ inches | 109.2 × 159.1 cm

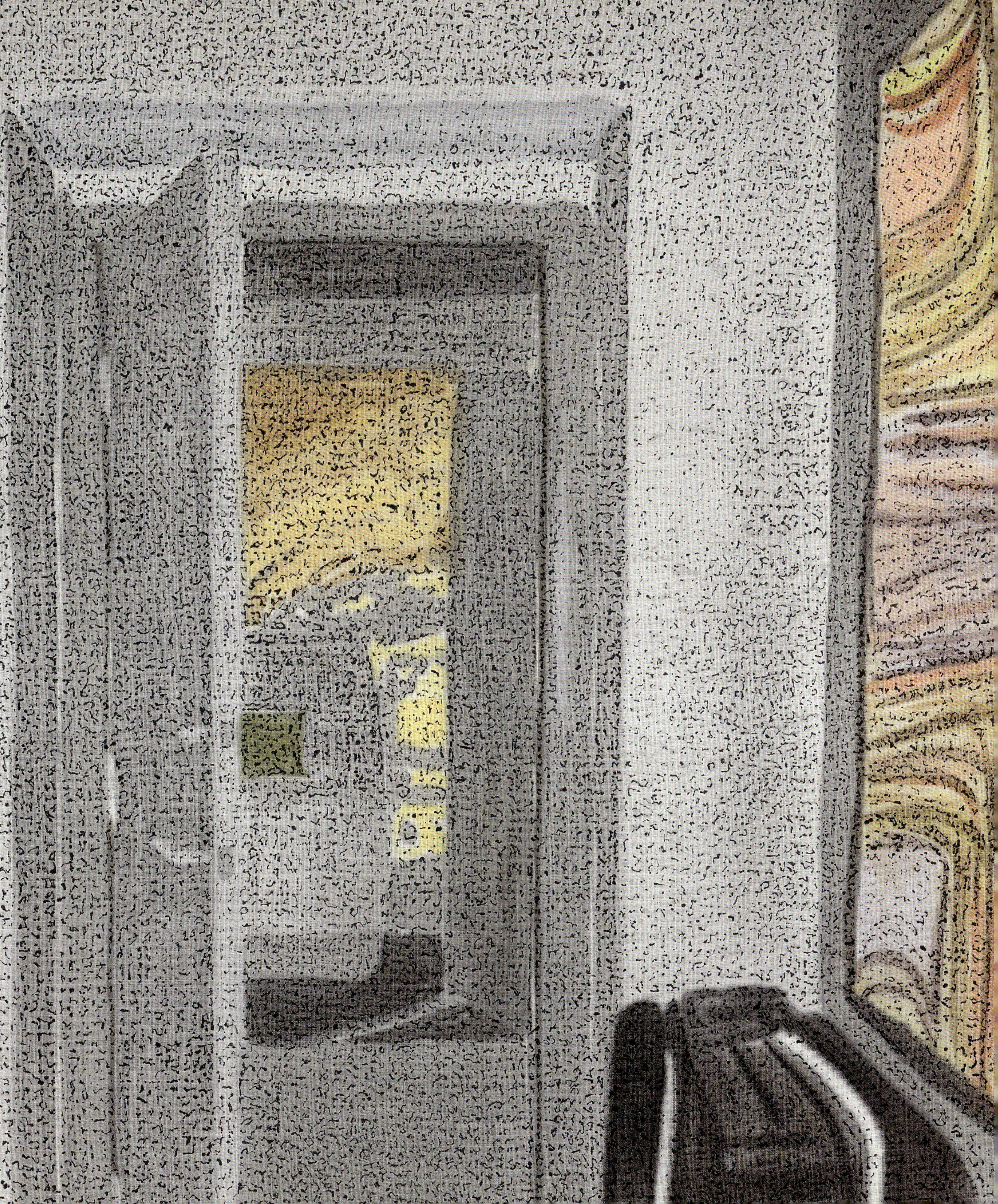

***Picture 10*, 2018** Oil and alkyd on linen, 72 ⅛ × 108 inches | 183.2 × 274.3 cm

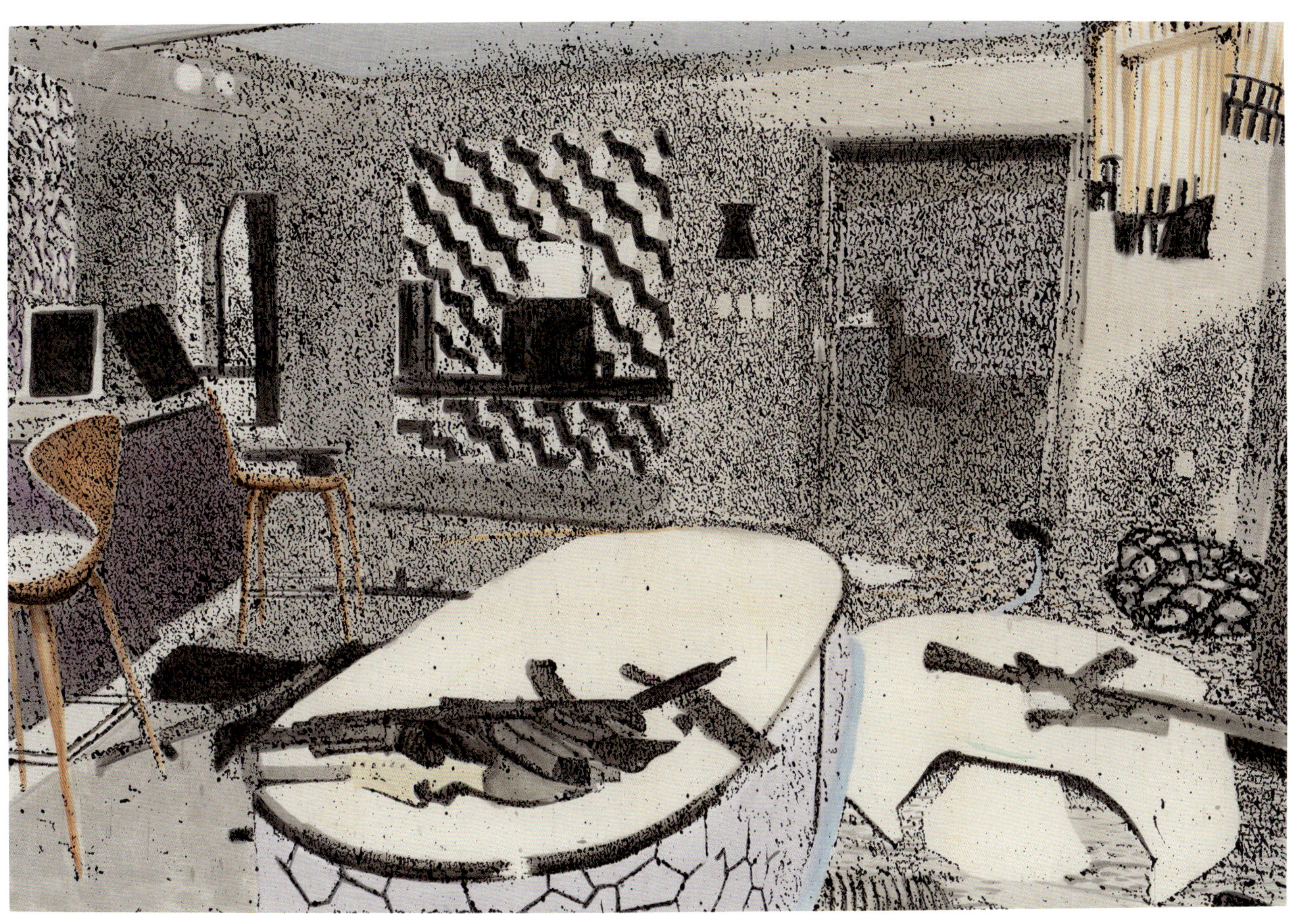

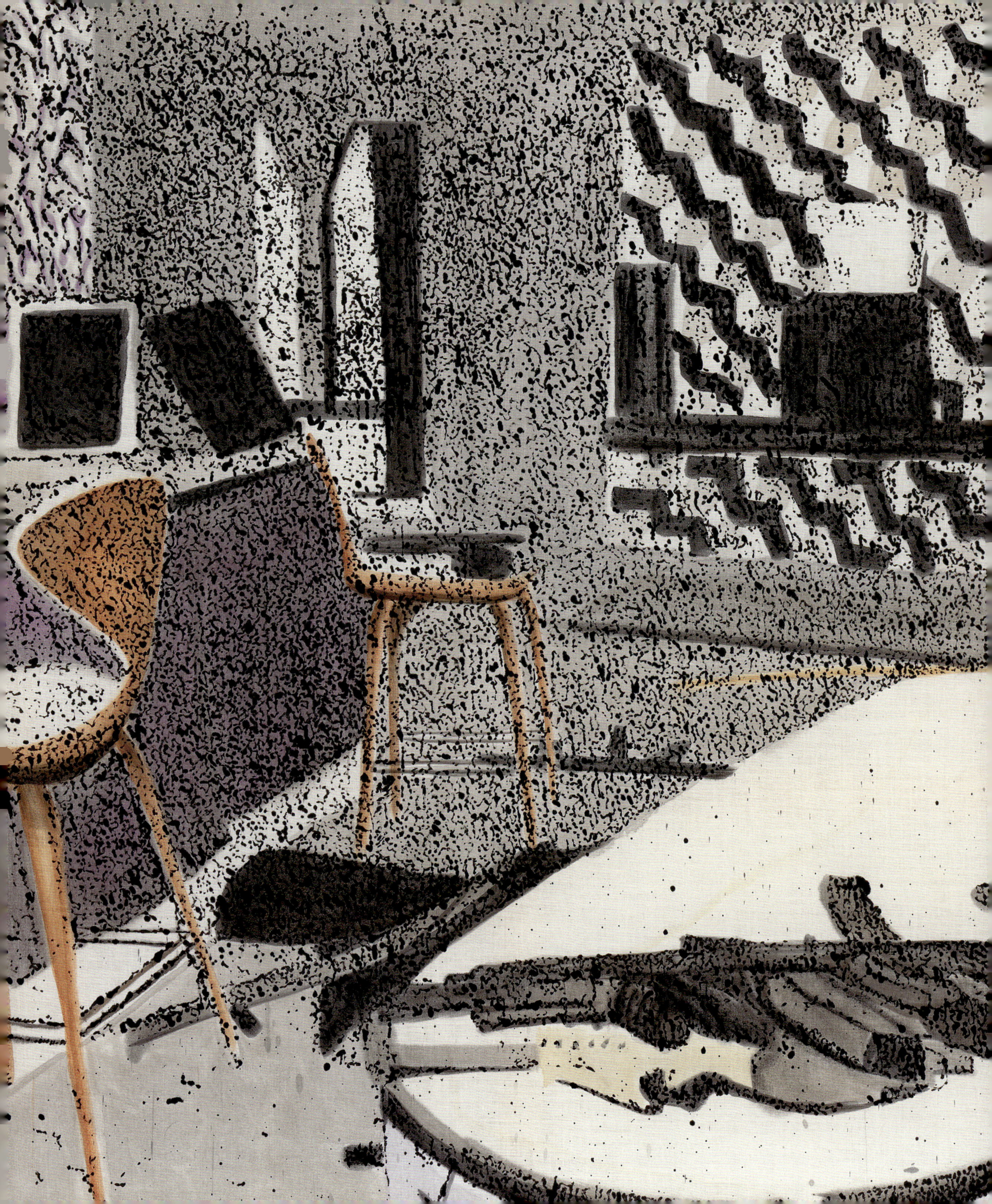

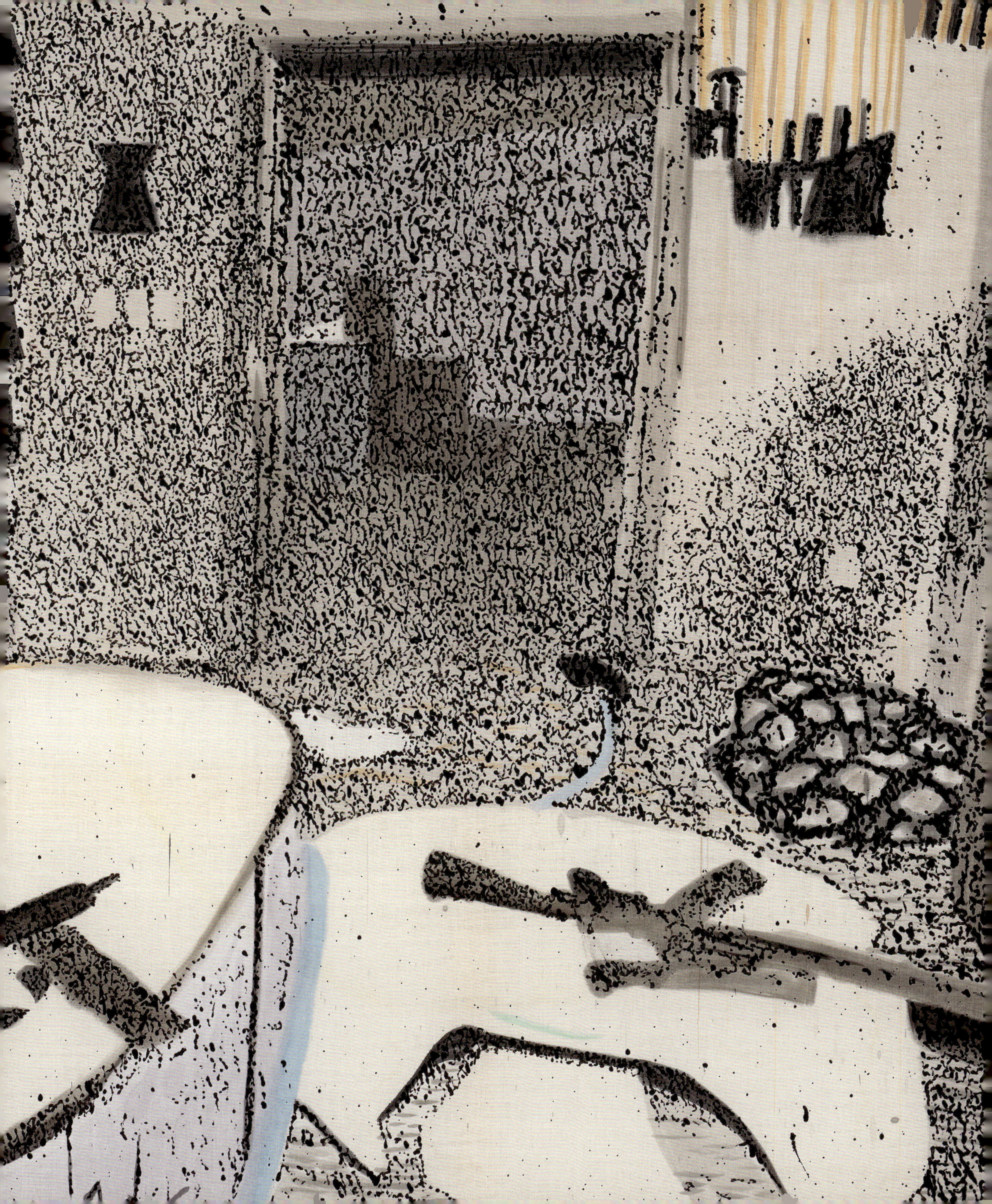

***Picture 6*, 2019** Oil and alkyd on linen, 87 × 132 inches | 221 × 335.3 cm

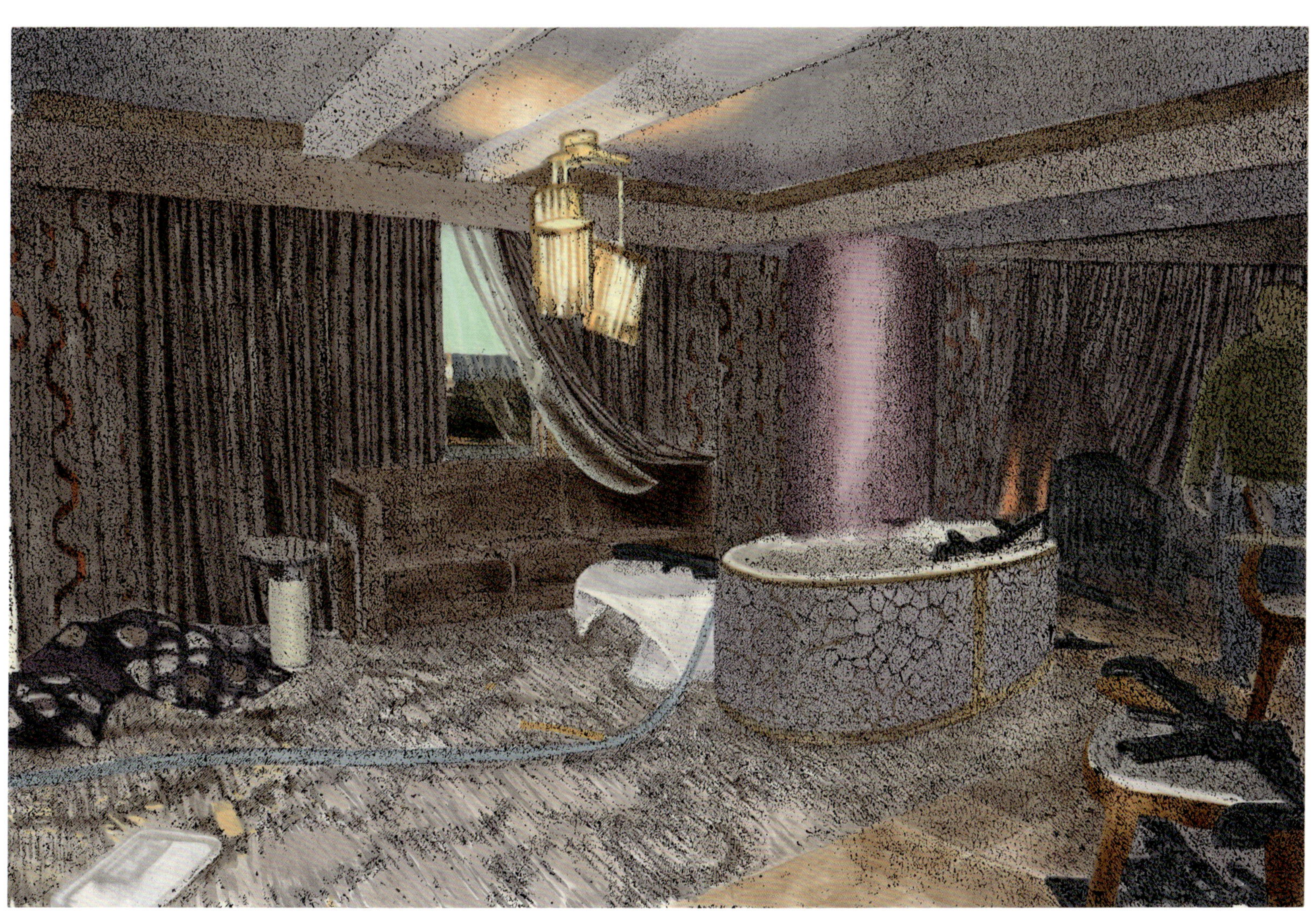

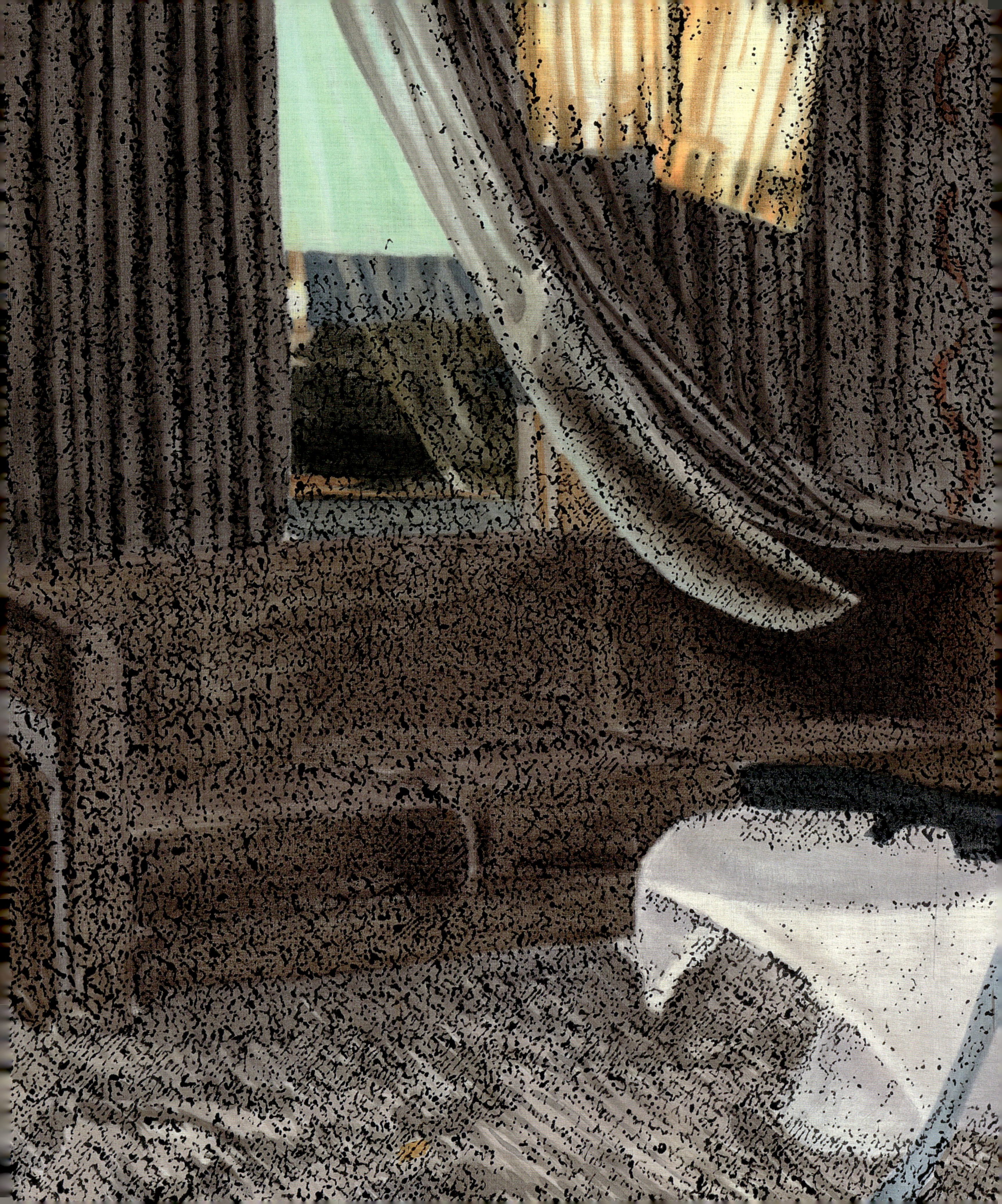

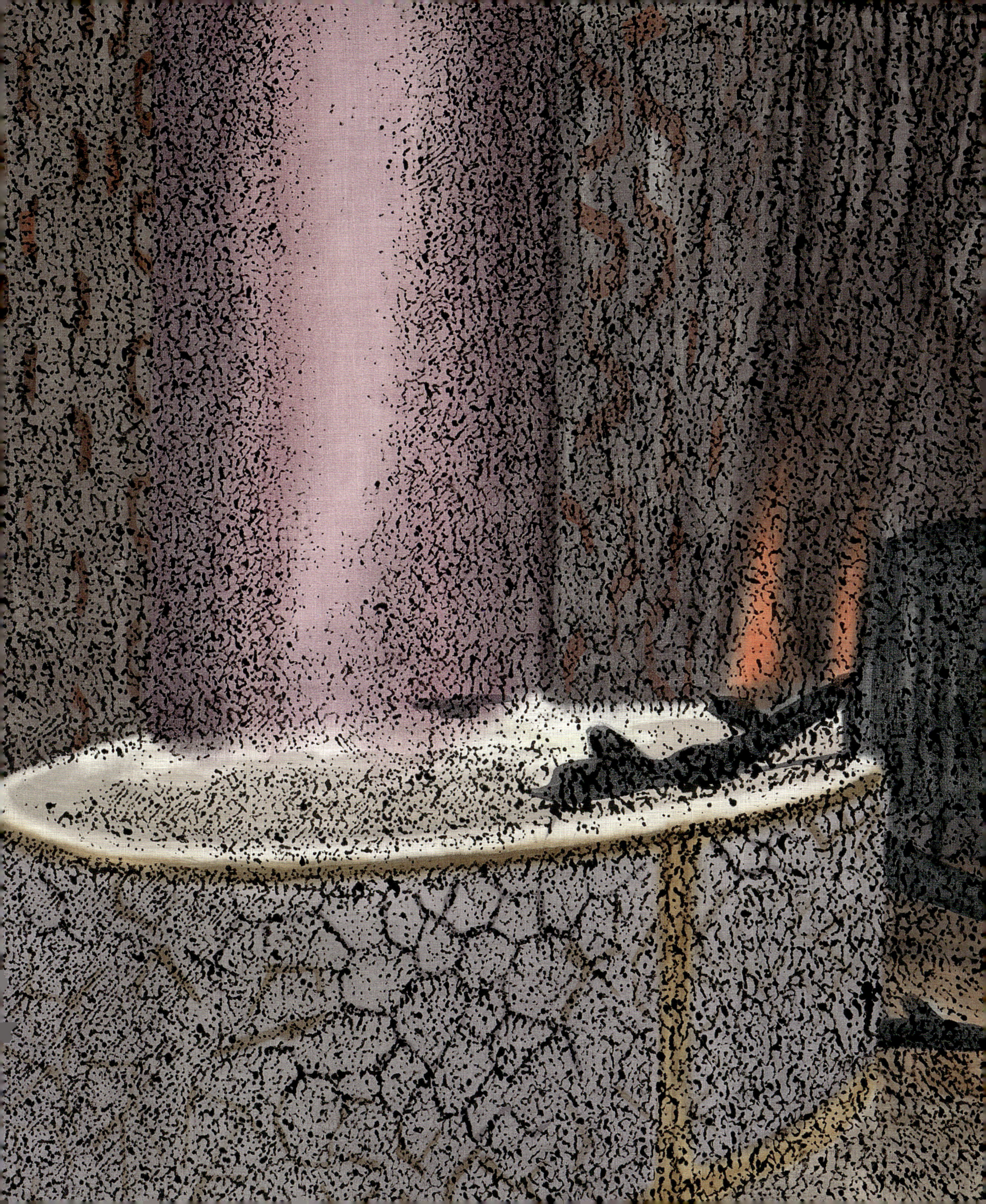

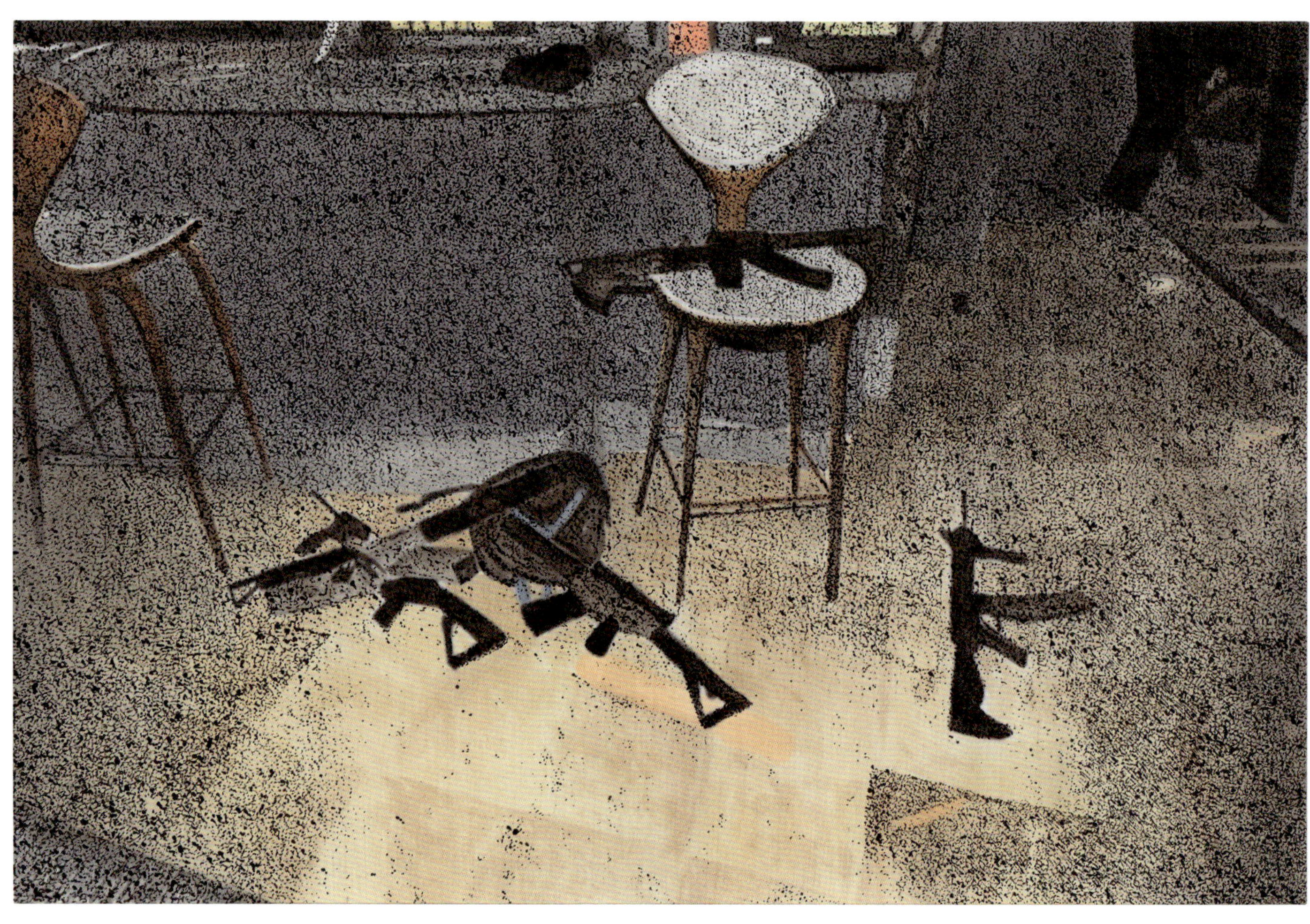

 ***Picture 9*, 2019** Oil and alkyd on linen, 44 × 67 inches | 111.8 × 170.2 cm

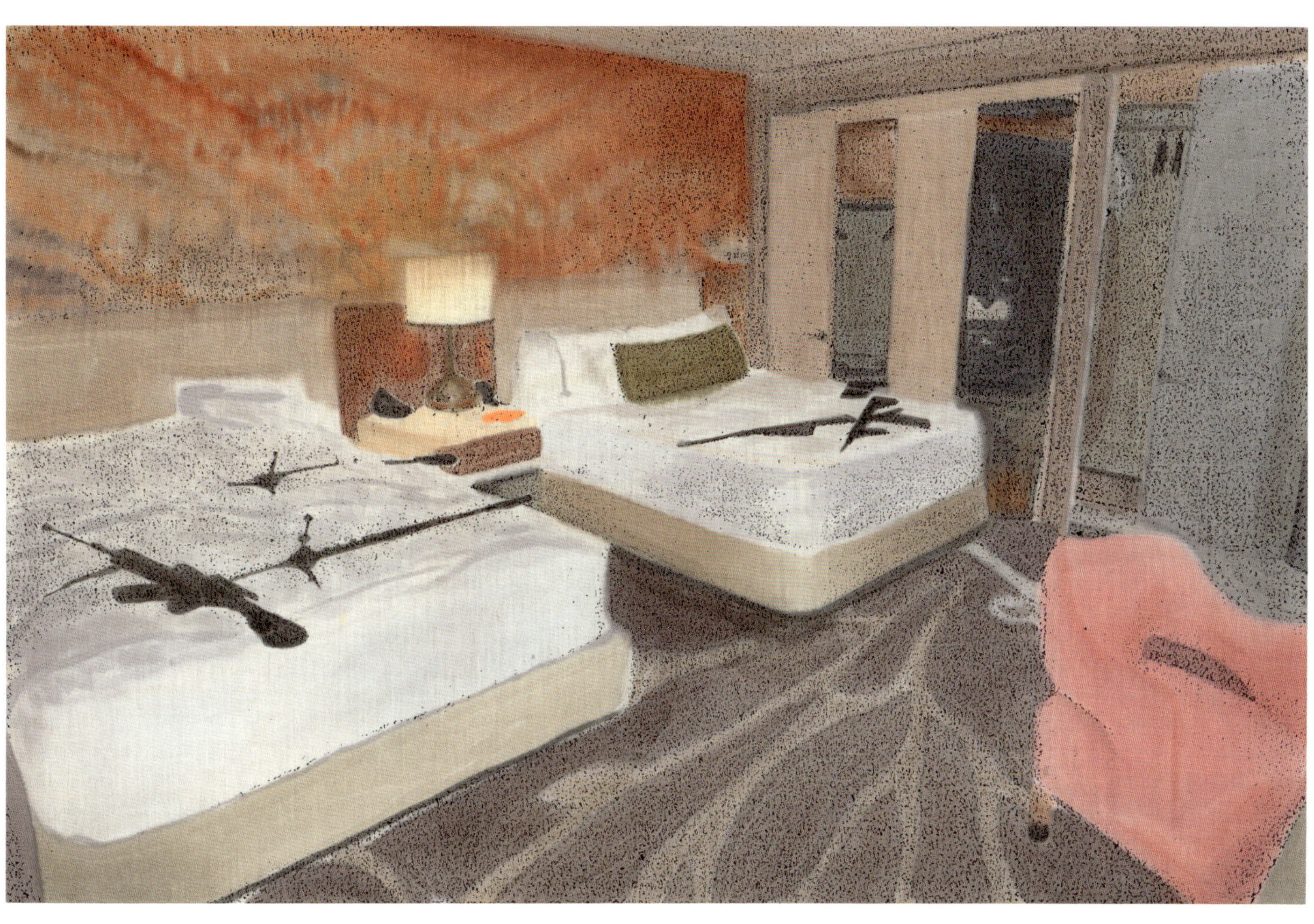

***Picture 20*, 2019** Oil and alkyd on linen, 47⅛ × 72⅛ inches | 119.7 × 183.2 cm

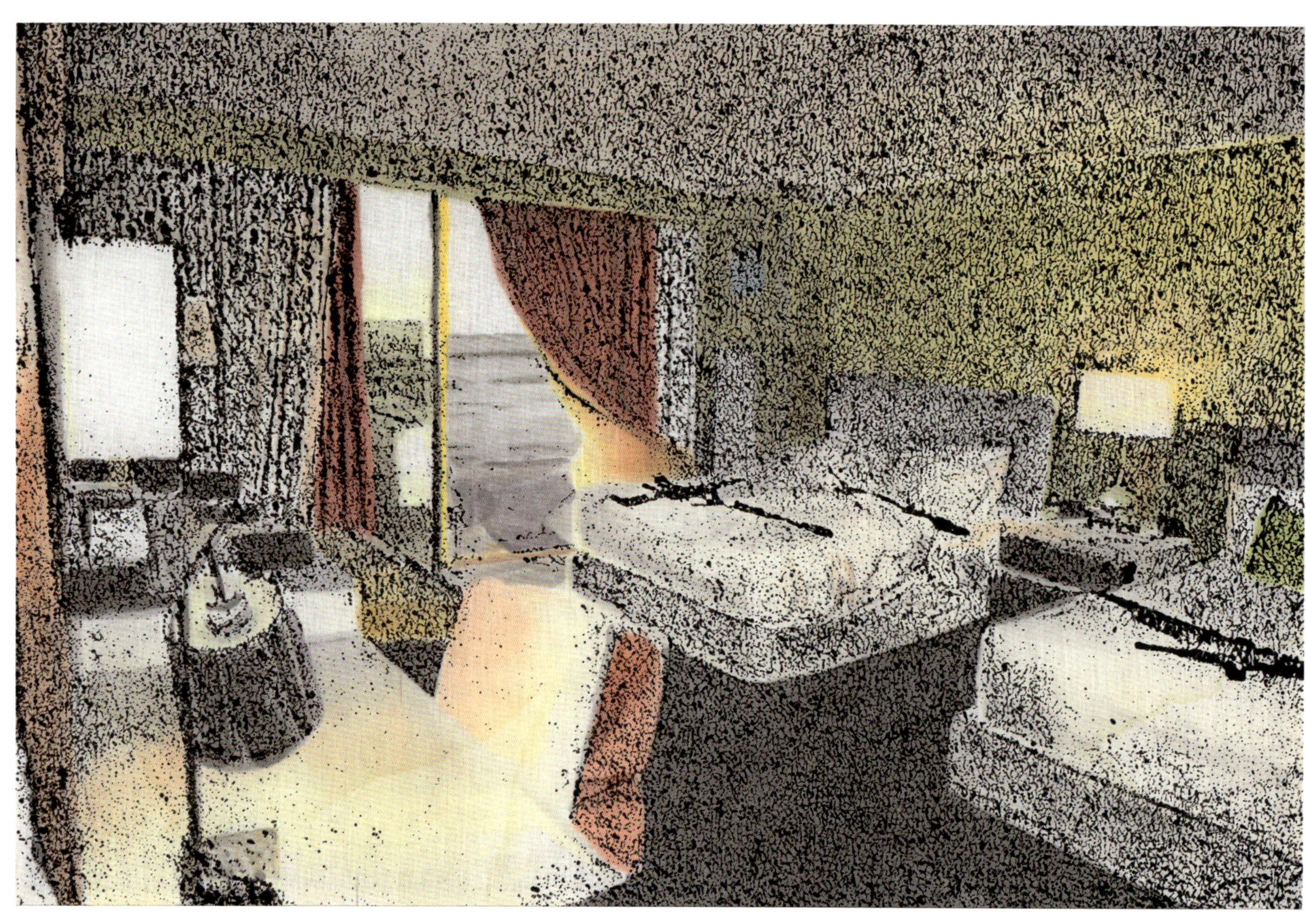

 ***Picture 19*, 2019** Oil and alkyd on linen, 47 5/8 × 71 5/8 inches | 121 × 181.9 cm

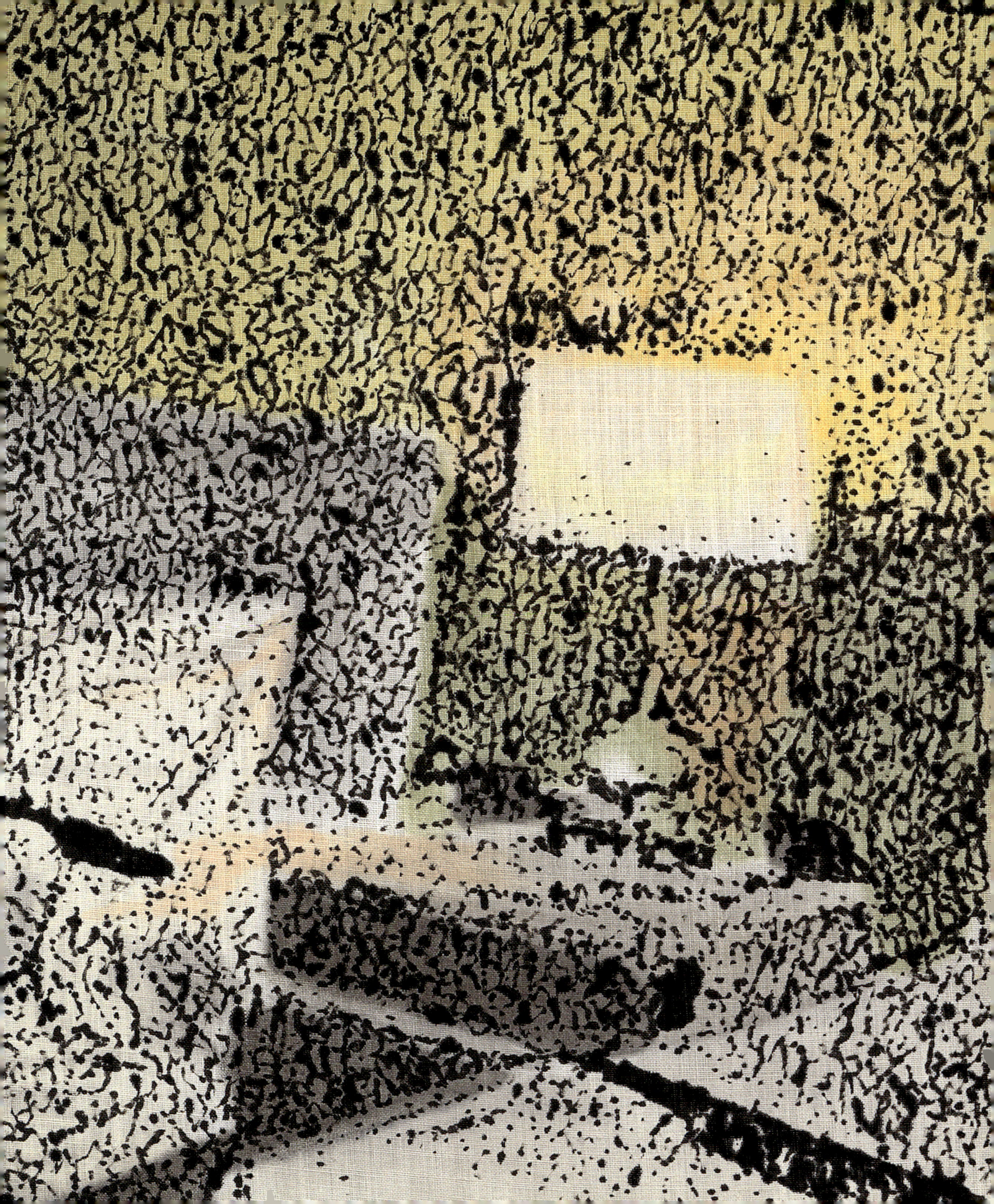

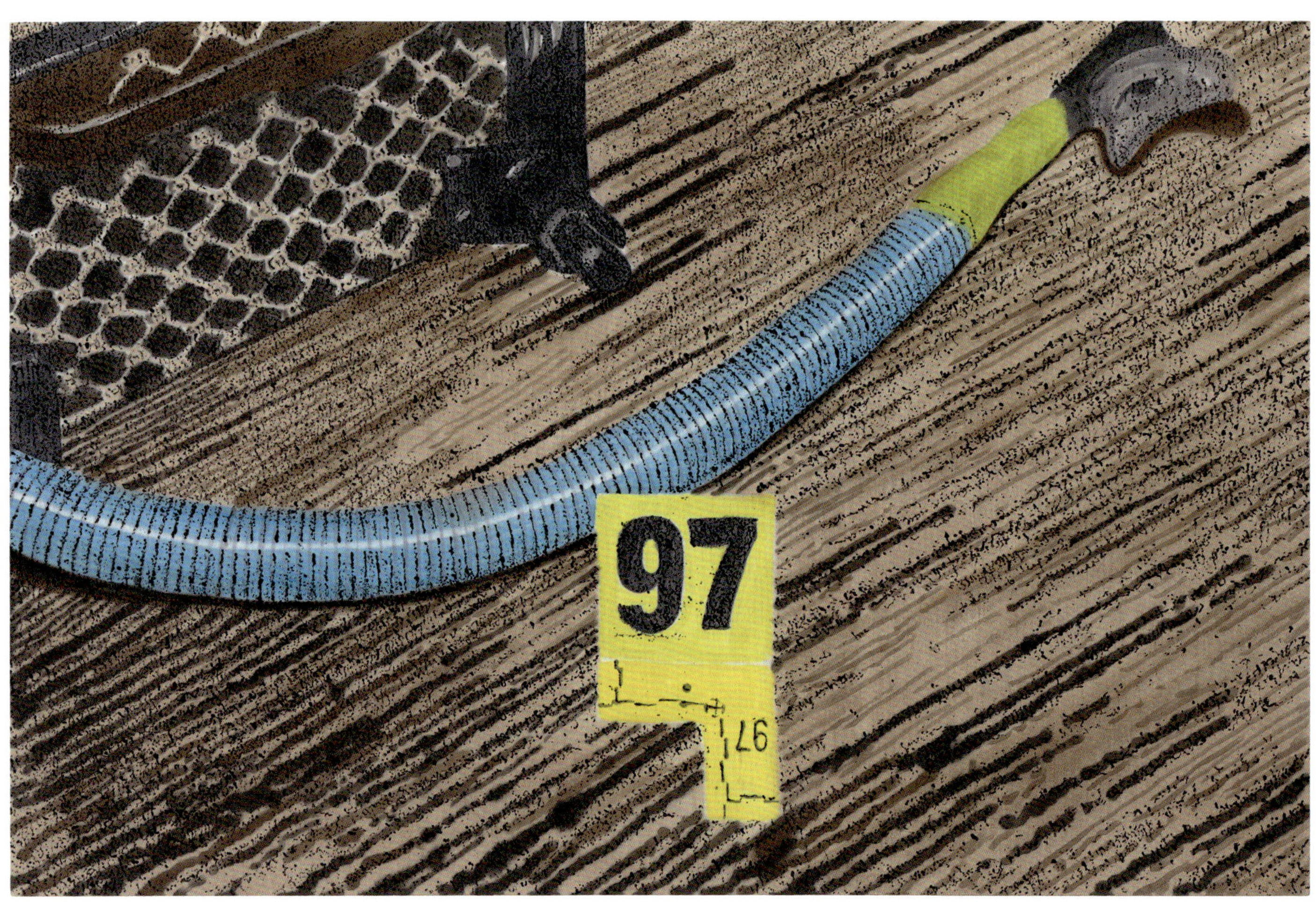

 ***Picture 12*, 2019** Oil and alkyd on linen, 45⅛ × 69⅛ inches | 114.6 × 175.6 cm

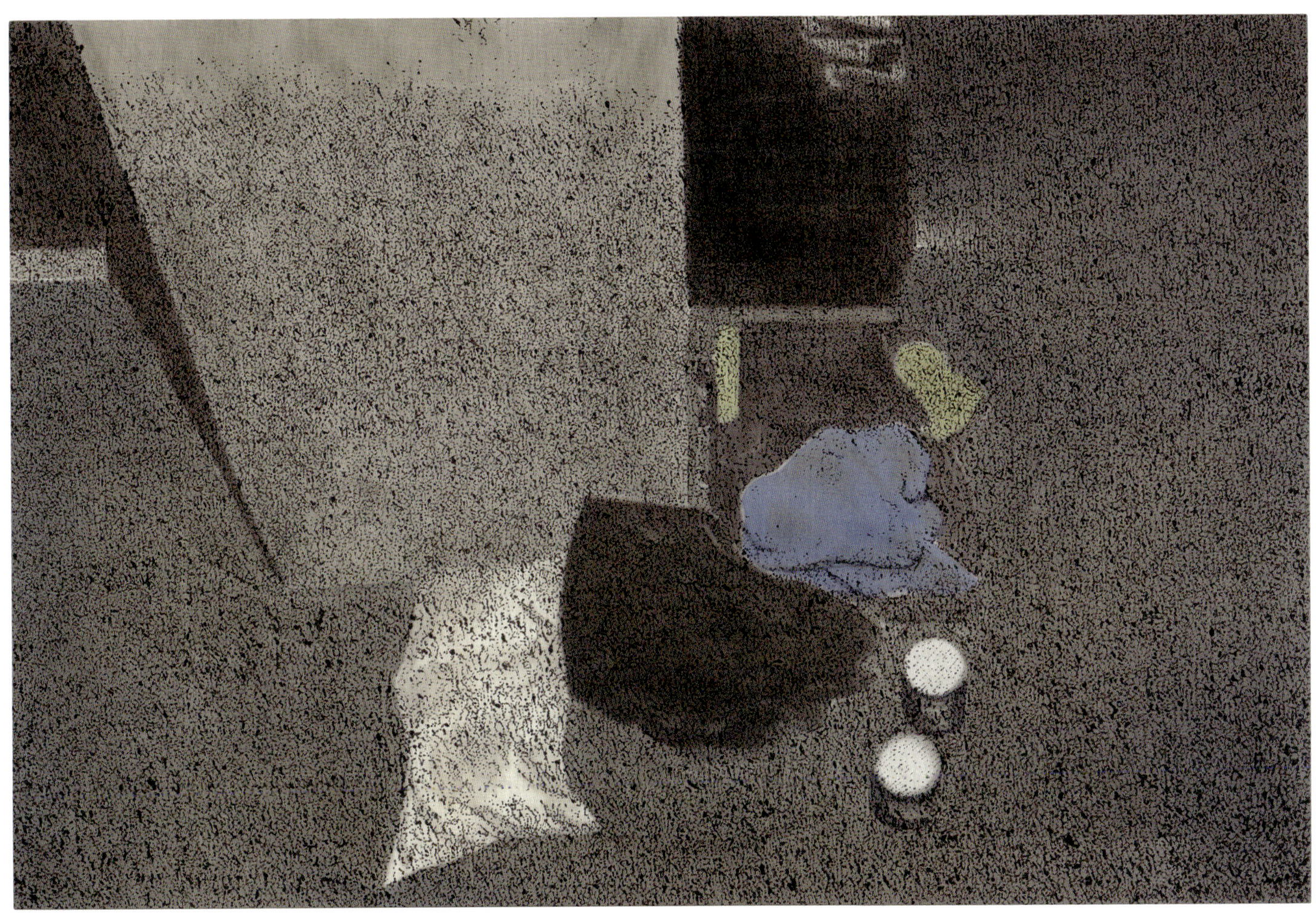

***Picture 23*, 2019** Oil and alkyd on linen, 48 ¼ × 73 inches | 122.6 × 185.4 cm

***Picture 18*, 2019** Oil and alkyd on linen, 48 × 72 inches | 121.9 × 182.9 cm

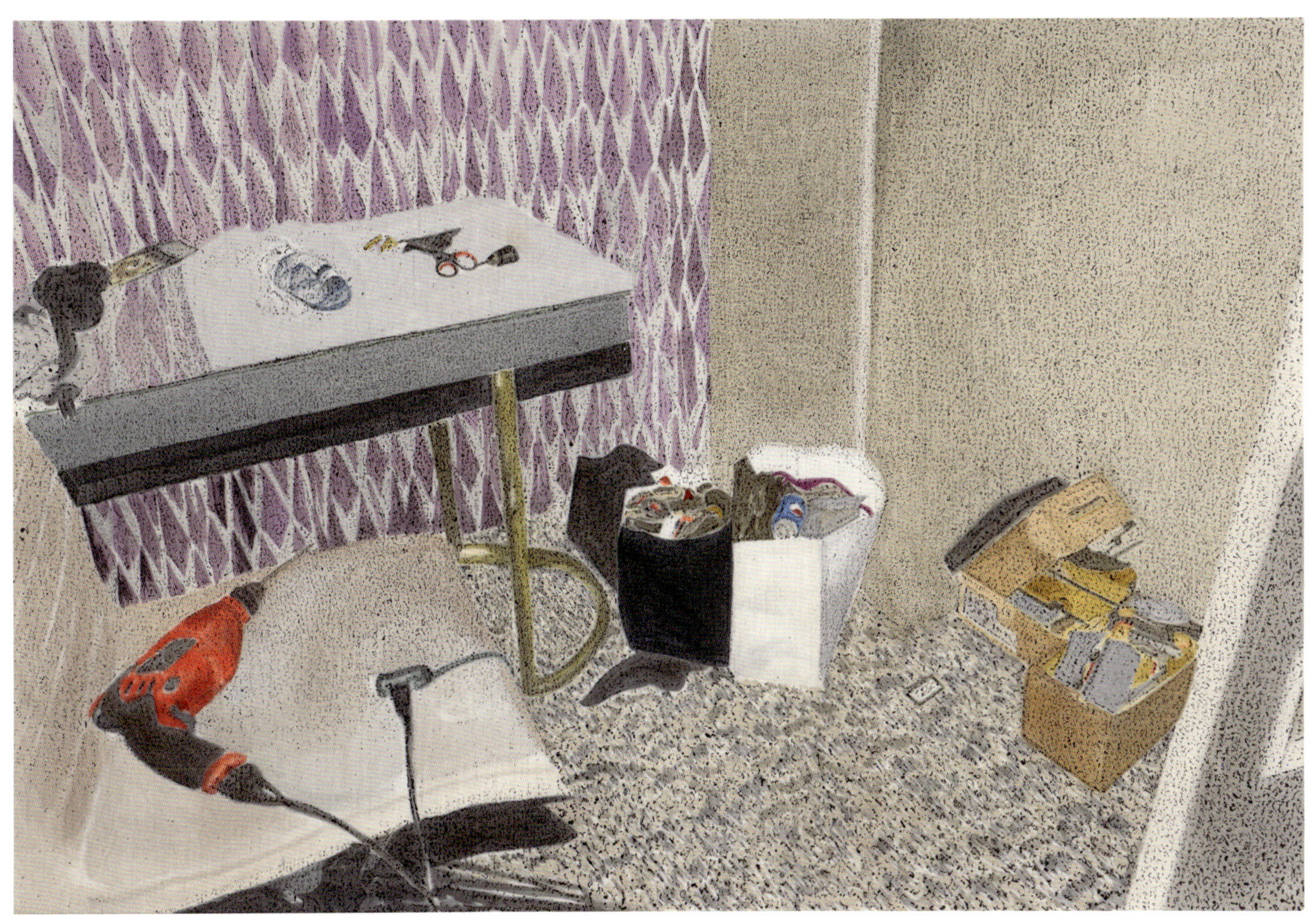

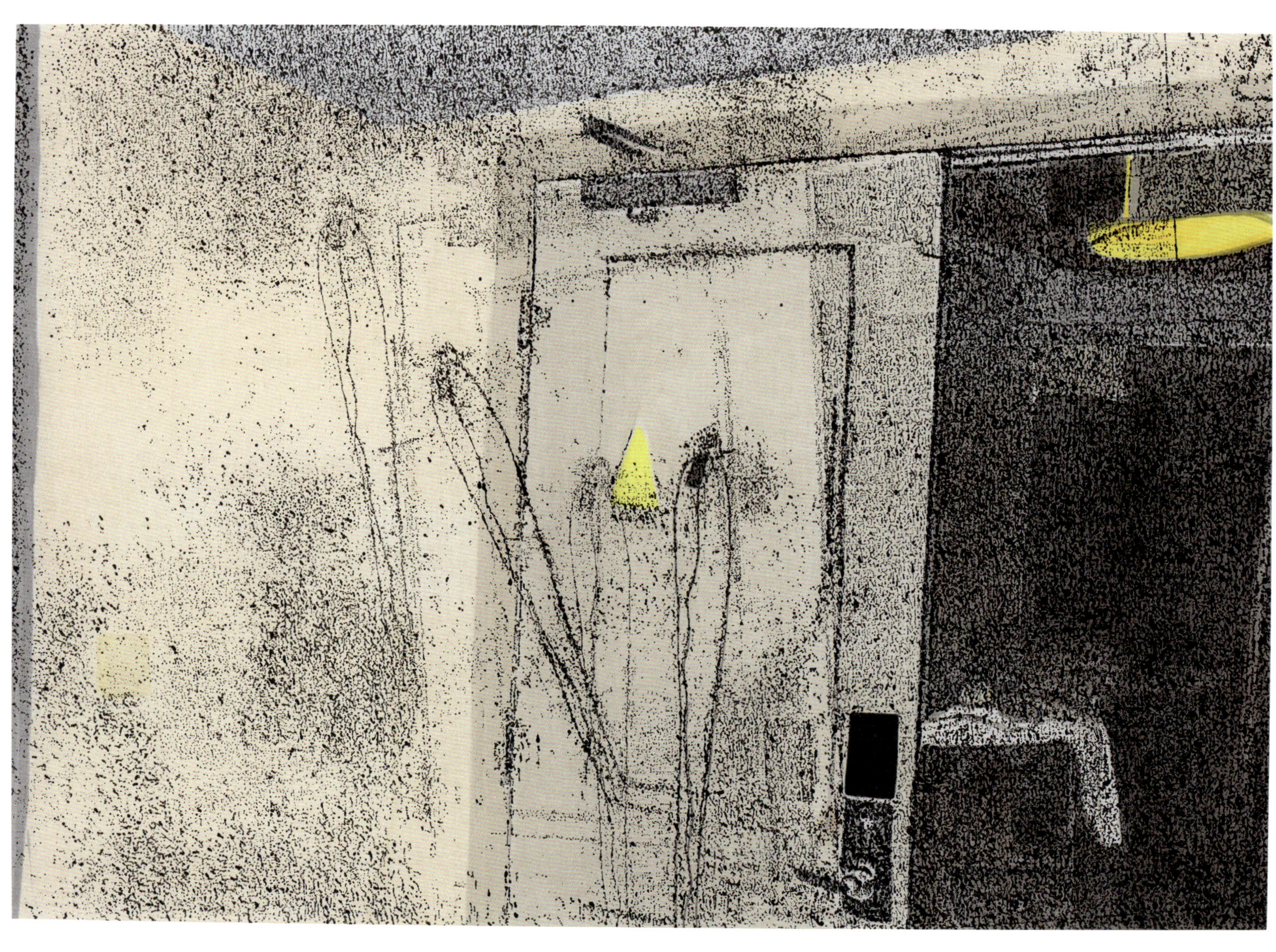

 ***Picture 13*, 2018** Oil and alkyd on linen, 66 × 96 inches | 167.6 × 243.8 cm

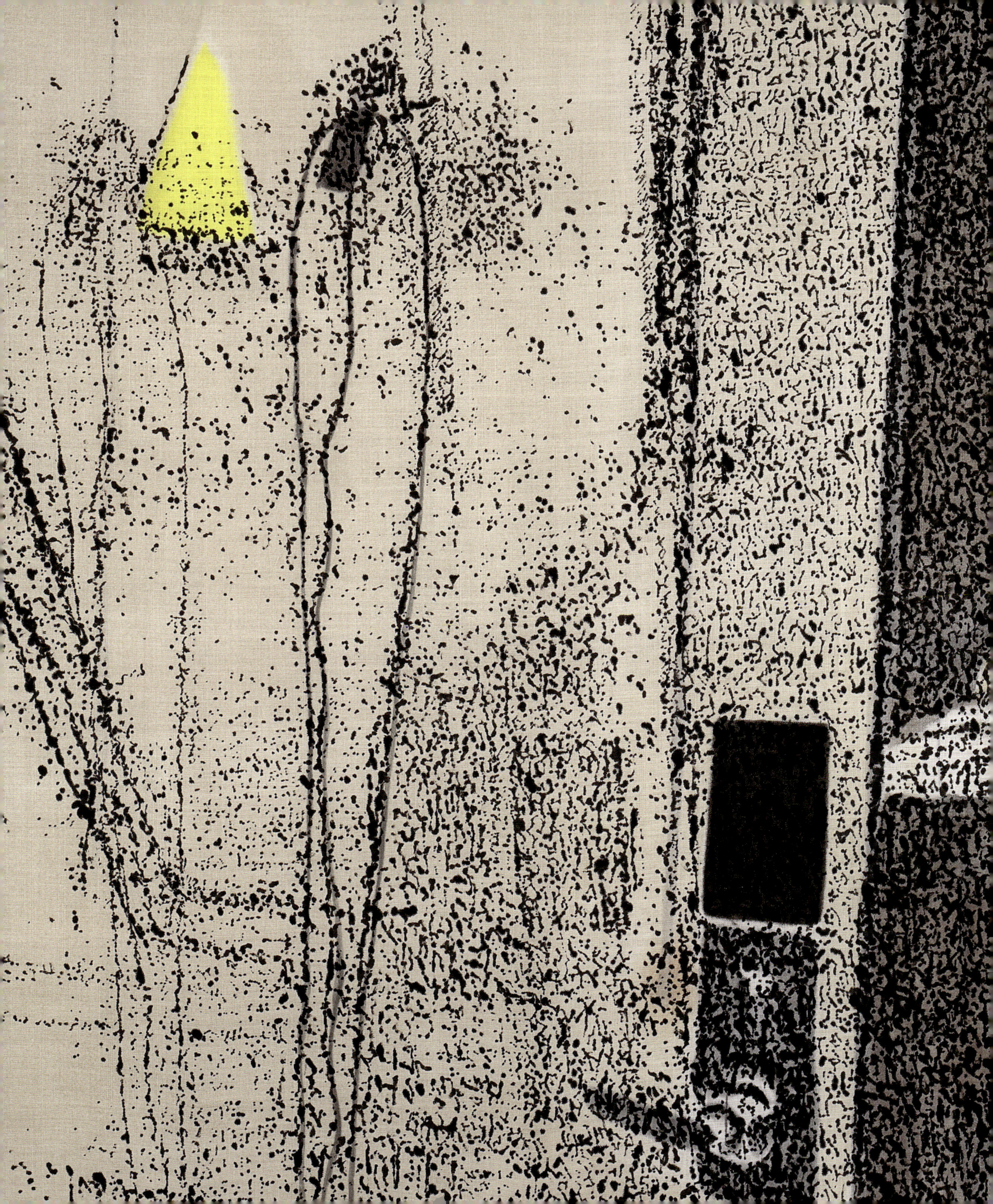

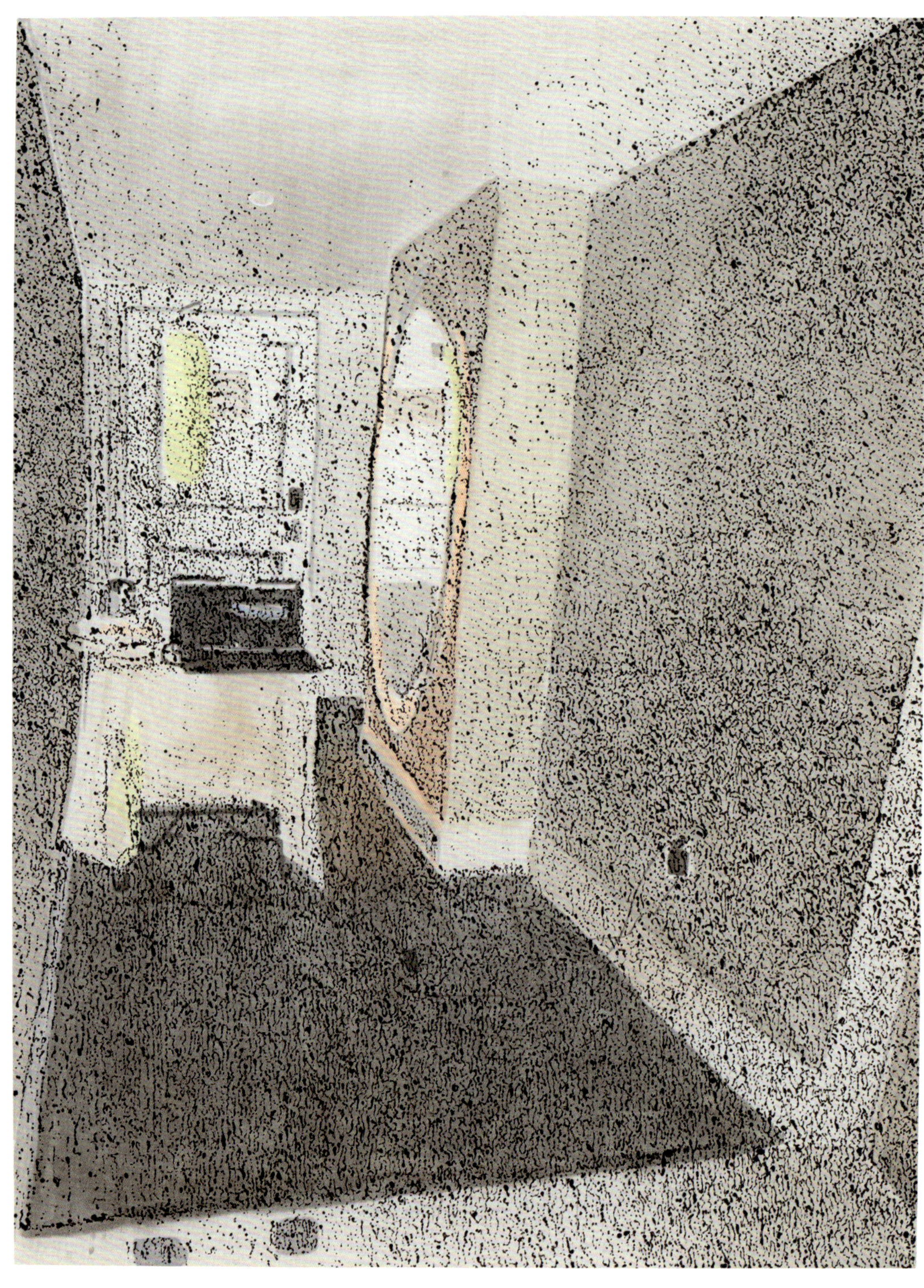

 ***Picture 21*, 2018** Oil and alkyd on linen, 65 × 48⅝ inches | 165.1 × 123.5 cm

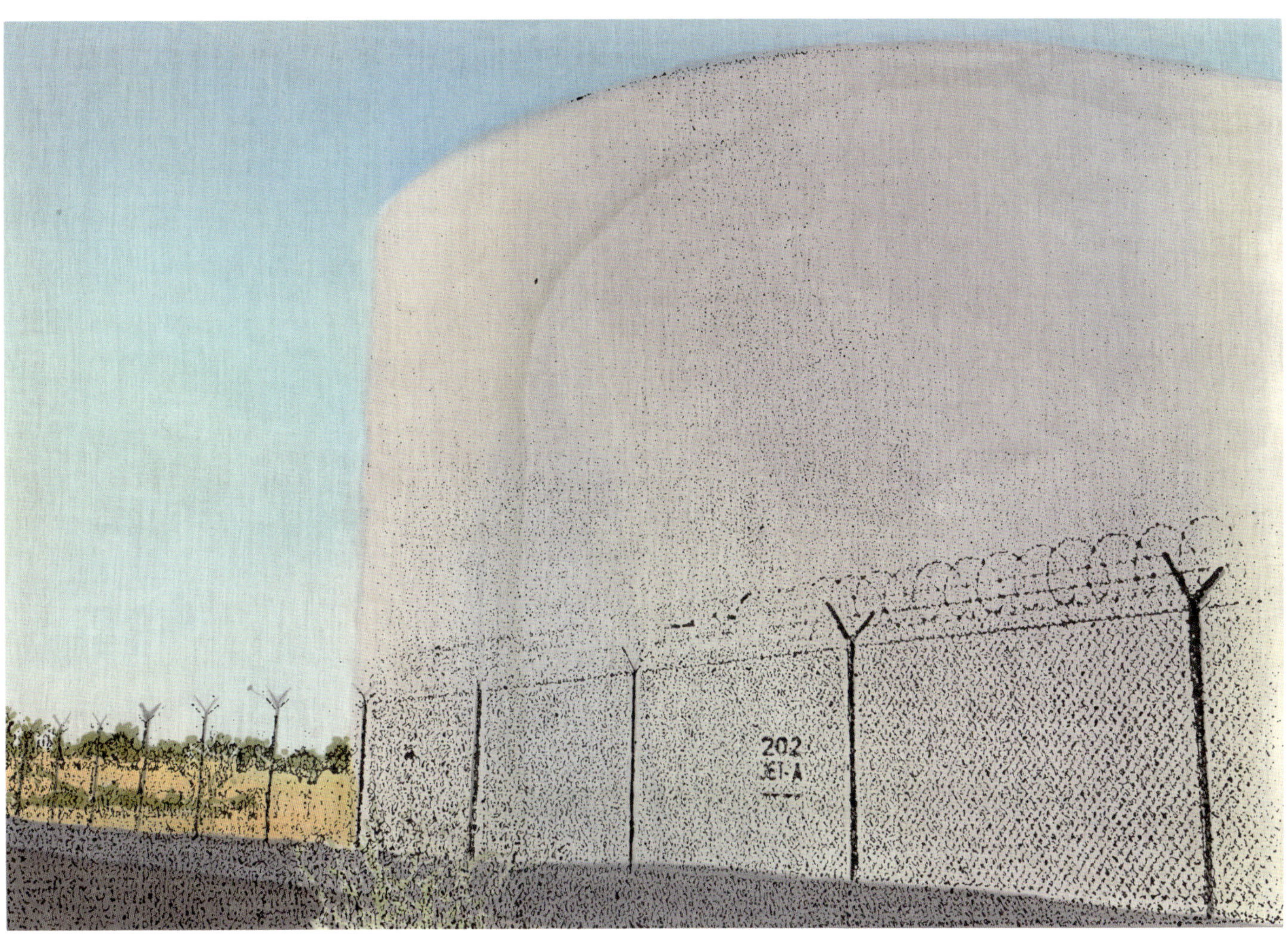

***Picture 25*, 2019** Oil and alkyd on linen, 47 3⁄8 × 69 1⁄8 inches | 120.3 × 175.6 cm

***Picture 28*, 2018** Oil and alkyd on linen, 30 × 43 ½ inches | 76.2 × 110.5 cm

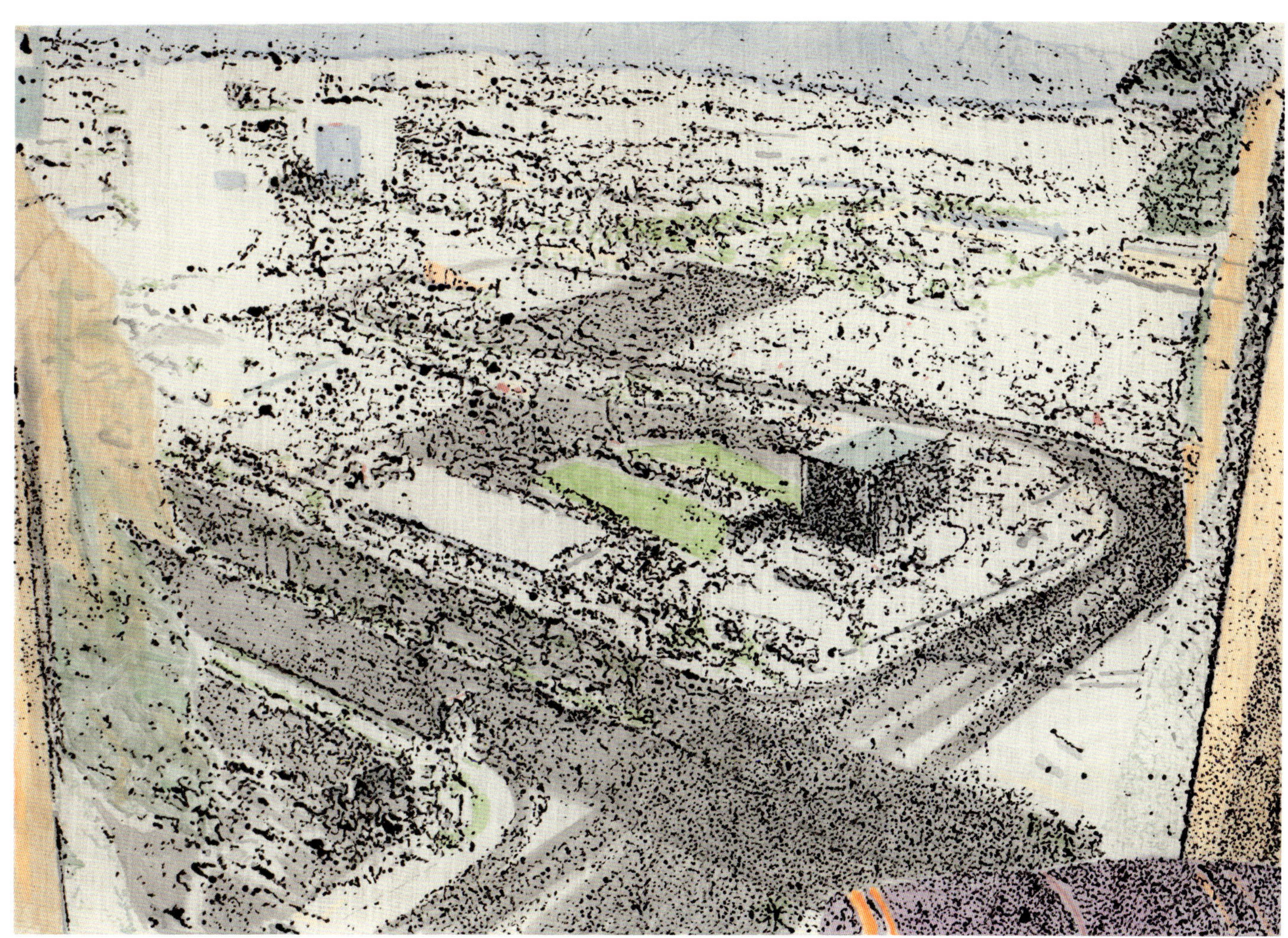

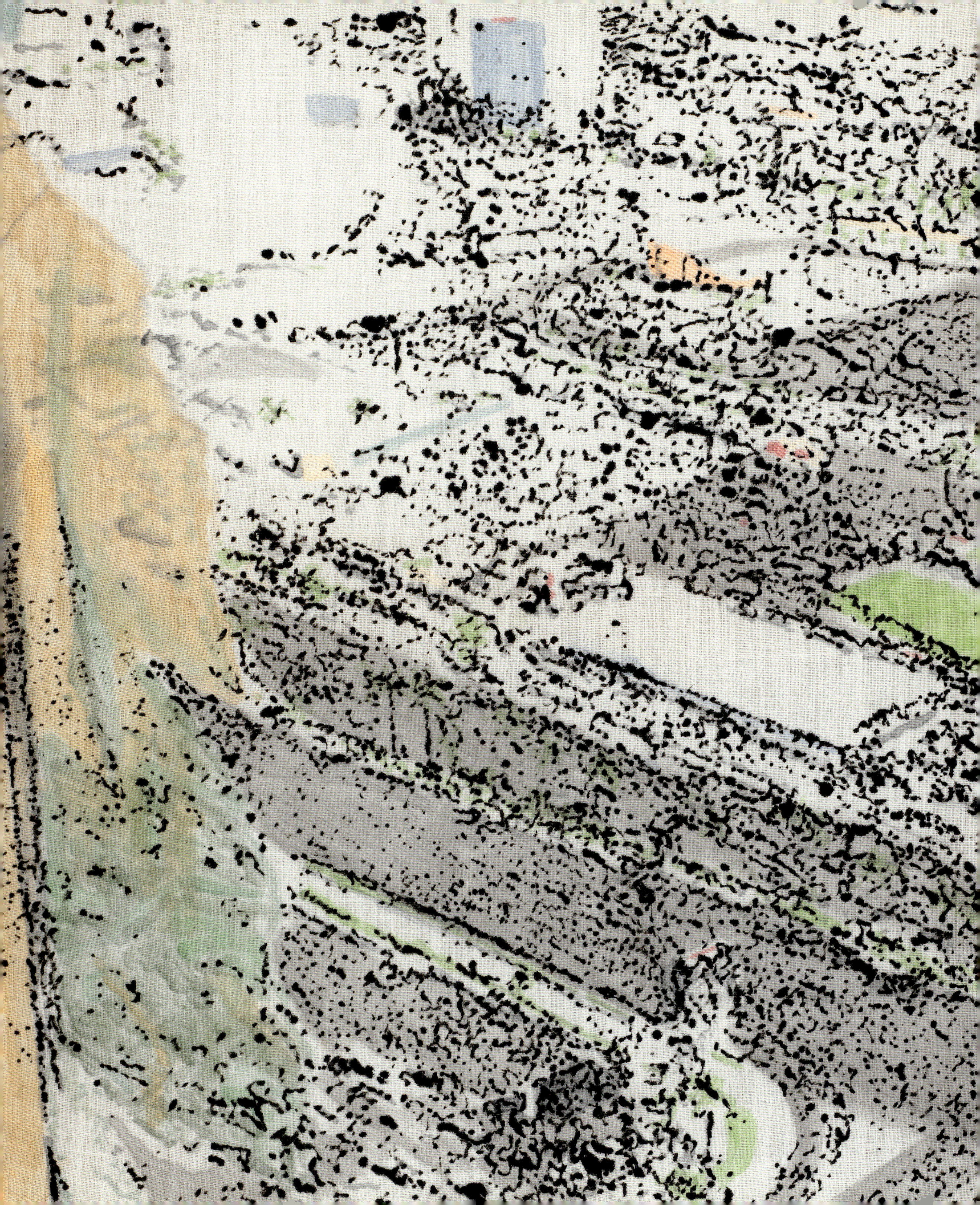

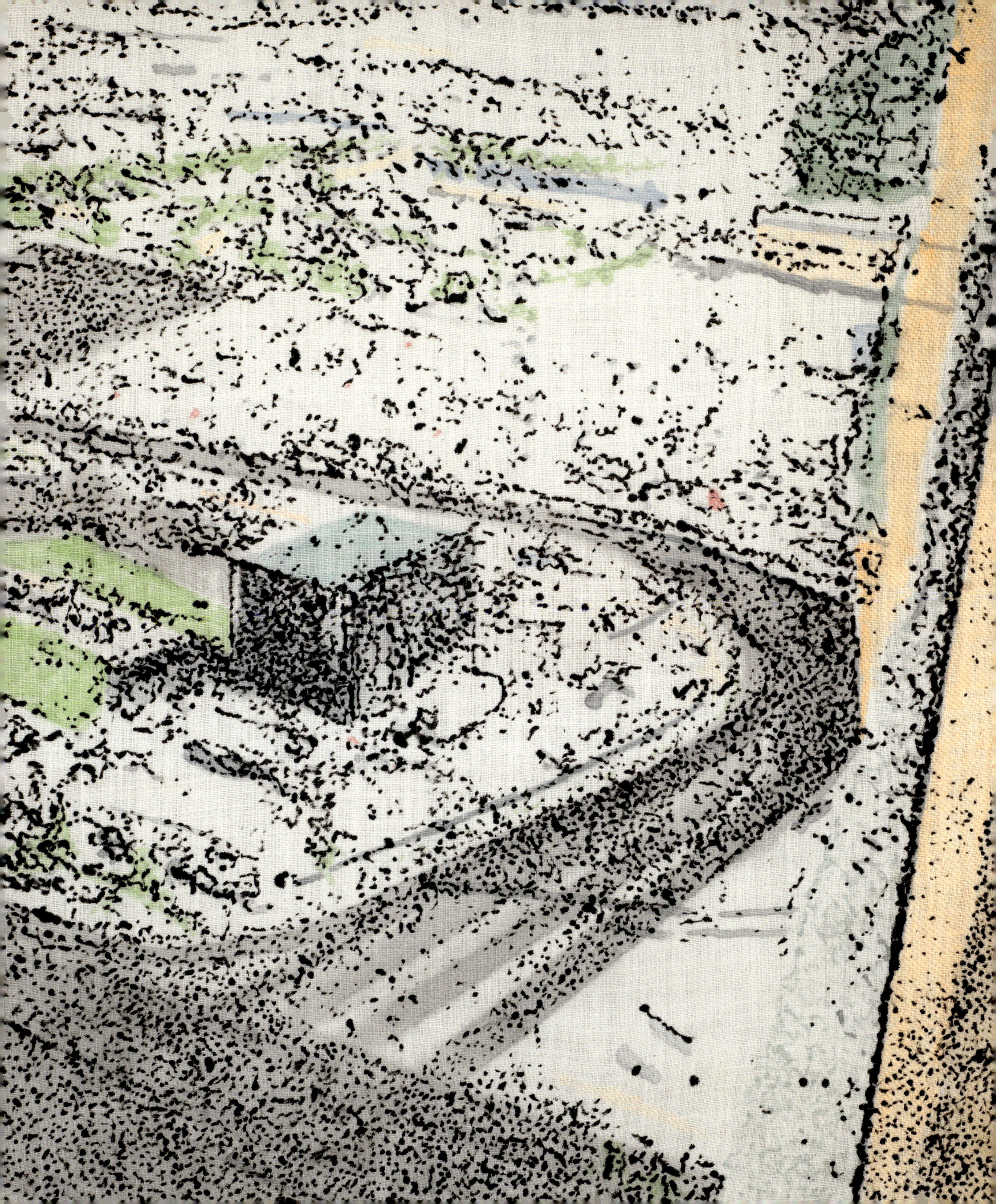

Installation views, *Nate Lowman: October 1, 2017*, David Zwirner, London, 2019

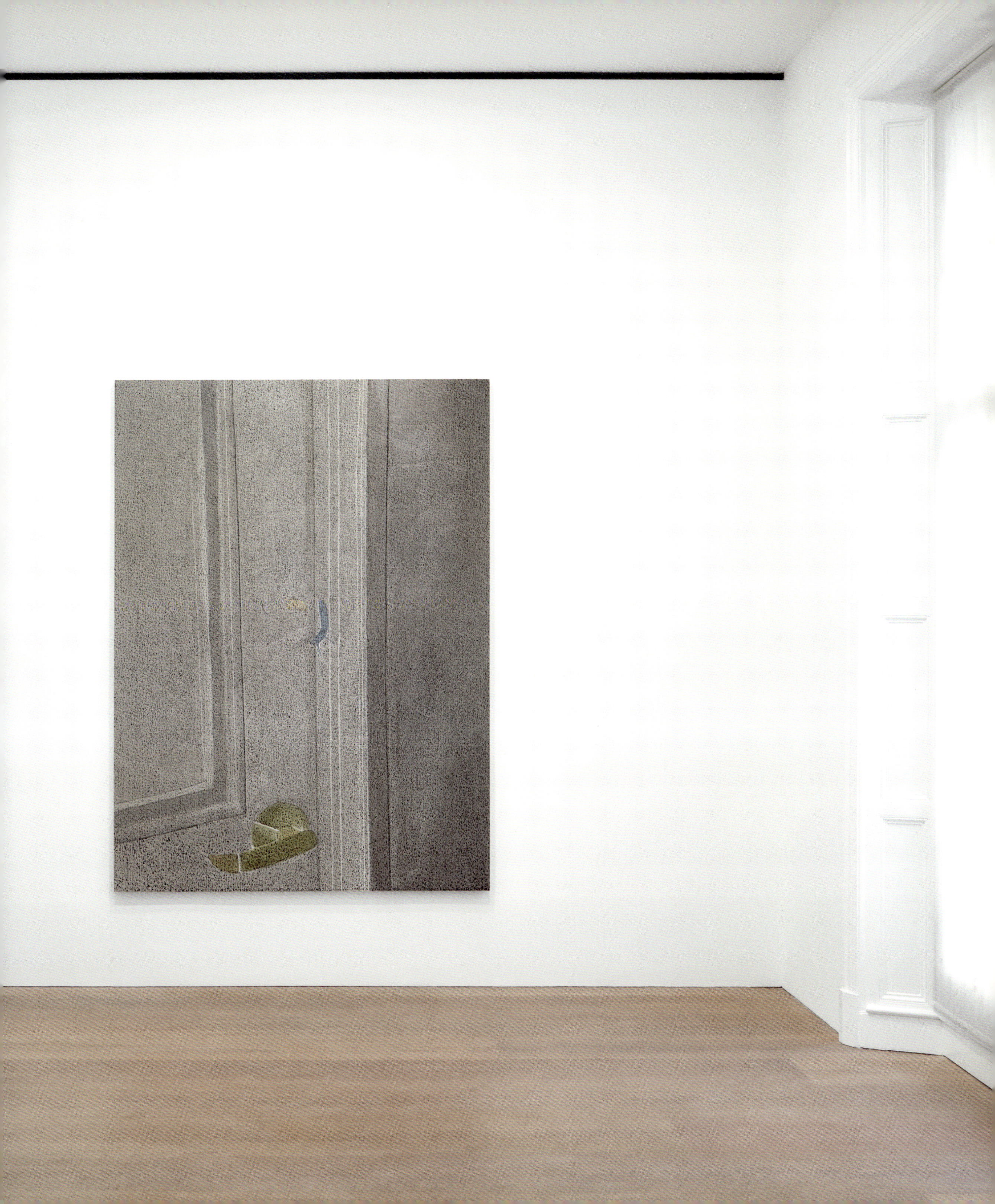

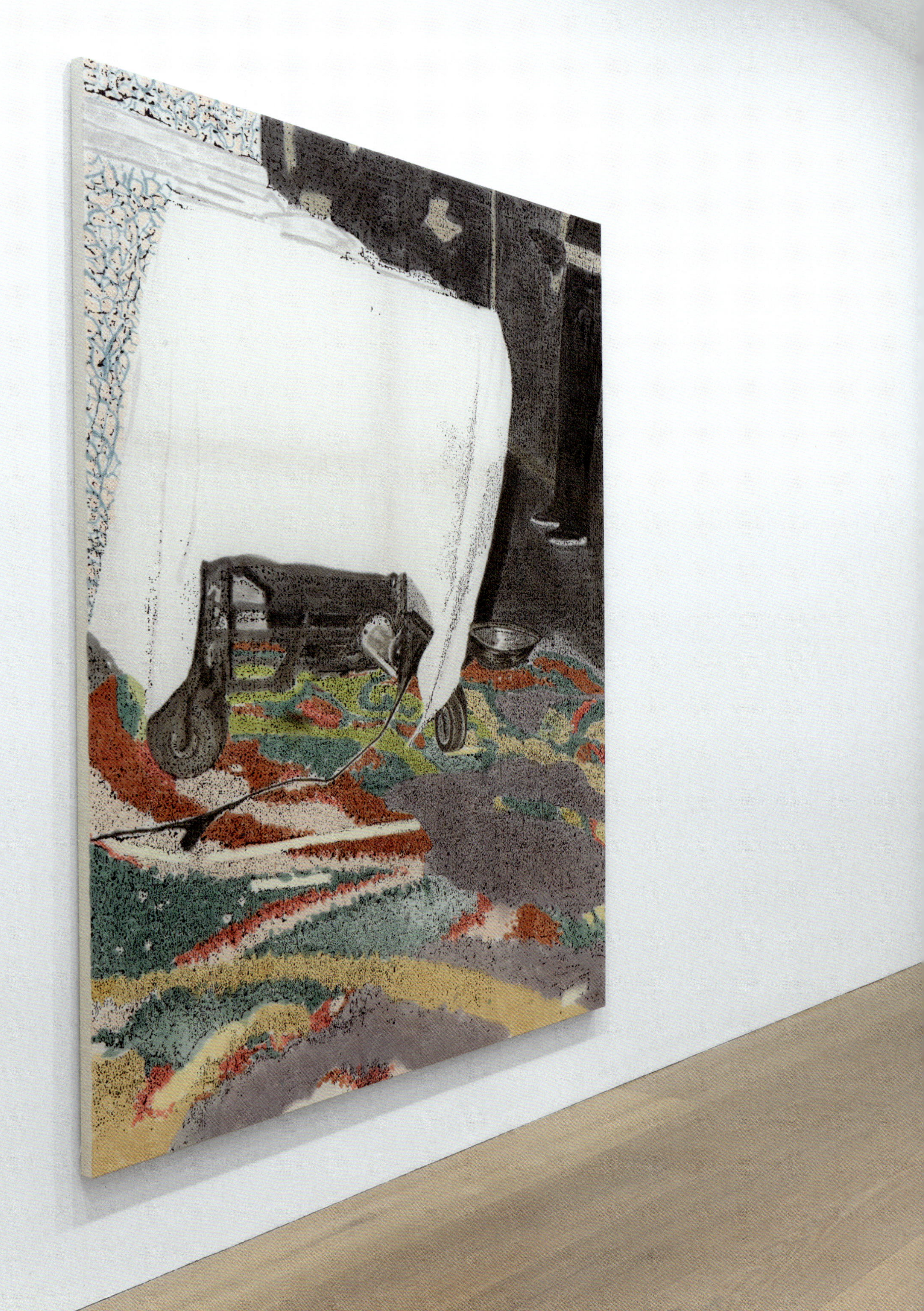

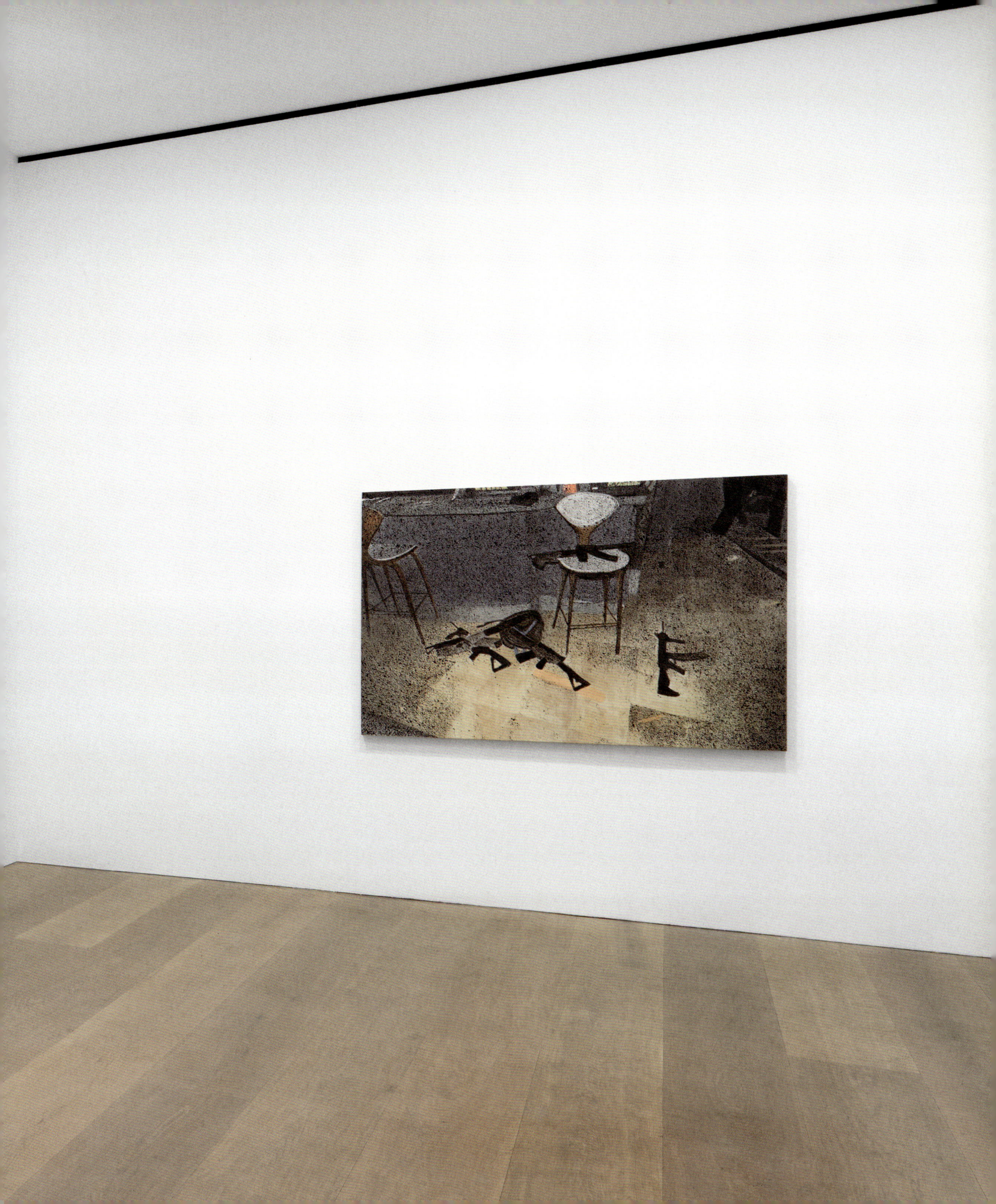

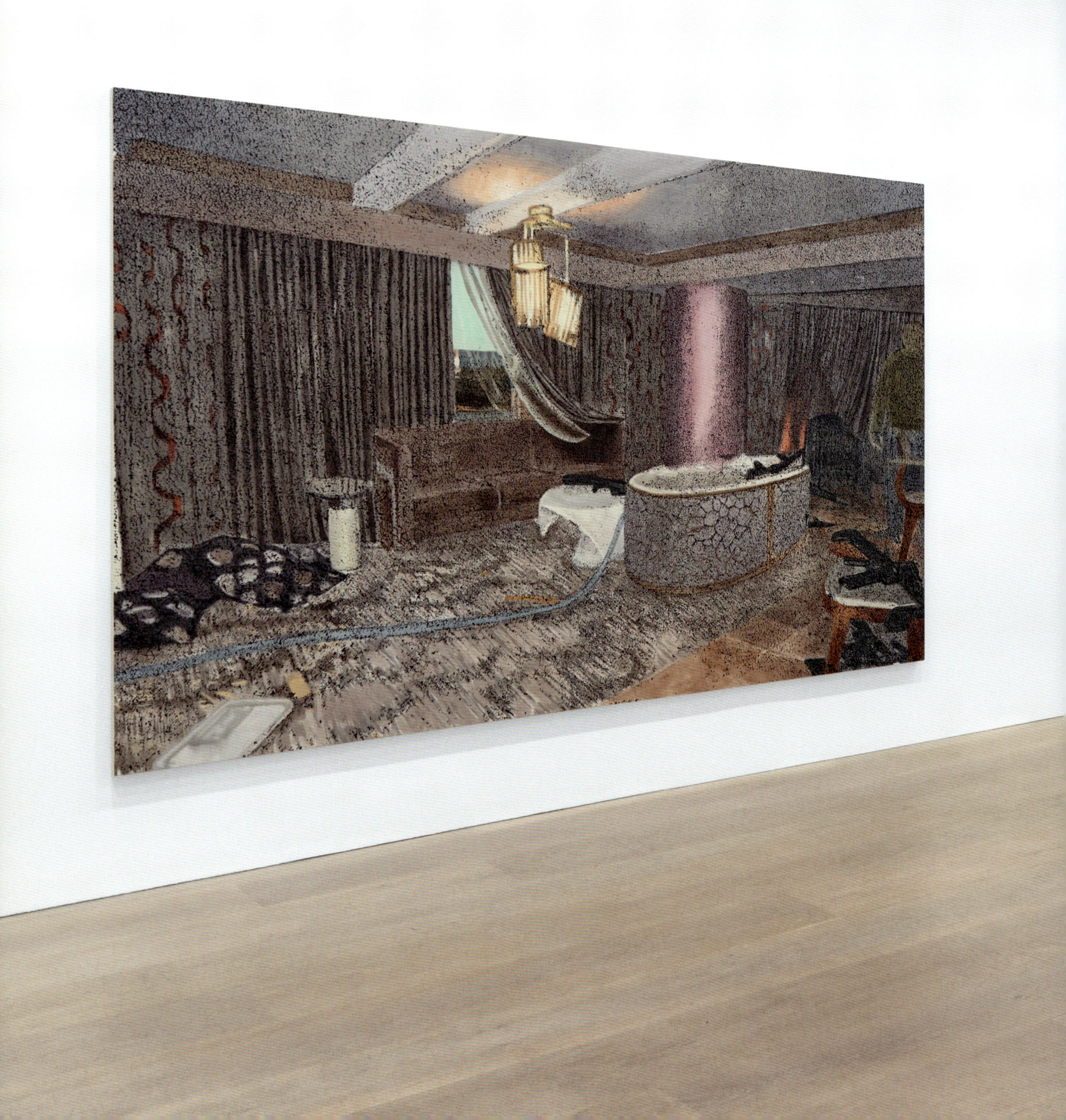

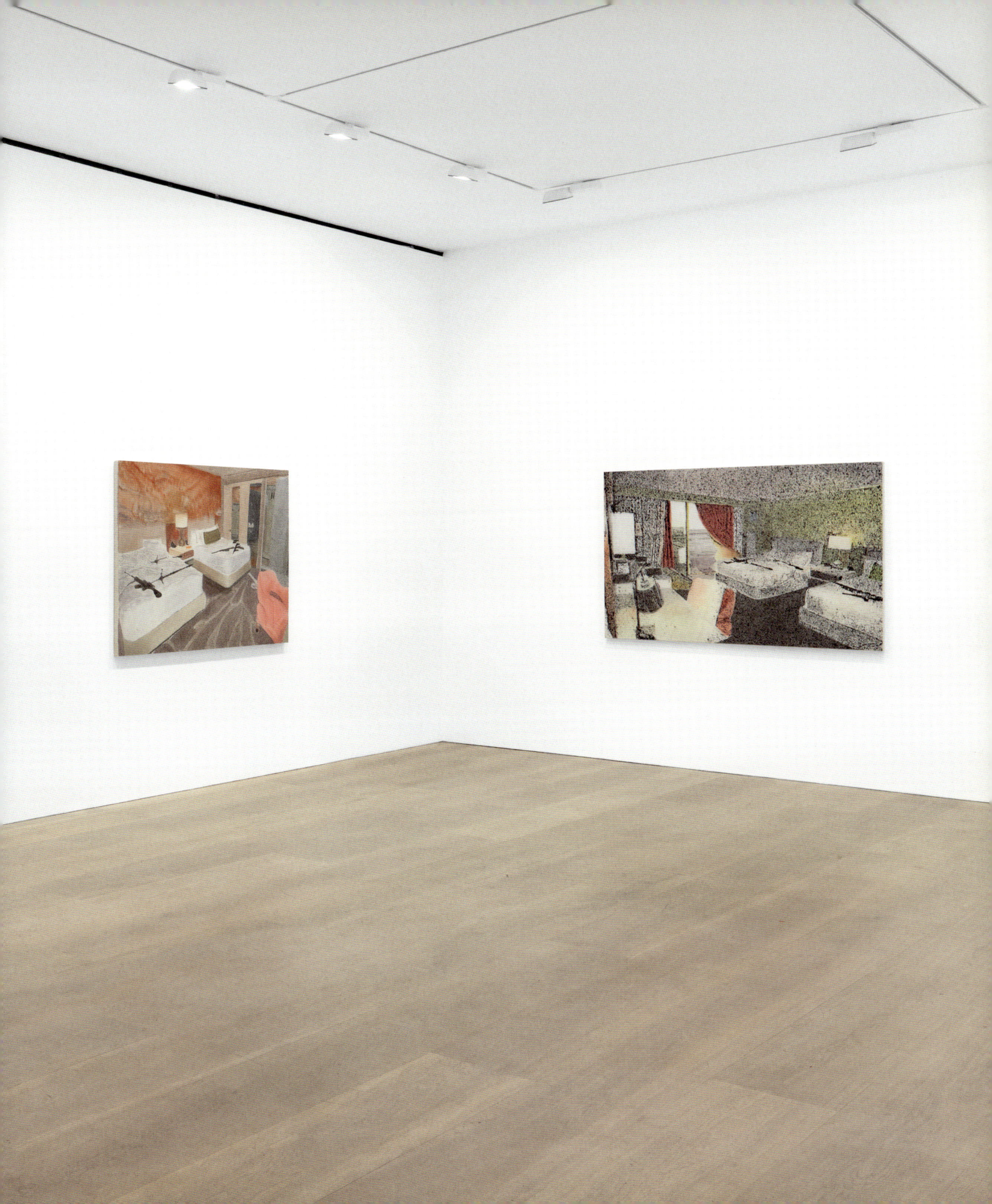

In Conversation

Nate Lowman and Andrew Woolbright

Andrew Woolbright: You've been called a child of Warhol in the past, but I think it's just as important to your development that you spent your formative years in Las Vegas, seeing the changeover that happens when you live in a city that's mostly meant to be experienced in a weekend.

Nate Lowman: Yeah, when I lived there in the eighties, Las Vegas was a small town that was also simultaneously the fastest-growing city in America. It was totally in flux—not a fixed thing. It still has a small-town vibe if you know people who live there or spend time there. In my adult life, I sometimes still meet people from Vegas and it turns out they know my dad or something. You know? It's that small, which is fascinating to me. But my relationship to Vegas is all in my memory now.

AW: Vegas already seems relevant in your earlier work, which engages with copies and ersatz languages. Some of it also just makes me think about being in a car and the drive-by simulacra produced by the Vegas strip. I still think about works like *The Wall* [2005–2012; fig. 1]. You use the tropes of the air freshener hanging on the rearview mirror and the bullet hole cartoon to engage with the ways that American culture gets filtered and passed along into inane representation.

NL: The bullet hole image is from a car decal. A friend of mine, the artist Chivas Clem, was visiting his family in Texas. He bought the decal at a truck stop there. He and I have a shared love of found imagery. I had a very extensive collection of bumper stickers, because after I moved from Vegas to Southern California—to a small town called Idyllwild—we were driving back and forth a lot. A lot of my childhood memories are of long car rides, through towns in the desert. I always found the strange poetry of bumper stickers quite intriguing, because it's the pinnacle of privatized travel. You're alone in your car with the windows rolled up—even if you're stuck in gridlock, you're still alone by yourself, shut off in what's essentially a mobile private unit. So then the one thing people choose to share in the form of a bumper sticker is that they love their cat or something. And it's actually very rare that you encounter just one bumper sticker, right? Usually you're confronted with a hundred and you're like, "Which one is me?" So I used to collect them, and a lot of my early paintings included bumper stickers collaged onto the surface of the paintings [fig. 2]. So when Chivas saw the decal, he was like, "Oh, this is so you." It took me quite a while to figure out what to do with it. The original decal is like the size of a coin.

AW: You have a way of zeroing in on subject matter that speaks to larger cultural pathologies and affects. I'm reminded of Cady Noland referring to the "American Gestalt." I think the bullet hole being reduced to a car sticker somehow gets at this underlying structure, at the gestalt—how gun violence has become synonymous with American life, while also being desired—weirdly—or romanticized, from a safe distance. The decal paintings,

Picture 27, 2019 (detail)

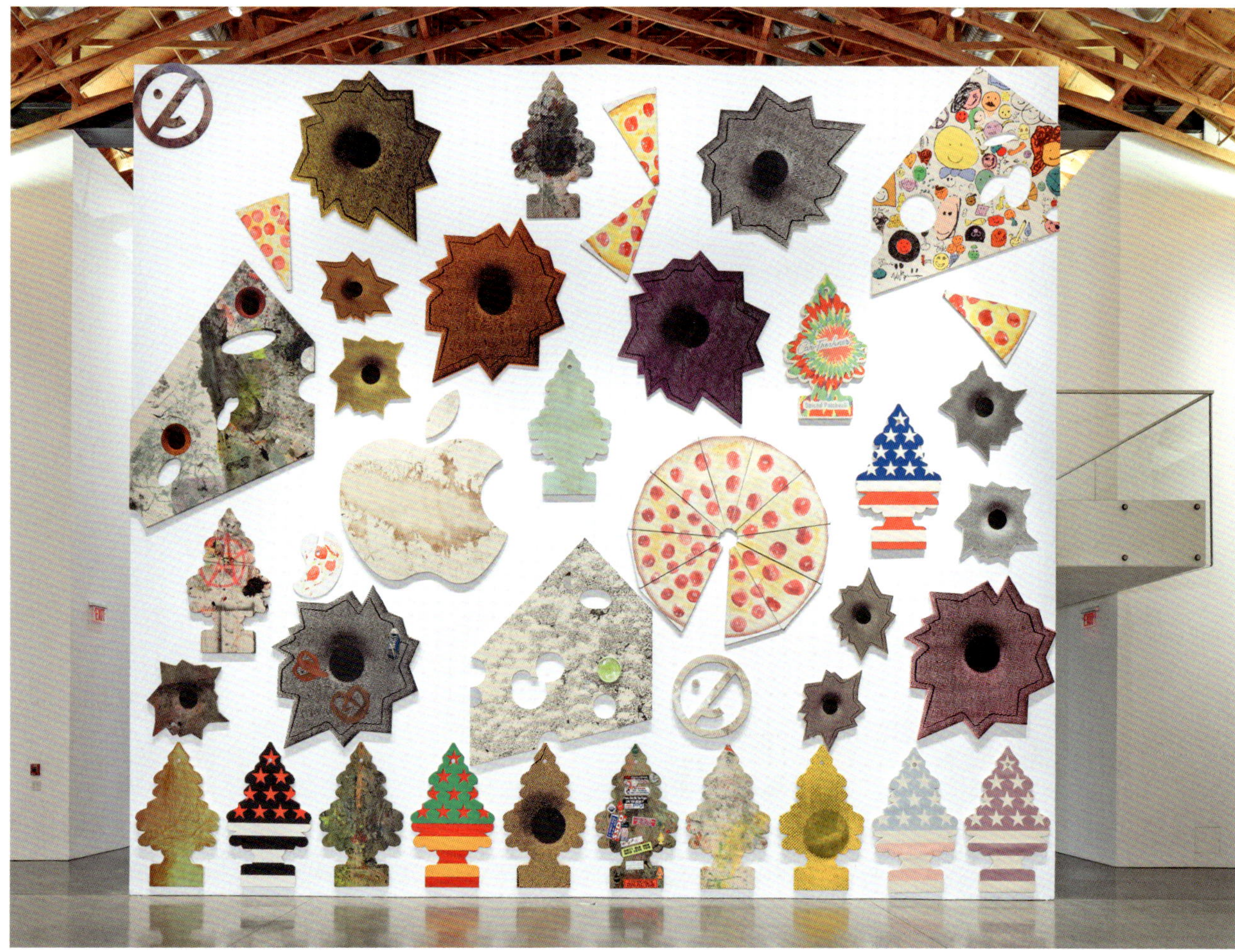

in general, engage with this doublespeak. These early works hold a tension between the image and the object. While they have a clear physical presence in space, they still evoke the way images feel on a screen. They feel compressed, or so graphic and precise that they appear hyperreal.

NL: The experience of viewing them in person is really different than looking at the work as an image. For example, if you look at the sides of the bullet hole works, you can see the cutting, folding, and gluing that goes into stretching the canvas around the wood panel [fig. 3]. I use the same decal silkscreen in other works but stretched around a flower shape. In some works, I pull the screens on top of the pieces of canvas that I leave on the floor to try to keep the floor clean while I paint other paintings.

AW: I like the speed of these. They initially feel clever, and their charm comes from feeling like you're being invited to be in on the joke. But then the joke reveals a deep channel, a fault line under our feet or an artery within us. They hit us quick but then unfurl into something slow—offering a way of looking at society from a distance that can only be achieved by being, on some level, alienated by it. This piece addresses both American violence as a societal texture while also dealing with the decal of it. I always associate these things with life in the suburbs, you know—I had friends who had this decal on their cars in farm-country Illinois. The person who puts that on their car is engaging with a complicated cycle of mediation, of self-mythology and self-parody, of fantasy and bathos.

1. *The Wall* (2005–2012), installed in *Nate Lowman: I Wanted to Be an Artist but All I Got Was This Lousy Career*, The Brant Foundation Art Study Center, Greenwich, Connecticut, 2012–2013

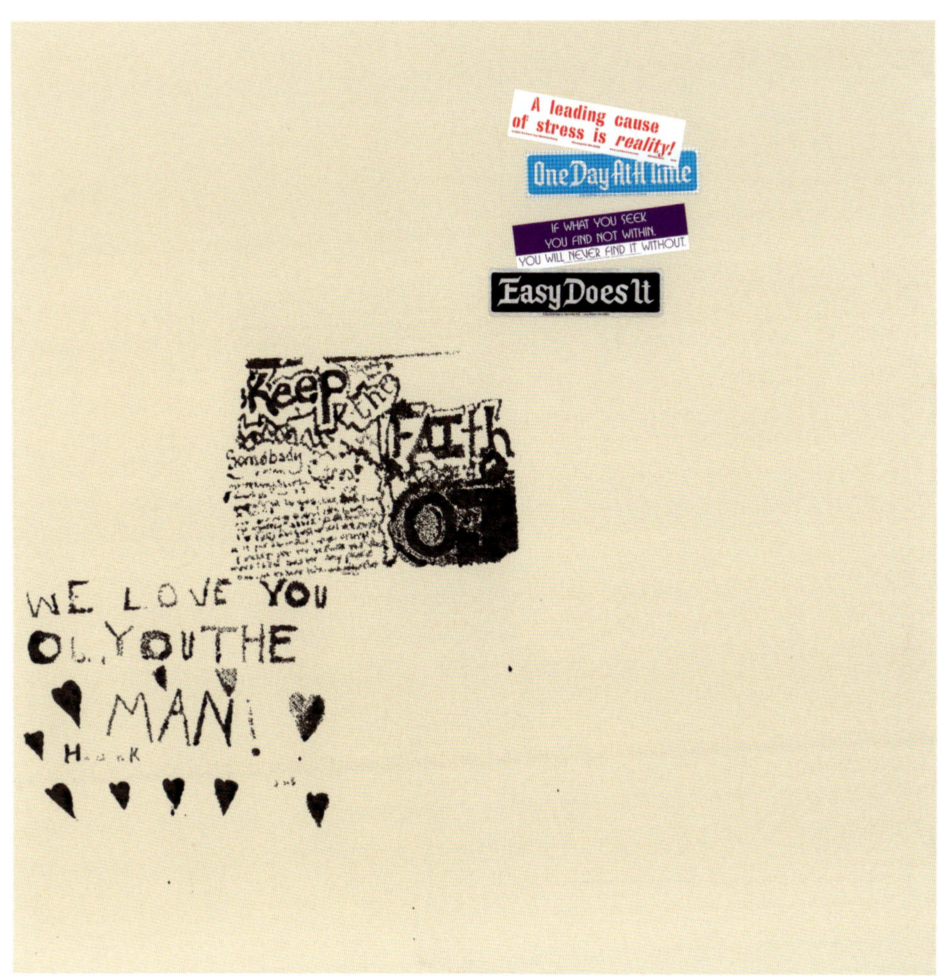

2. *Keep the Faith*, 2005. Alkyd and bumper stickers on canvas, 60 × 60 inches | 152.4 × 152.4 cm

NL: I find that because I'm from an extremely American place like Las Vegas, my artwork is totally prone to being about violence. It's the foundation of the country that we live in. It's this—

AW: Bedrock.

NL: So, for me, it's like, "Well, shit, I have to talk about violence"—the avenue naturally leads to humor, because otherwise it's too hard.

AW: The first time I ever encountered your work was in 2019, fourteen years after you made the first bullet hole paintings, when friends of mine kept sending me images of your show *October 1, 2017*, at David Zwirner in London, in which you used the crime scene images from the Las Vegas mass shooting as direct source material for the paintings [pp. 15–54; figs. 5, 6]. I'm interested to hear how you felt about this process of leaving behind irony and humor to get straight to the source.

NL: When that incident occurred in Las Vegas, I was traveling. I was in London, so it was in the middle of the afternoon when I started to find out about it. I was waiting to go to the opening of a friend's exhibition and was sitting by myself at my hotel—and you know how it is when the news alert appears on your phone unsolicited, sort of like an SOS? I was very upset. At that time, I had more family still in Vegas, so I was trying to reach them.

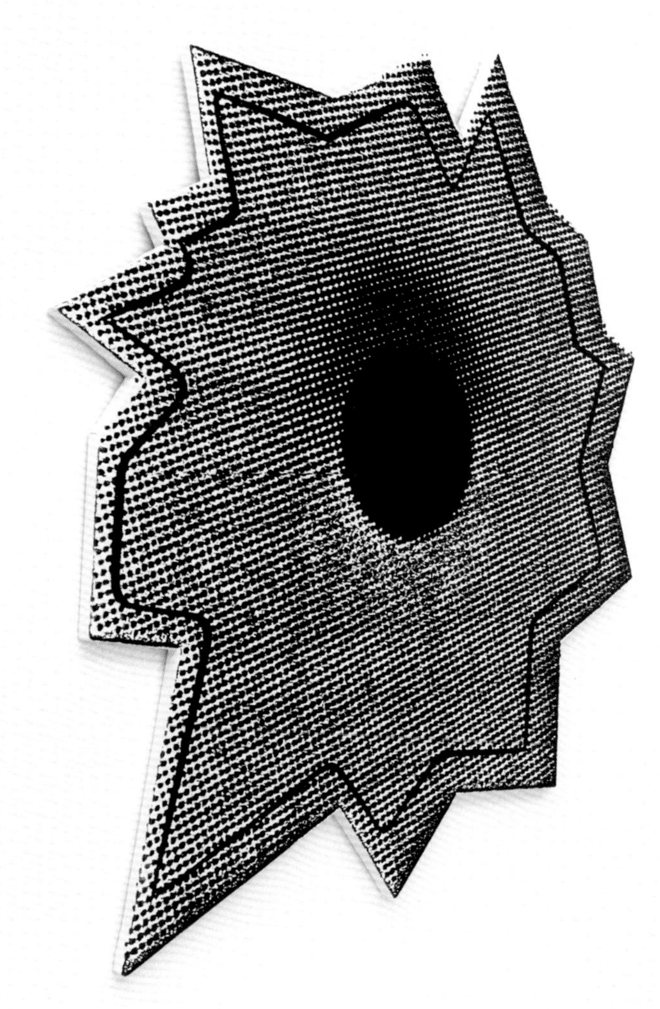

Before this, I hadn't engaged in artworks with that particular level of direct emotional connection. It would usually take many years of reflection and processing for me to work on something so close to home. But I was about to travel to Milan to look at a gallery where I was going to make an exhibition a few months later; by the time I got there, the Las Vegas shooting was all I could think about. I was staring at this beautiful room where I was supposed to make a show of new paintings, and all I could think about was the bullet hole paintings I had made. It didn't make sense though since this was twelve years after I had made them the first time. It wouldn't have made any sense for me to make them and show them again.

At that point, I started doing research about private gun collections—people who own a lot of guns and share pictures of their guns with each other in chat rooms—enthusiasts, collectors, whatever. For some reason, the images you find are often of guns laid out on a bed, as if people who own more than five guns don't also own tables. It's such a wild, striking image to see a mattress with all that heavy metal on it. So I was collecting images like that because I wanted to paint some weird intimate scenes that were also taking on the challenge of this kind of amateur photography—shots taken on a phone in order to share them with somebody [pp. 78, 79]. It only has to capture what it is, it doesn't have to be a good photo. I was interested in the challenge of this: Can you make an interesting, beautiful painting from this kind of source image?

3. Side view of *Escalade*, 2005. Silkscreen ink on canvas on wood panel, 59 × 62 inches | 149.9 × 157.5 cm

4. Installation view, *Nate Lowman: Before and After*, Aspen Art Museum, Colorado, 2017–2018. Left to right: *Bathing Tourist* (2013); *Rear End* (2017); *Bail Bonds, Temecula* (2016)

While I was working on that show, the Vegas police department published their initial report on the October 1 incident. It was six months after the fact but they were still investigating. The shooting had affected so many people that they were just still trying to find out why he did it, which they never did. But they released these images, which were also strikingly amateur in their execution. They were probably working in a great flurry and rush when they were taken that night, because of the insane magnitude of the incident. On the other hand, it's a large, historic event and you would have thought that they would bring in the forensic team to really document everything. But these were definitely just taken on somebody's phone.

AW: When I was doing research for this talk, I looked up the word "forensic." I was surprised to find that its etymology comes from the word "forum," suggesting that sites of trauma become public spaces of interpretation. Though these crime scene photos were taken quickly, many of us ended up pouring over them for months and months trying to find the details. It became a semi-public space in which we were all trying to find the meaning in all of this. But through your hand and the slowness you're able to get through painting, I was able to see things in your works that I had missed when I saw the report.

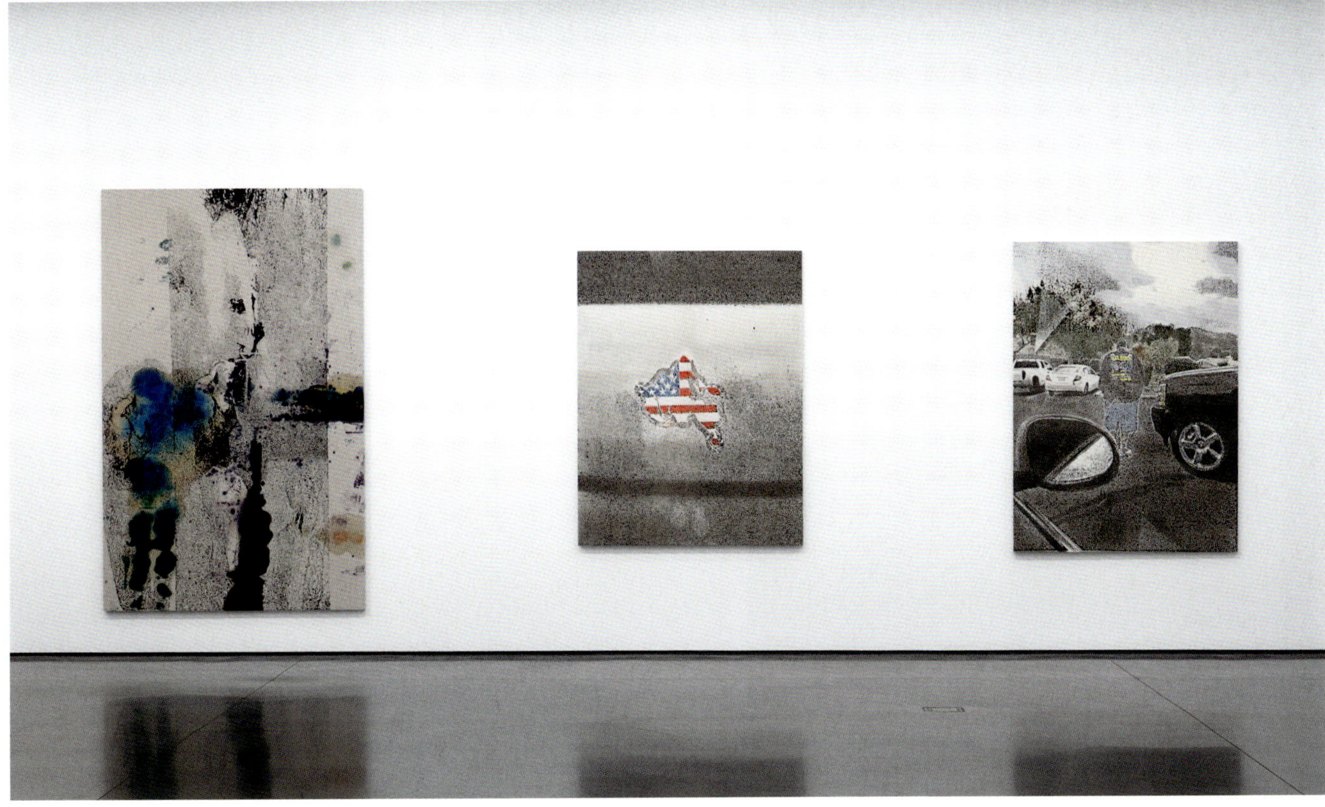

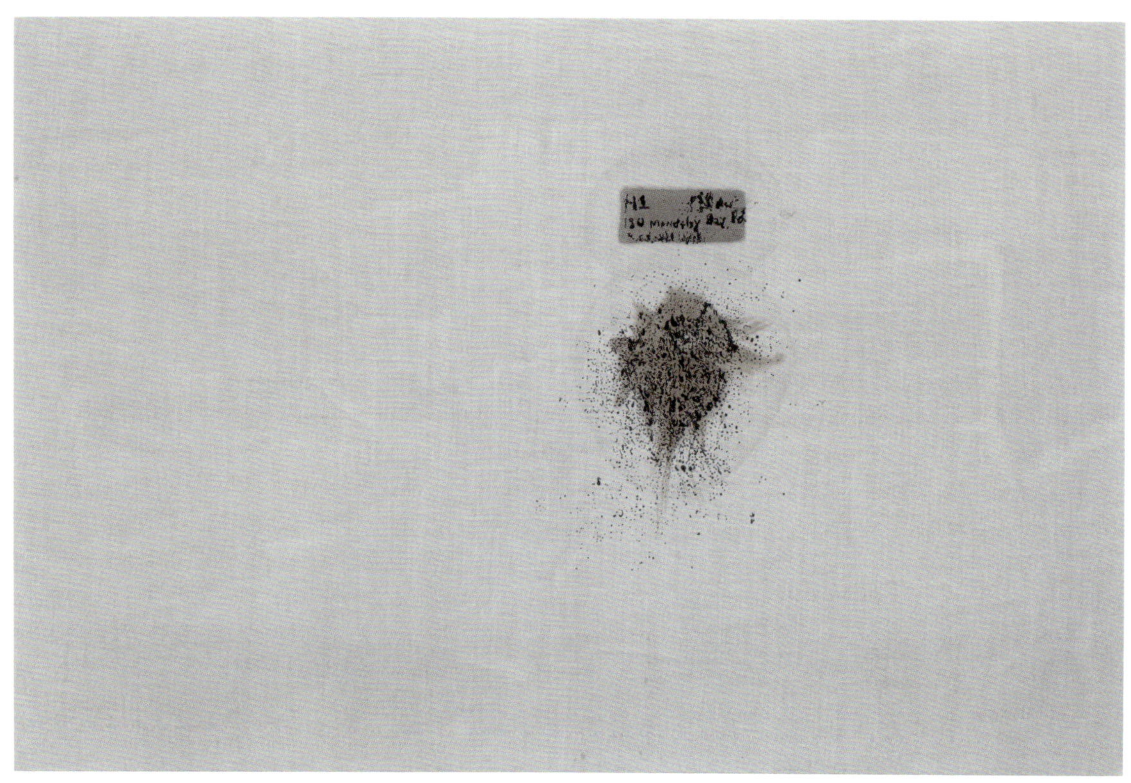

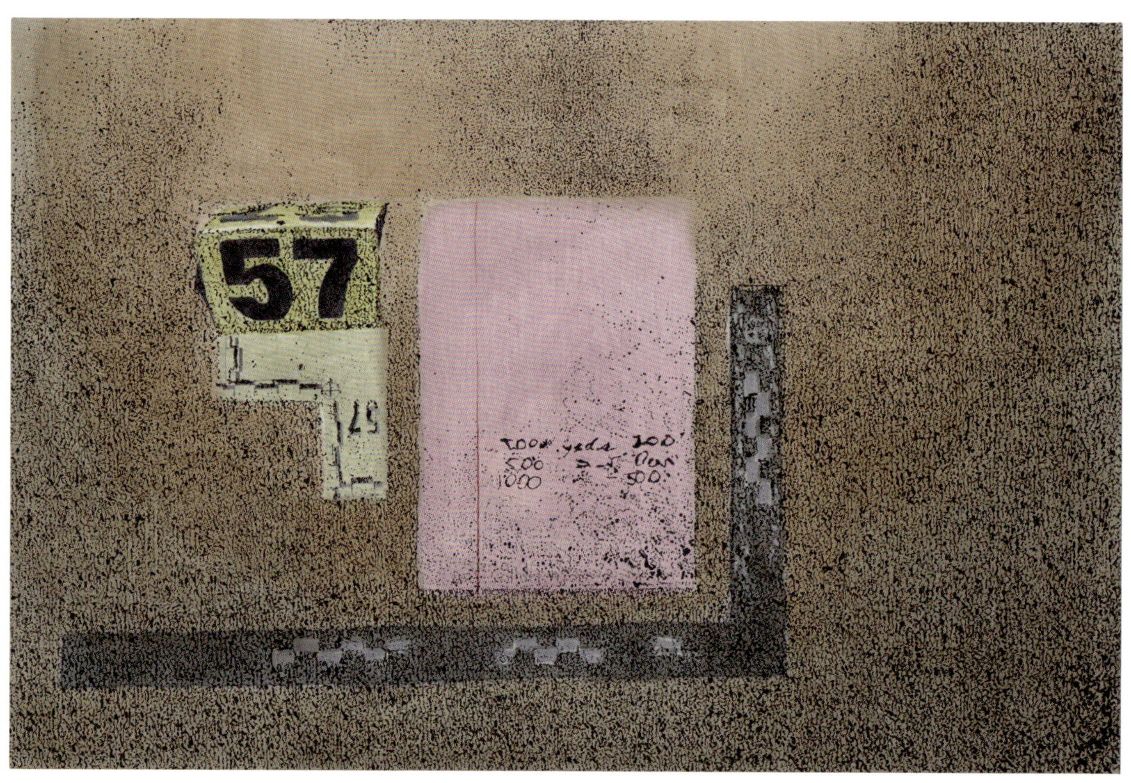
57

NL: Right. There's a scale shift and then it's like a treasure hunt—all this stuff comes out. You discover things—like this guy in black with the glove on [in *Picture 4*, 2018; p. 17], I didn't really see him in the original image before I painted him.

I found that the light is so different in every image. He had broken the window, so there's all the designed interior lighting of this giant, fancy Vegas suite mixed with this blue daylight, the desert sunshine. And the light changes every few feet, so each painting has a totally complex and unreal kind of atmospheric shift within it. Painting all the different textures of the wallpaper and the carpet and then that light was a totally unique experience. Spending all this time with this horrible imagery also meant learning to enjoy the weirdness of painting these insane elements, which became the only way to deal with doing it.

This painting with the tablecloth [*Picture 4*] is from the first image I saw. I was sitting around in the middle of the night literally watching paint dry, waiting to work on something, and I noticed that the Vegas police department had published this thing. I knew within like half of one second that I was going to paint that image.

AW: Wow.

NL: At first I had a lot of mental inertia, thinking, "I probably shouldn't do that," or "Do I really want to do that?" but I already knew that I was going to do it. It felt completely inevitable. I'm not saying it felt great either. I was just like, "Fuck, I've got to paint this now." You know? So in this first painting what you see there is a cord on the floor, and on top of that room service tray, there was a camera that was recording who was coming and going in the hallway so that the guy could see. To me it was just such a quintessential crime scene image—the white light of the tablecloth takes up maybe 20 percent of the painting. That's a really unpainted painting.

AW: You once told me that you don't necessarily identify as a painter, that you have a conceptual education. It reminded me of how Josephine Halvorson says, "To this day, I don't think of myself as a painter. I do think of the painting as a kind of record of the time spent with this thing in its environment. How do you make the conditions to have a really long uninterrupted time with something? . . . I would never spend twelve hours just standing in front of something. But I do because of painting." There's this incredible force to your Las Vegas paintings—this impact that comes from your commitment to spending time with the crime scene images. I think of Roberto Bolaño's model of the artist as a detective. He talks about how the artist, just like the detective, isn't necessarily the smartest or most gifted individual in society, they are simply the ones who can tolerate the crime scene longer than anyone else. You're not flinching. You're staying with these images long enough to paint them, which means that you're really considering everything within each image. It's an idea of painting that is shared by artists like [Gerhard] Richter and [Luc] Tuymans,

5. *Picture 27*, 2019. Oil and alkyd on linen, 38¼ × 58¾ inches | 97.2 × 149.2 cm

6. *Picture 15*, 2019. Oil and alkyd on linen, 36⅛ × 55 inches | 91.8 × 139.7 cm

who feel compelled to engage with cultural trauma. I can only imagine how challenging it was to make these paintings and stay with this subject matter.

NL: Yeah, I work with a handful of studio assistants and I don't know if it was good for us to share that journey or not, you know what I mean? It's funny that you brought up Luc Tuymans. Right before the pandemic started, he had a conversation with Helen Molesworth at the Morgan Library and she more or less said, "I think of you as a Pictures Generation person who just happens to be a really good painter." Obviously he's a great painter, but the framework is about being image-based—the collection, the editing, and the fact that the images come from the world around the artist. You know, not necessarily from within.

AW: This really comes across for me in your current show, *Let's Go*. The hurricane paintings [pp. 115–155; figs. 22, 23] deal with images, as well as with this idea of recording something that is cataclysmic yet also in danger of being forgotten after it is over. Your gesture, your brushwork borders on pointillism in these paintings. There are these really stunning calligraphic marks. The paintings incorporate and store so many techniques that are familiar from different types of abstract painting, but you're using the marks to keep us engaged. It's an interesting conceptual practice that employs pastiche so that we linger, so that we look longer. We can see these virtuosic marks, the kind of gestures associated with painters like Joan Mitchell, but now they make us think about meteorology and the visual expressions of data. We have to consider how Doppler radar images quantify the catastrophic event of a hurricane through color; and then how the hurricane itself is a metonym of climate collapse. It's a really incredible trick.

NL: I realized recently that one of my goals—unknowingly at first, when I was younger—is to merge the dominant expressive languages of painting, especially American painting. Combining the wild abstraction—the pleasurable uses of paint, such as gesture, color, and articulations—with the sort of humorous, tight industrial component of pop depiction at the other end of the spectrum [figs. 7–10]. I guess this whole time I was just trying to do both of those things at once because I like them both. To me, when two languages are so far apart, they essentially become the same, you know? Because they occupy an end. I figured out that I was trying to do this by copying someone else's painting. I was copying a painting by [Willem] de Kooning [figs. 8, 9]. So I was doing his marks. Copying them and then painting a printed image of that same painting on top of the thing. Then I did it many, many more times, so there are variations, but it's like a handmade mass production. The bullet hole paintings are the only time I really use silkscreen. All the rest of the paintings—all the dots and little marks on these—are done by hand, but the marks sink into the material so that you don't see the gesture of my hand reflected in a brushstroke, because it's absorbed. I didn't want people to get distracted by my own fingerprints on top

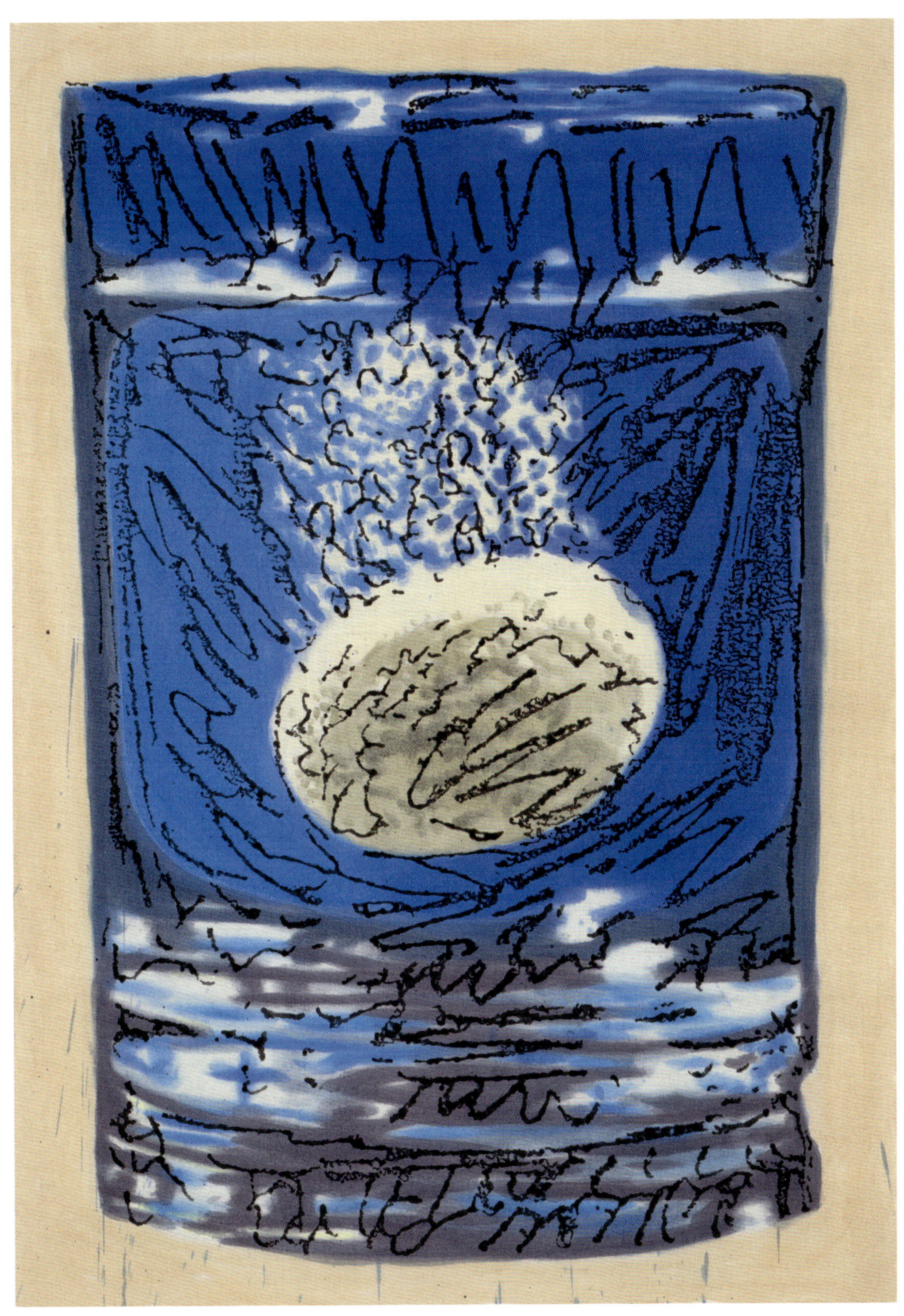

7. *Kill the Pain No. 2*, 2021. Oil and alkyd on linen,
58⅛ × 41⅝ inches | 147.6 × 105.7 cm

of the marks. It's like you know someone painted it, but the evidence has been withdrawn. I like that because it confuses people, and when people are confused, they look longer.

AW: Cecily Brown talks about how we can kind of store other artists in our mind. That when we copy a mark or a gesture by another person, when we do it four or five times, we no longer have to think about it. We've just kind of taken that muscle memory or hand memory and made it our own. [David] Hockney does the same thing—he keeps sketchbooks of "French marks" and different kinds of marks. You've found a parallel between the storage system of your archive and the way that the painting itself becomes a storage system of marks.

NL: I like to try to do things that probably aren't going to come out right with painting. Like these images of hurricanes, you would never paint with these colors in these combinations. Some of these colors you might not even want to paint in the first place. They're completely crazy. It's similar to that amateur shitty photo thing—I'm wondering, if you examine imagery through a painting process, can it be interesting? Can it be beautiful? When I started painting these images, I really thought that it was fifty-fifty. There were some that felt like disasters and others that came out, that felt like, "Oh my gosh, that was so easy." [*Laughs.*]

AW: How do you feel about the paintings now and the difficulty of the process?

NL: Having this exhibition felt like a great opportunity because moving them out of the studio and into this beautiful room, and being able to look at them all at the same time, provides a very unique experience. Even though they're all the same, right? They're all this same sort of approximation. We understand what the hurricane imagery is because we've all been experiencing it. It's probably not real, but we all know what it means and agree upon it somehow.

AW: The conditions of the images are speed and exhaustion; for me it connects to your interest in iPhone crime scene photos and bumper stickers. These images aren't valued for formal qualities; they are just a medium to illustrate information. They pose themselves as literal events, without any subtext to them, and once we digest them, once the event that they represent has passed, we don't feel the need to revisit them. Each Doppler radar image is replaced by an update that makes it irrelevant; you recognize that since they project themselves as objective, they reveal ideology.

NL: When I embarked on this series, I thought that I would eventually learn what all the colors meant, seeking out the images and finding the ones that I wanted to paint. But then I realized I was purposefully avoiding learning what the colors meant in terms of the

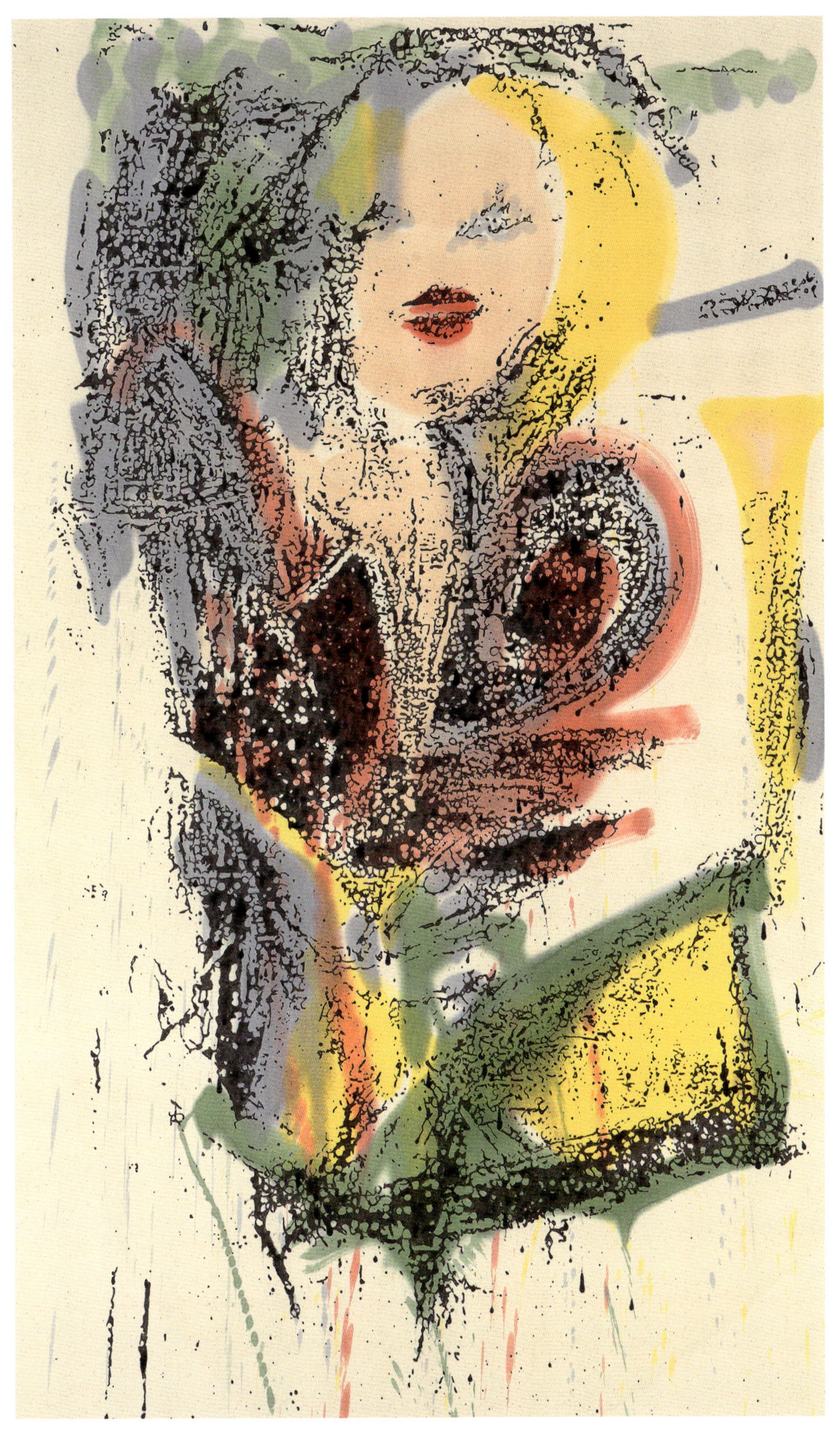

8. *Trash Landing Marilyn #4*, 2011. Oil and alkyd on canvas, 74 × 44 inches | 188 × 111.8 cm

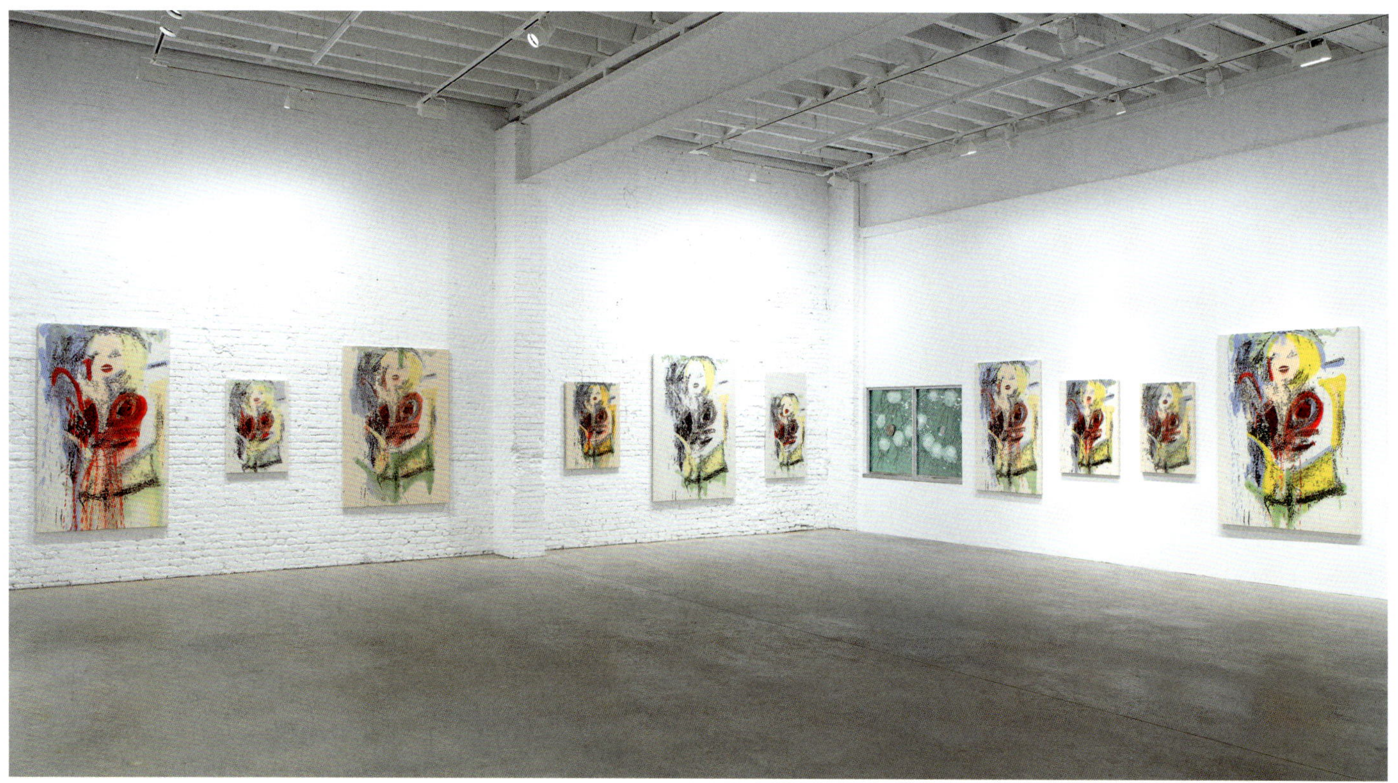

qualities of the storm—then I wondered, why do I not want to know this? Because it's obviously interesting. I realized that knowing the meaning of some of those hurricane colors would add a layer of responsibility that would have been totally distracting for me. I still don't know what any of the colors in these paintings mean.

AW: There are so many alkyd marks—the black calligraphic markings—and yet they don't become repetitive. Each mark is slightly different. There's a primacy to everything you're laying down. How does it feel when you're making these? How long are you able to spend on them at a time—does it become a meditative process? Does it become a material thing? Or do your eyes start to lose focus enough that you have to step away?

NL: On the good days you get great rhythm—it's awesome. I also have assistants who help me paint the dots, because if I painted all the dots, these paintings would not exist. It takes a lot of time to do. They are massive, 90 by 126 inches. When we embarked on this one [*Irma* (2022), p. 139], I wasn't sure that it was going to work out because I didn't have that much experience painting with those grayscale colors. I thought I was in over my head—just from an ability standpoint—and all those darker pink parts had to land in exactly the right place. There's this whole vast area in the center of the painting that has very few of the alkyd marks. This particular image was one of the first ones to introduce that pink color—lucky me, because pink's my favorite color. It was just so joyous to have a color that I like among all these insane, bright colors that don't go together.

AW: One thing that's consistent across your work is how the collection and archiving of images forms relationships amongst the images, from one to the next. While narrative might have a role within your work, it comes from each image implying that it has a *before* and *after*. It comes from each image suggesting it's part of a sequence.

NL: Yeah. Narrative has always been a central part of my practice. Well, it's just *engagement* with narrative. Narrative itself is not something I practice. As you say, it comes out of collecting and archiving imagery and, say, re-proposing it, whether it's in painting or any other kind of image-making—using other technologies. Re-presenting imagery always proposes alternate narratives for all of us. These hurricane paintings probably have less to do with narrative in and of itself than they do with the fluctuating historical narrative that they signify and stand for, which, like I said, remains unfixed.

AW: There's a meme or a tweet I saw that's someone saying, "The wind is shaking the windows of our apartment, and my husband is looking up 'wind' on Wikipedia." Staying informed has become a coping strategy; translating a natural event into language is a way for us to reduce it to something we can comprehend and have more control over. What does it mean to type the word "hurricane" into Google while the real thing approaches? And then, once it passes, we drop it and move on. A lot of the images you've addressed across your practice have this dramatic sense of temporality. They were the most important images in the world to us, for a time, making everything else recede, but then they become completely meaningless. You're trying to see if something happens when you bring them back from attention exile.

NL: Yeah. I used to call it the anti-amnesia machine. I turned to the imagery of hurricanes for the first time in 2011 because I was doing a show here in New York and the exhibition was a suite of paintings of moments of disasters and disaster landscapes—one was of that volcano that erupted in Iceland that suspended all air travel for a while [*Volcano (Iceland)* (2011); pp. 72–73]. There were various historical images and I also really wanted to make a landscape painting that had to do with Hurricane Katrina. It was impossible for me to approach the actual documentation—it was too vast, and I didn't have any personal criteria for how to engage with any of those images. It occurred to me to try to paint the hurricane graphic [*We Are Seeing People We Didn't Know Exist* (2011); p. 115].

When you put something into the language of oil paint, it takes a very broad step; painting is a place where people go to look and think. It's invigorating and/or disarming, but when you hang a painting on the wall, the painting actually negates the wall; where there was a wall, there's now a place that you can go and look. The level of abstraction that that storm graphic held became the avenue for me to engage with that historical moment. It was also a challenge from a technical artistic standpoint—like, "Can I paint that?" Then after the first Katrina painting it was six years before I returned to paint hurricane imagery again. It had started out as this one isolated way of approaching an historic event, but in 2017 there were three particularly devastating hurricanes almost all at once—Harvey, Irma, and Maria—so I got interested again. The overwhelming magnitude of that year just swept me back into it, and I started looking at the imagery and remembering the weird journey it was to paint that first graphic. I wanted to see if it would be interesting to pursue these new ones.

9. Installation view, *Nate Lowman: Trash Landing*, Maccarone, New York, 2011

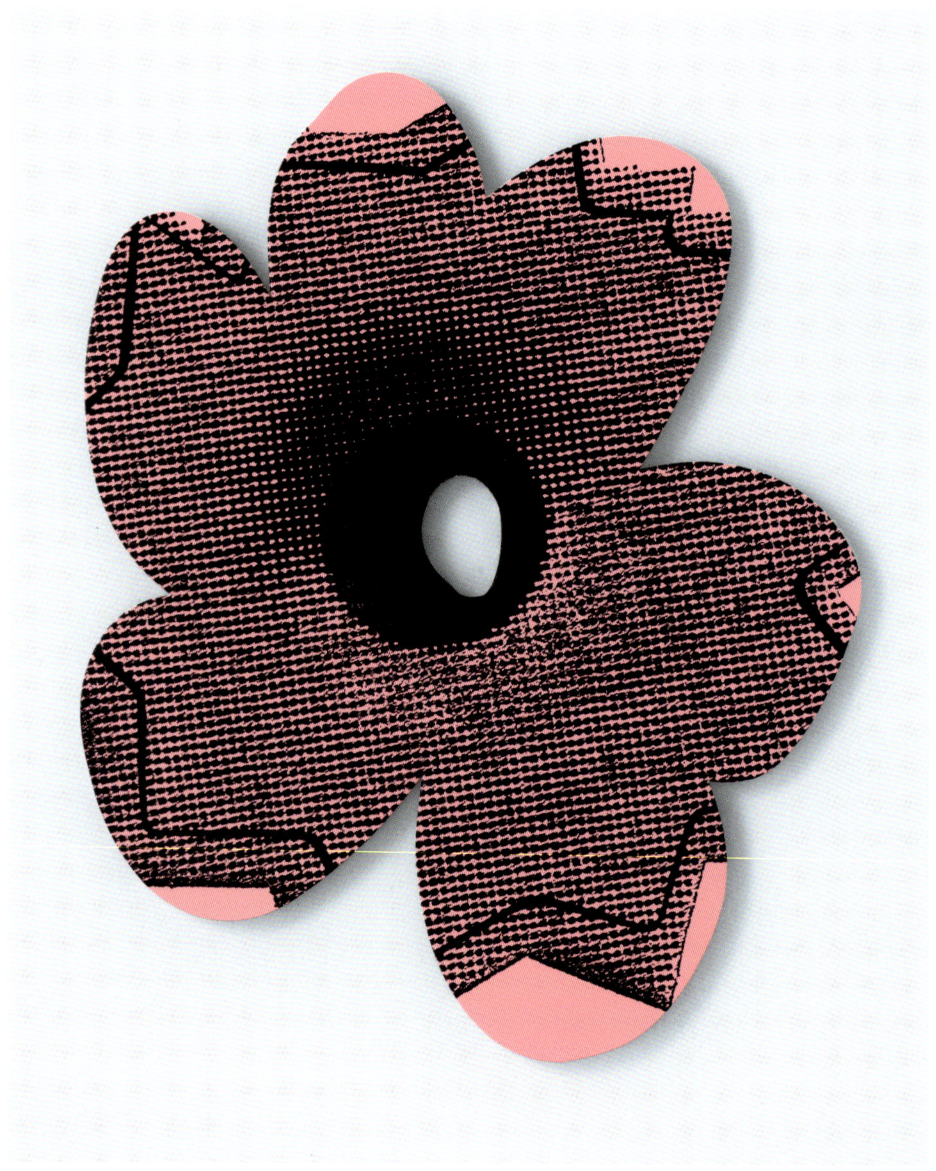

10. *Carpel/Void (Pink No. 2)*, 2021.
Oil and alkyd on linen on wood panel,
56 ¾ × 47 ½ inches | 144.1 × 120.7 cm

AW: In your exhibition at Zwirner, there is a group of works in a side room, smaller oil paintings on watercolor paper [pp. 148–151]. For me, the scale shift is really important because you're reducing and scaling down. In *Irma Paper* [2022; p. 148], the scale of the black mark, done in oil rather than alkyd, is approximately the same as in the larger paintings, but then the hurricane image itself is smaller.

NL: I needed a new solution for these smaller ones because if I were to paint those little dots over it, they would obliterate the image; the marks would have had to be excruciatingly miniscule. The black marks come from a little drawing I made of each storm. These small oils were fun for me. They aren't studies for the bigger paintings. I did them afterward, using the leftover paint. The paper I used is made for oil paint, so it has this quality that, like the linen that I use for the big paintings, absorbs the paint; the paint has so much solvent mixed with it that the solvent instantly spreads, pools out. The paper is almost like the equivalent of a semi-primed surface. It's very cool. It absorbs a little bit, but you can just glide and keep going, it doesn't trap the solvent, which then repels the paint that you're trying to put on next. So I can paint these little ones all at once. When I was finalizing the exhibition, I would set aside six hours to try to do one in one sitting. It was really joyous to redo the larger painting in an intimate scale, all at once, because it was a totally new way of processing the same experience. The large ones are a real undertaking.

AW: Also in that gallery is a second Hurricane Sandy painting, this time on a flower-shaped canvas [*Sandy Poppy* (2022); fig. 23]. You've been making these flower-shaped works for years, as far back as 2005, when you first transformed the bullet hole bumper sticker into a flower. At first those works contained a certain amount of humor, but with this recent work there's little or no humor. As you mature as an artist, there seems to be more subtlety in your choice of subject matter. It's carefully directing us to something we are speeding by: this moment where the bullet hole becomes the flower, which in turn becomes the radar or meteorological depiction of the hurricane. The visual language continues to shift; but each time the shape morphs, it keeps the charge of what it came from. The flower keeps the radar, which keeps the forensic, which keeps the impact of the bullet hole.

NL: This for me was one hundred percent just a playful experiment. I was trying to figure out a narrative counterpoint for all these storm paintings. I'd made a handful of paintings with this poppy-flower shape. I had this canvas unpainted and stretched in the studio; it was hanging on the wall unpainted next to the desk where I sit when I think. I was in the middle of painting a larger version with this same storm graphic of Hurricane Sandy and I decided to do a Sandy poppy. I was like, "What if it's fun?" There was so much control involved in making these paintings. I'm matching the color of the original thing, matching all of the marks, rendering something as closely as I can, following a course. So it was interesting just to do something off that course, with no resolute, meaningful goal either . . . because the poppy has nothing to do with a hurricane. It's not even a flower that grows where hurricanes happen. It's a totally idiosyncratic shape for the image to be transposed on and that felt totally dangerous, in a fun way, for me.

This conversation took place on March 29, 2022, as an online event hosted by *The Brooklyn Rail*.

Selected Works, 2011–2021

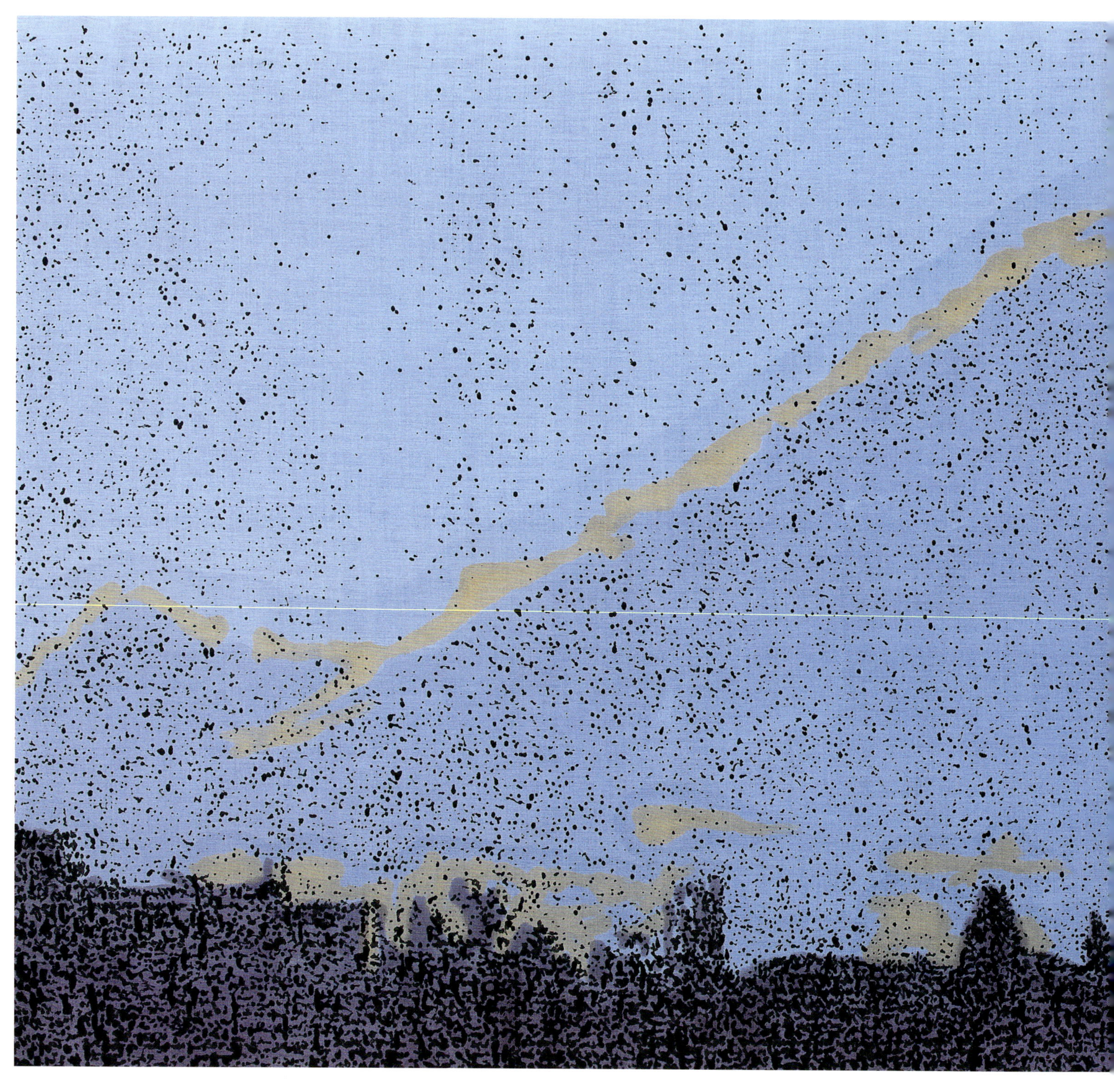

***Volcano (Iceland)*, 2011** Oil and alkyd on linen, 49 ½ × 108 ¾ inches | 125.7 × 276.2 cm

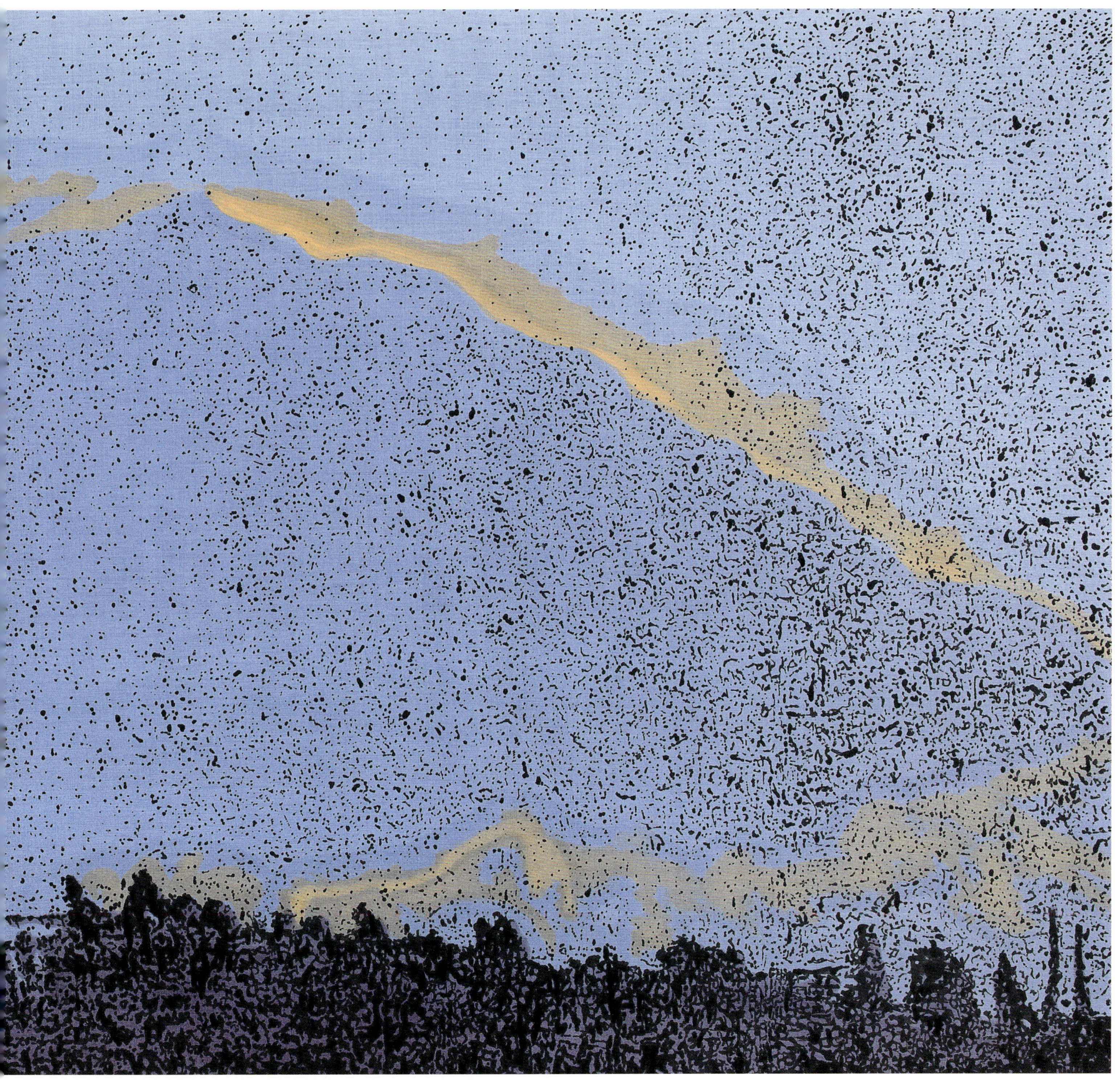

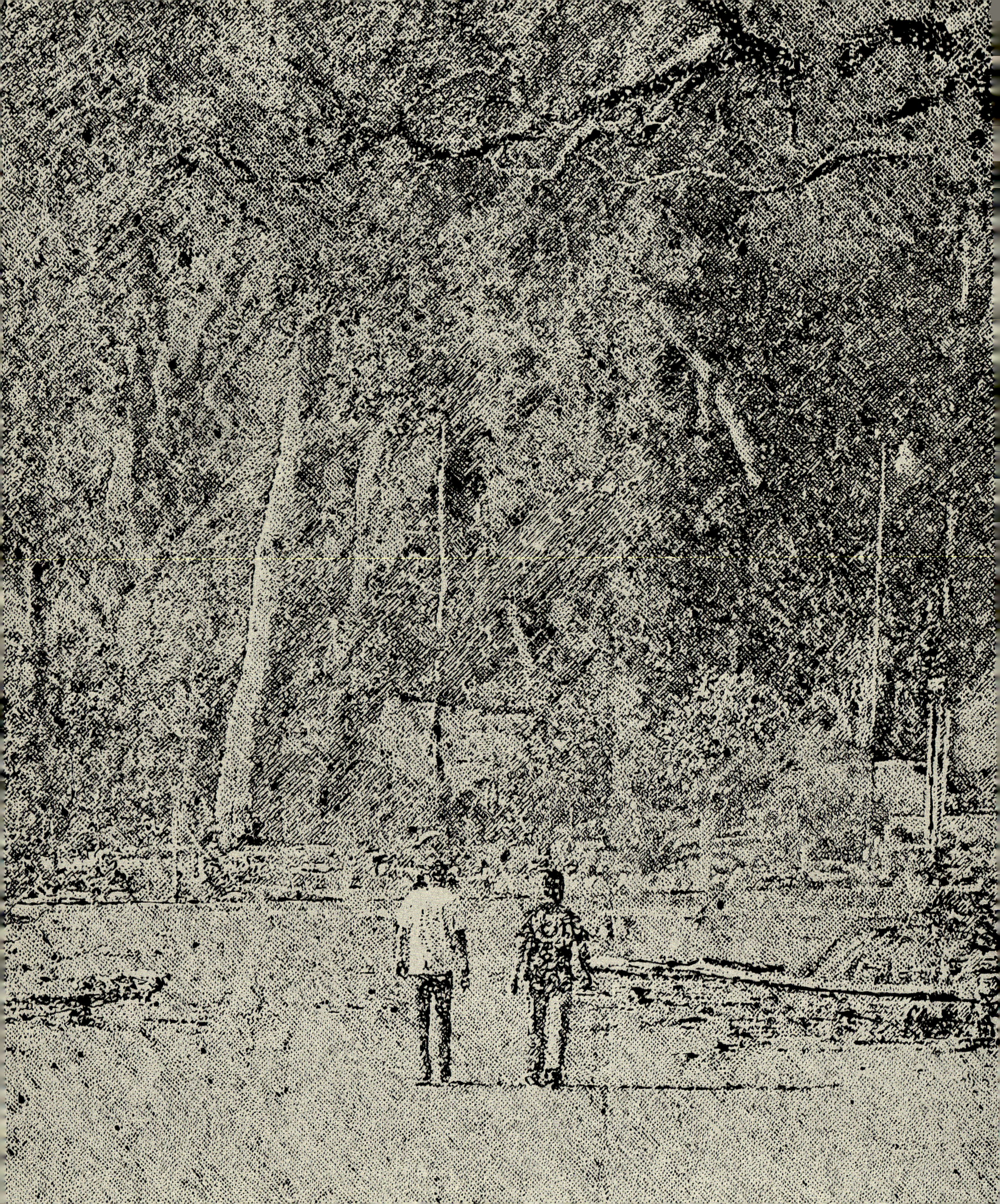

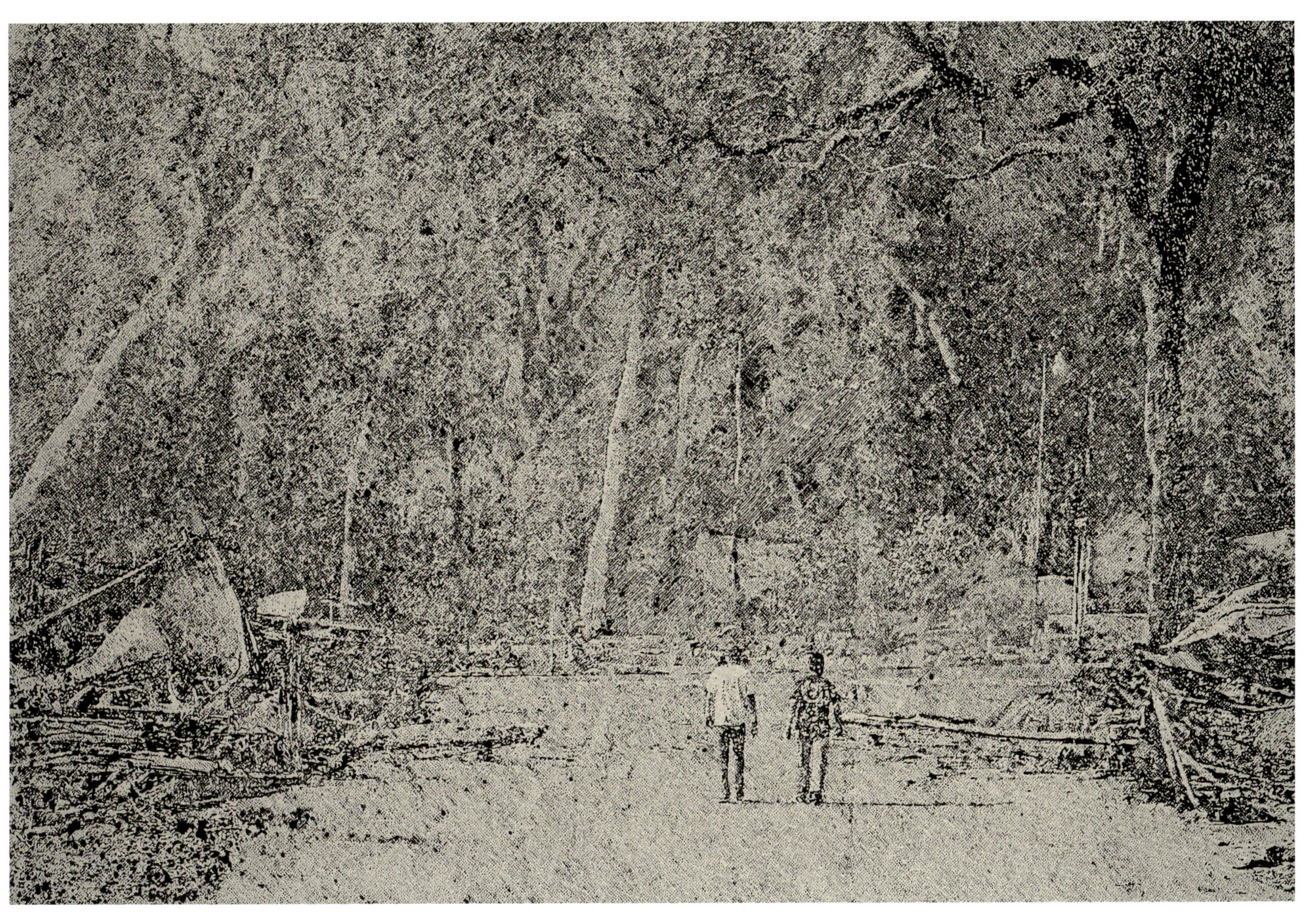

***Fire (Temecula)*, 2011** Alkyd on canvas, 42 × 63 inches | 106.7 × 160 cm

 ***Traffic*, 2011** Oil and alkyd on linen, 60 × 56 inches | 152.4 × 142.2 cm

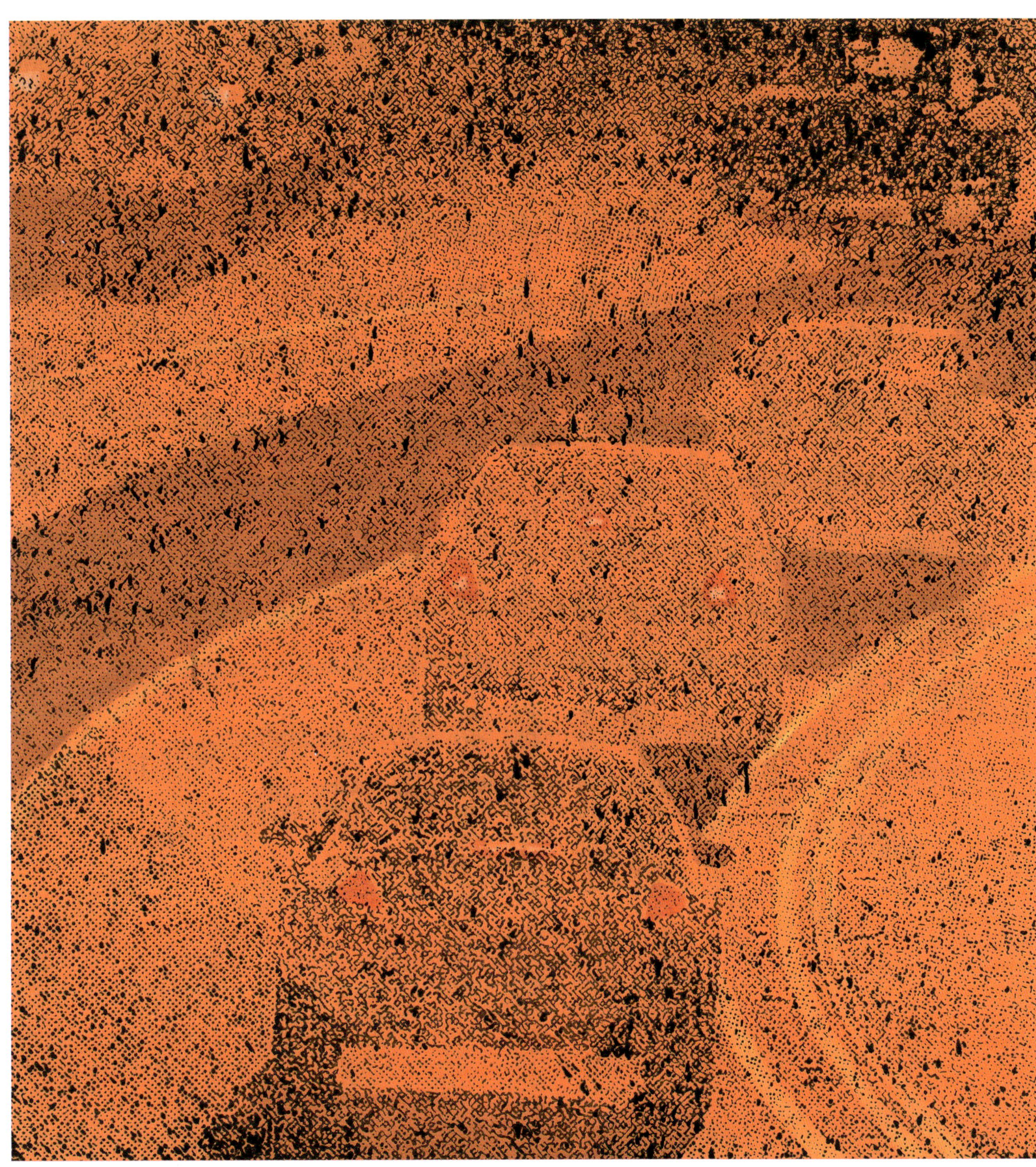

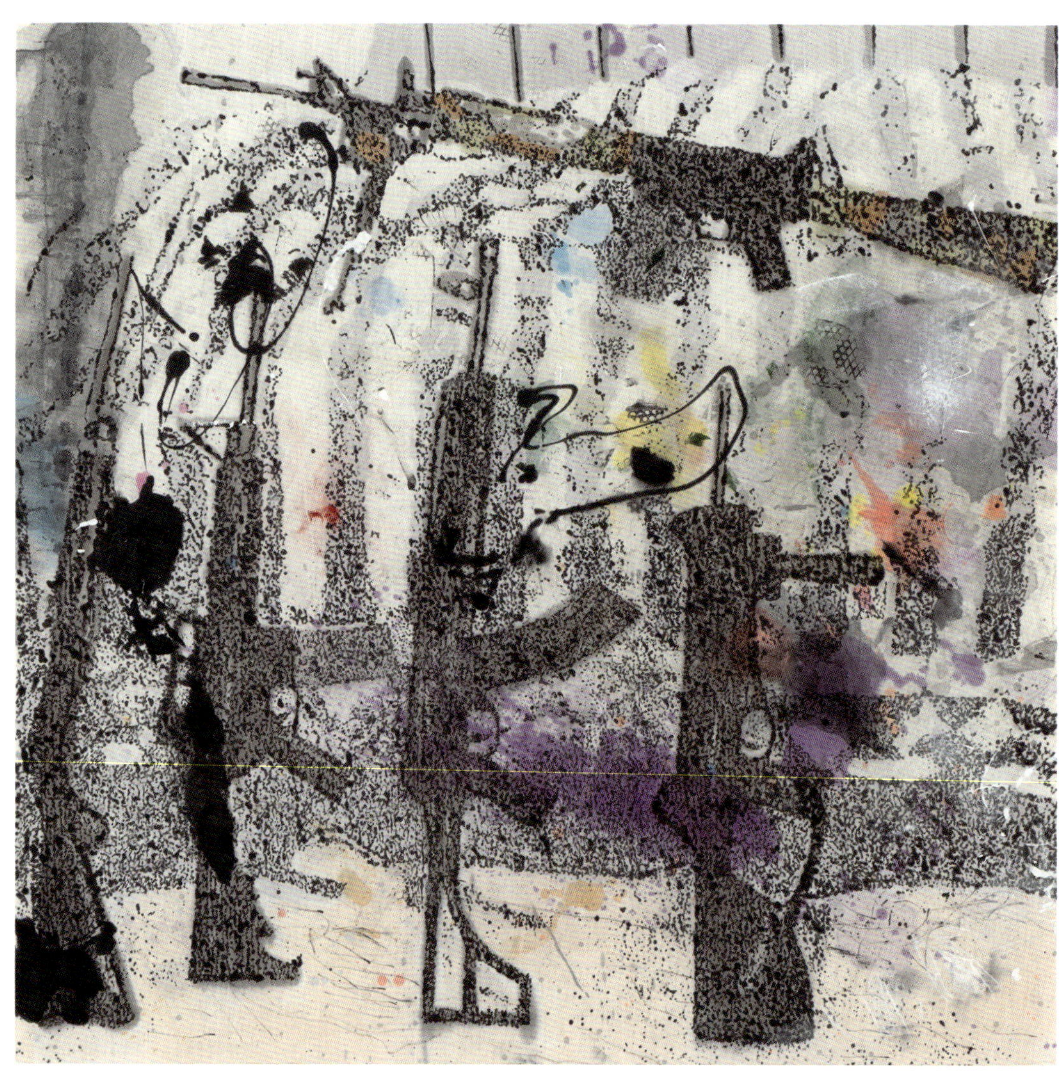

 ***Collection*, 2018** Oil, alkyd, and dirt on linen, 60 × 62 inches | 152.4 × 157.5 cm

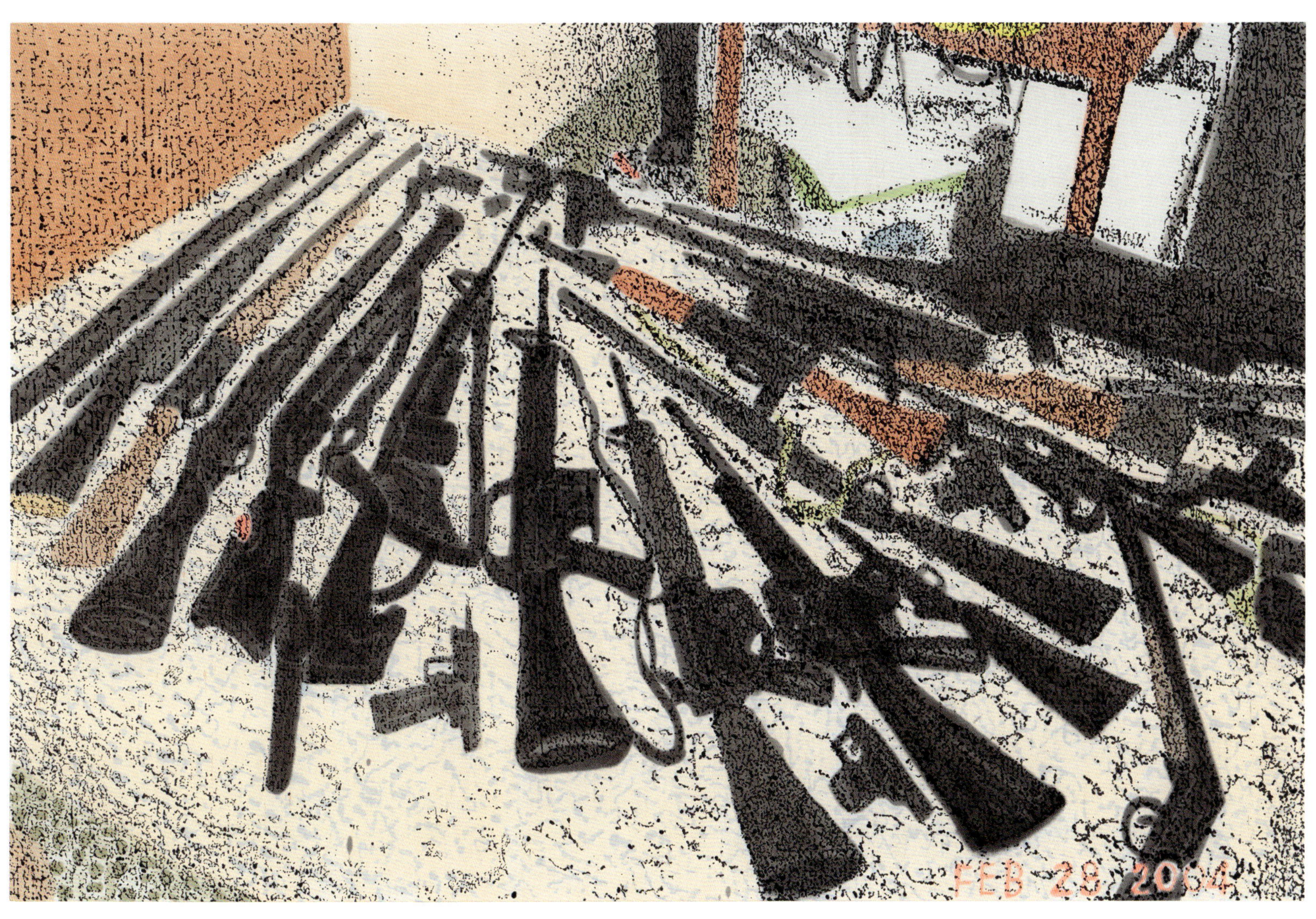

***You Live at Home with Your Mom*, 2018** Oil and alkyd on linen, 63½ × 96 inches | 161.3 × 243.8 cm

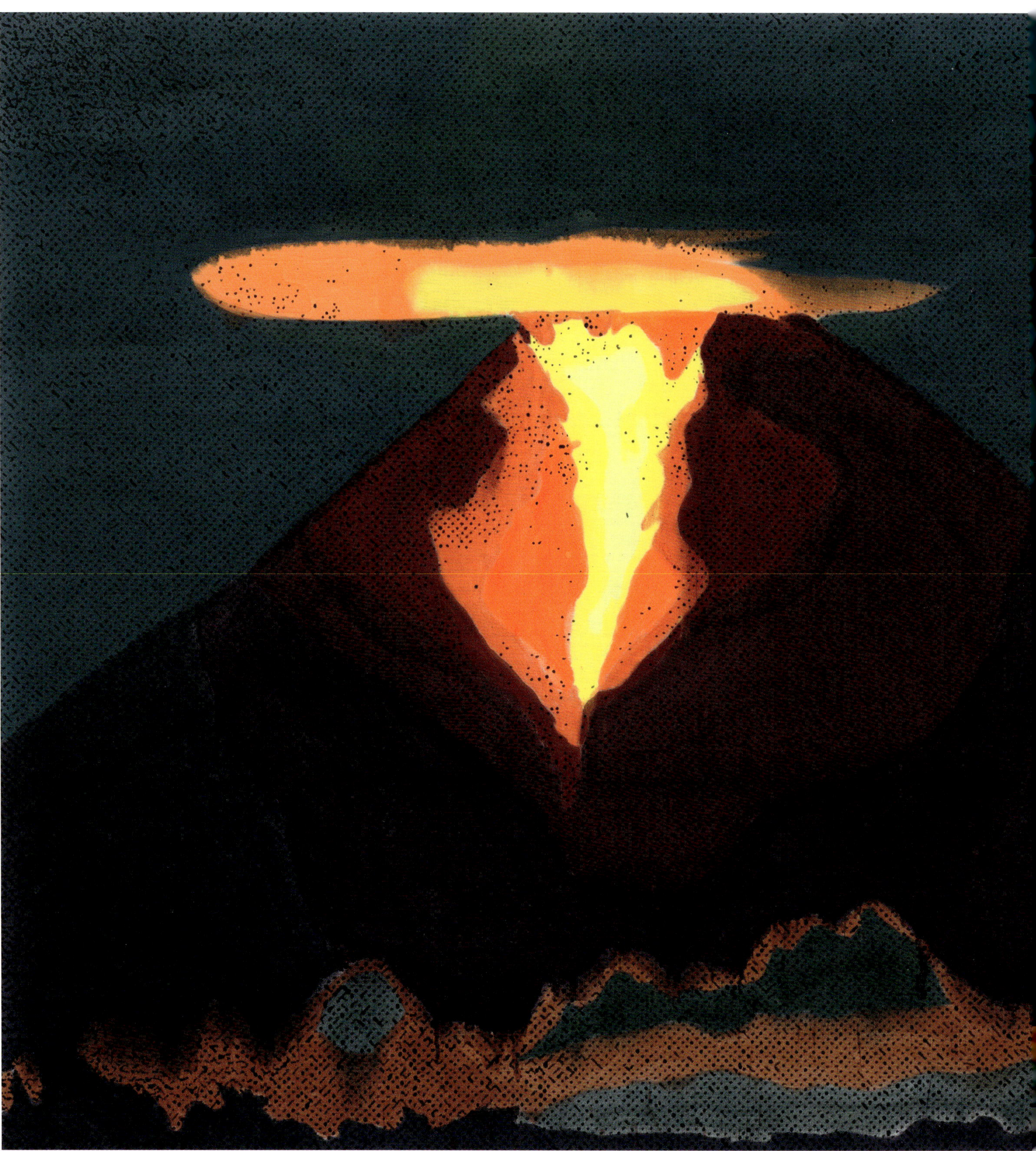

***Stratovolcano (Merapi)*, 2021** Oil and alkyd on linen, 84 × 120 inches | 213.4 × 304.8 cm

***Merapi/Cutouts*, 2021** Oil on canvas on wood panel in two parts, 63 ¾ × 60 inches | 161.9 × 152.4 cm

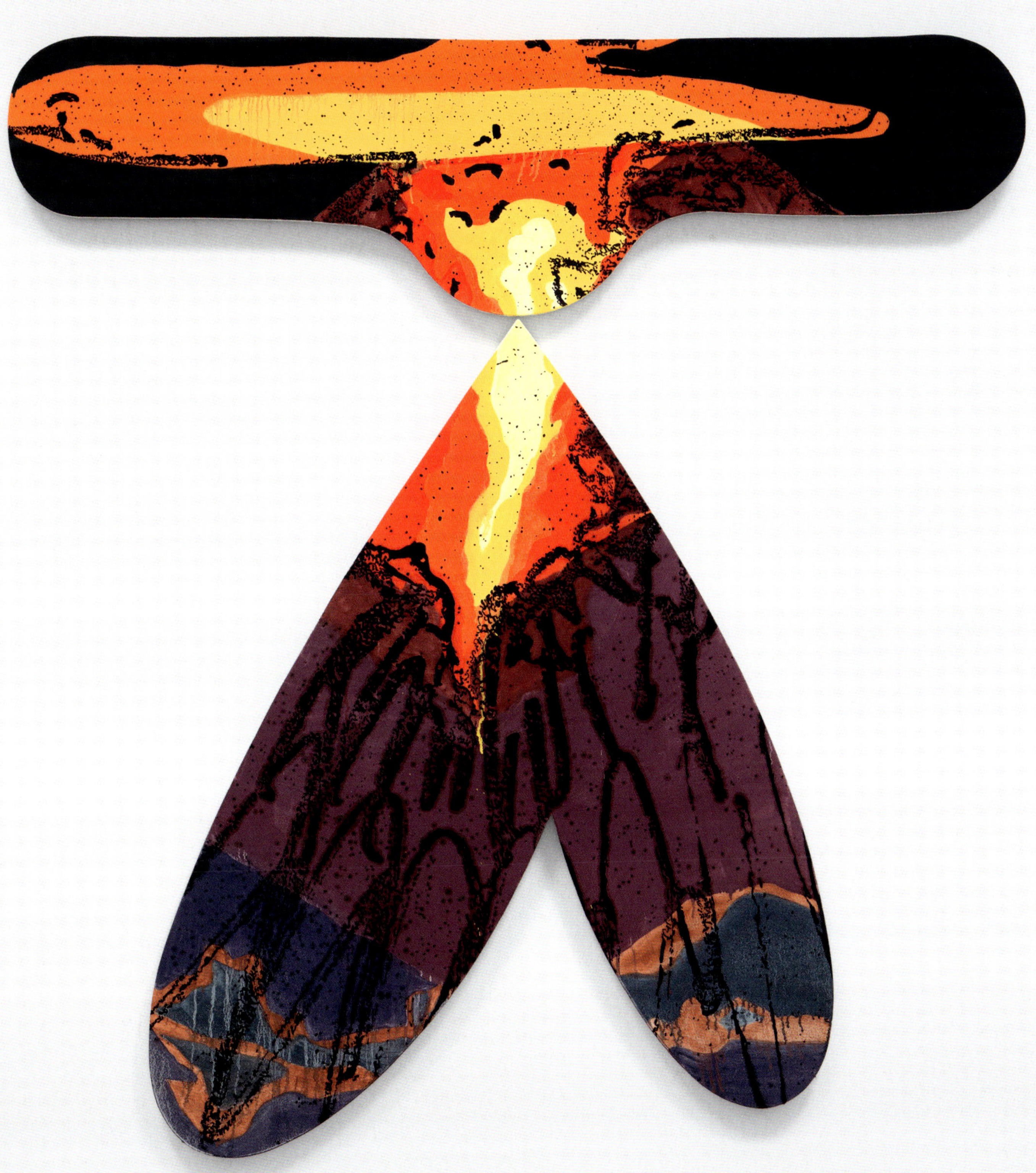

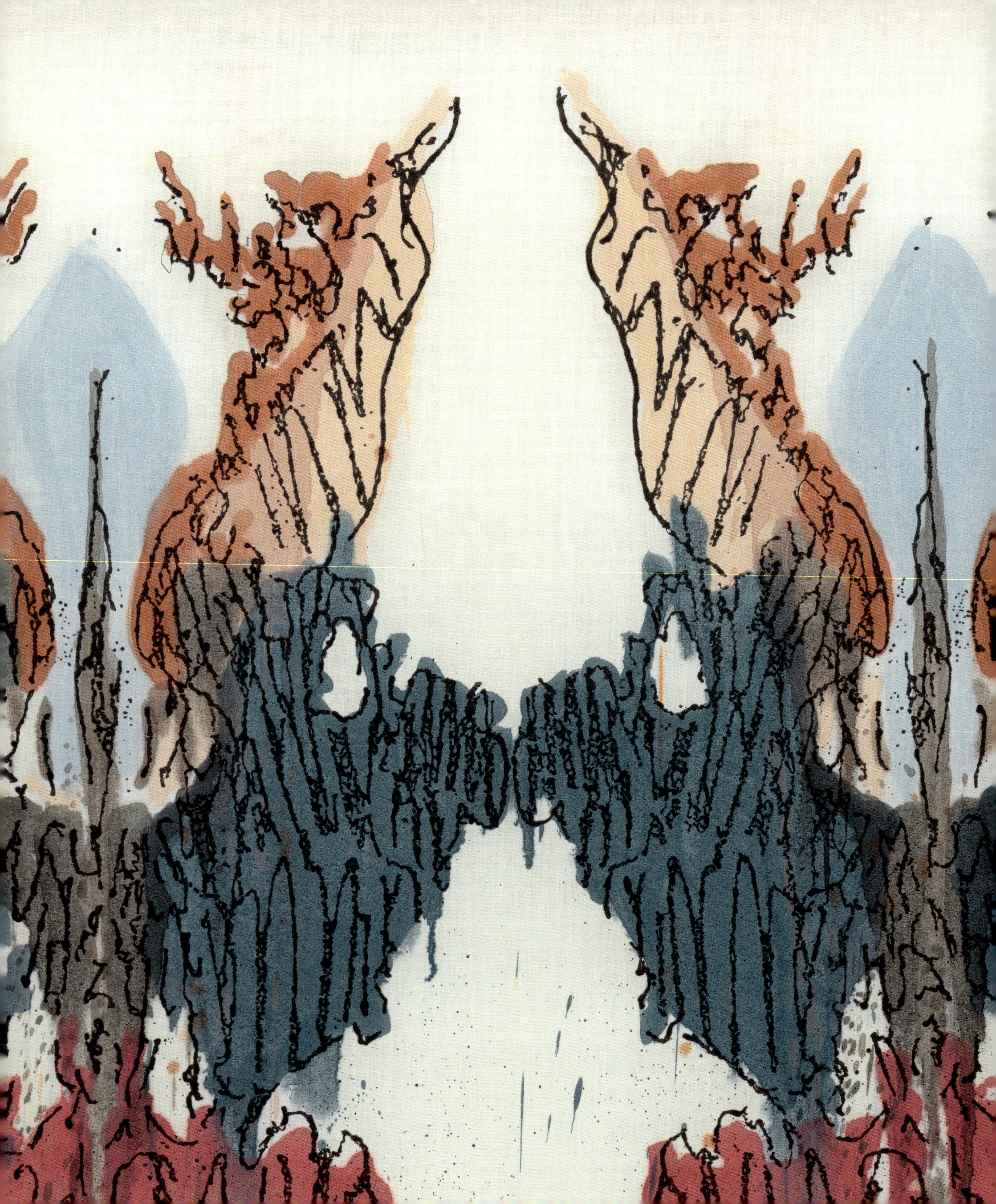

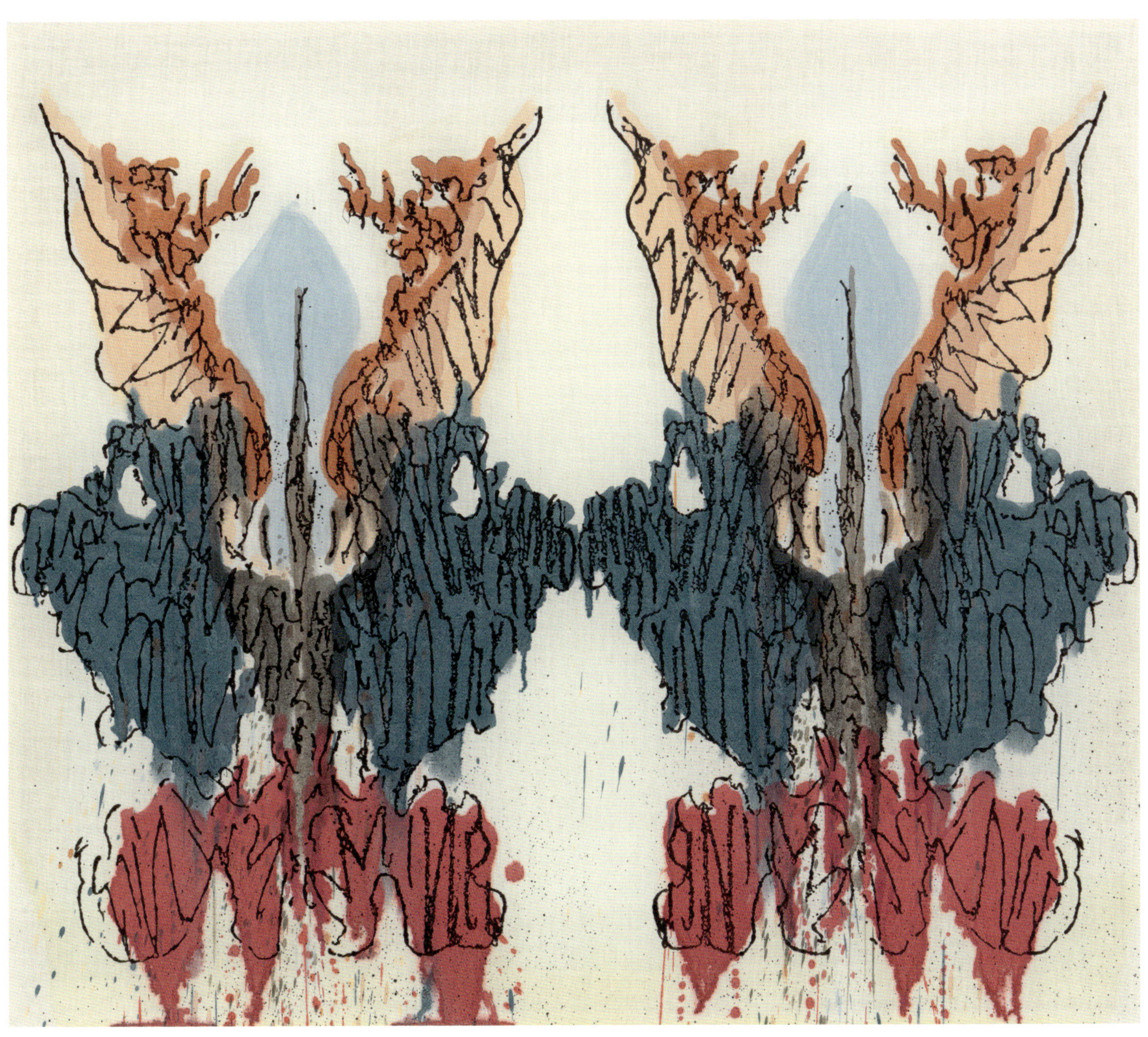

***You Can't Win*, 2021** Oil and alkyd on linen, 62⅛ × 72⅛ inches | 157.8 × 183.2 cm

 ***Bikini Atoll March 1, 1954*, 2021** Oil and alkyd on linen, 48 × 84 inches | 121.9 × 213.4 cm

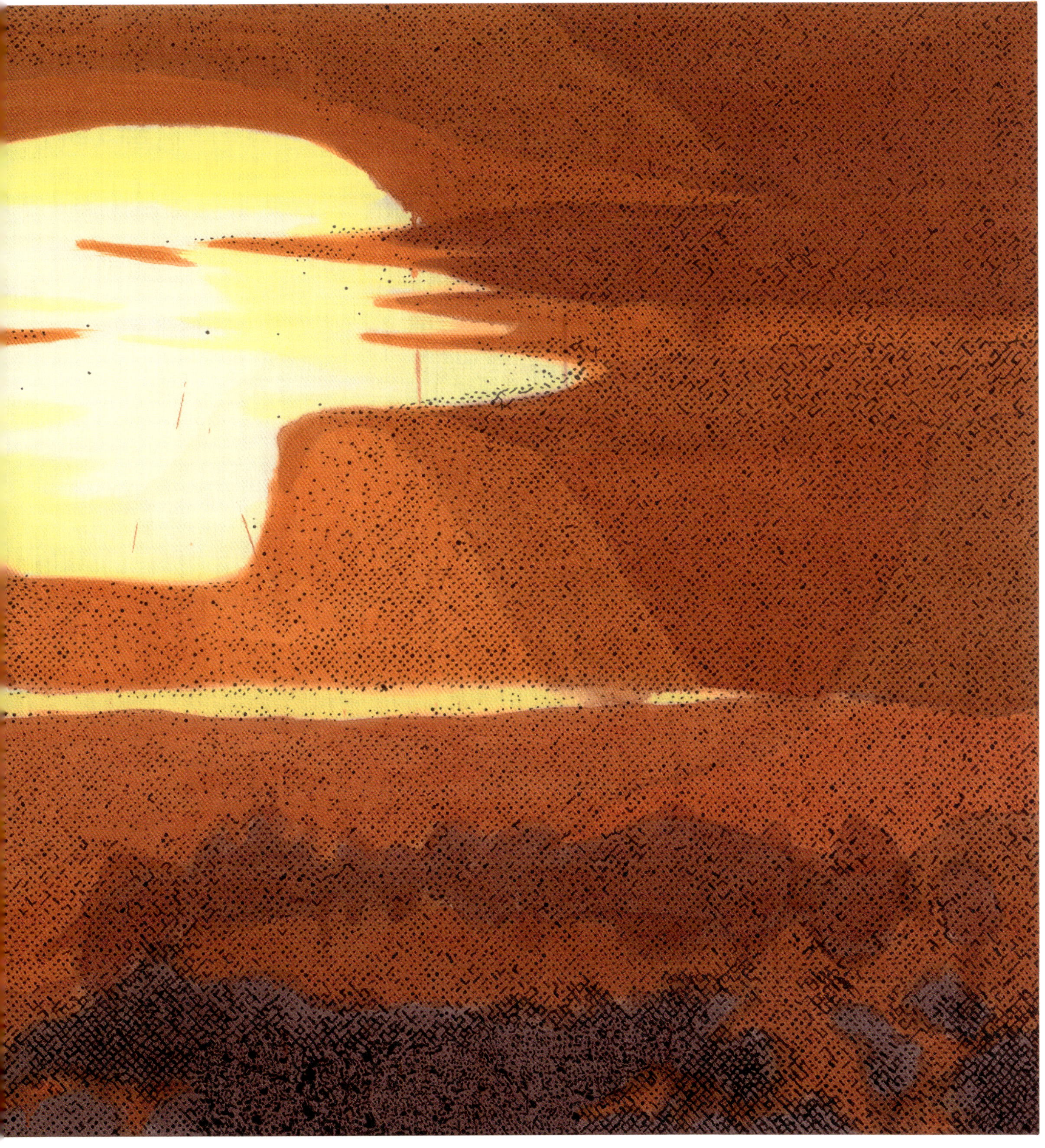

***Post-Apocalypse Now*, 2020** Oil on canvas on wood panel, 36 ¼ × 21 ¾ inches | 92.1 × 55.3 cm

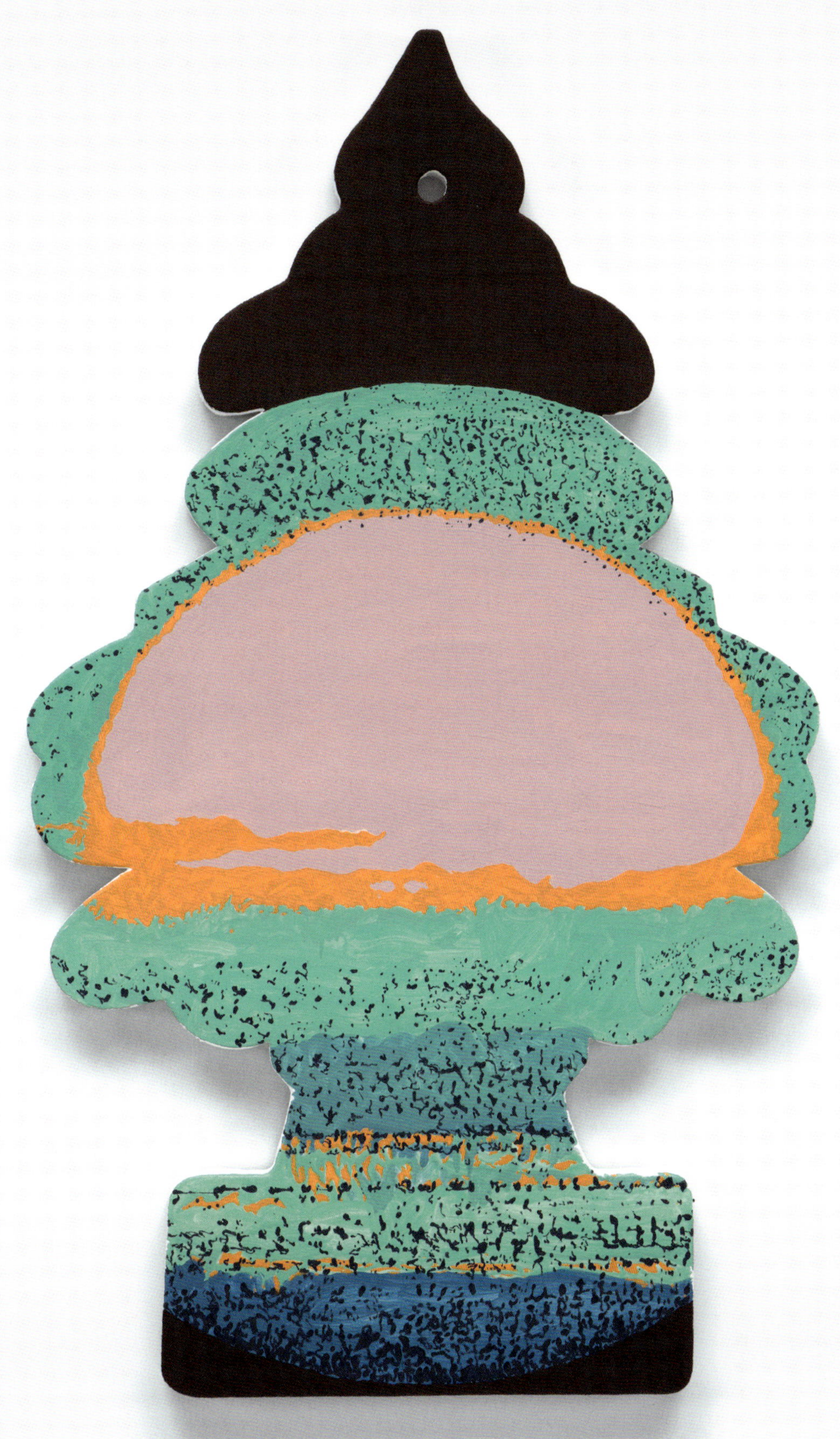

***San Andreas Fault*, 2021** Oil and alkyd on linen, 79 × 53 inches | 200.7 × 134.6 cm

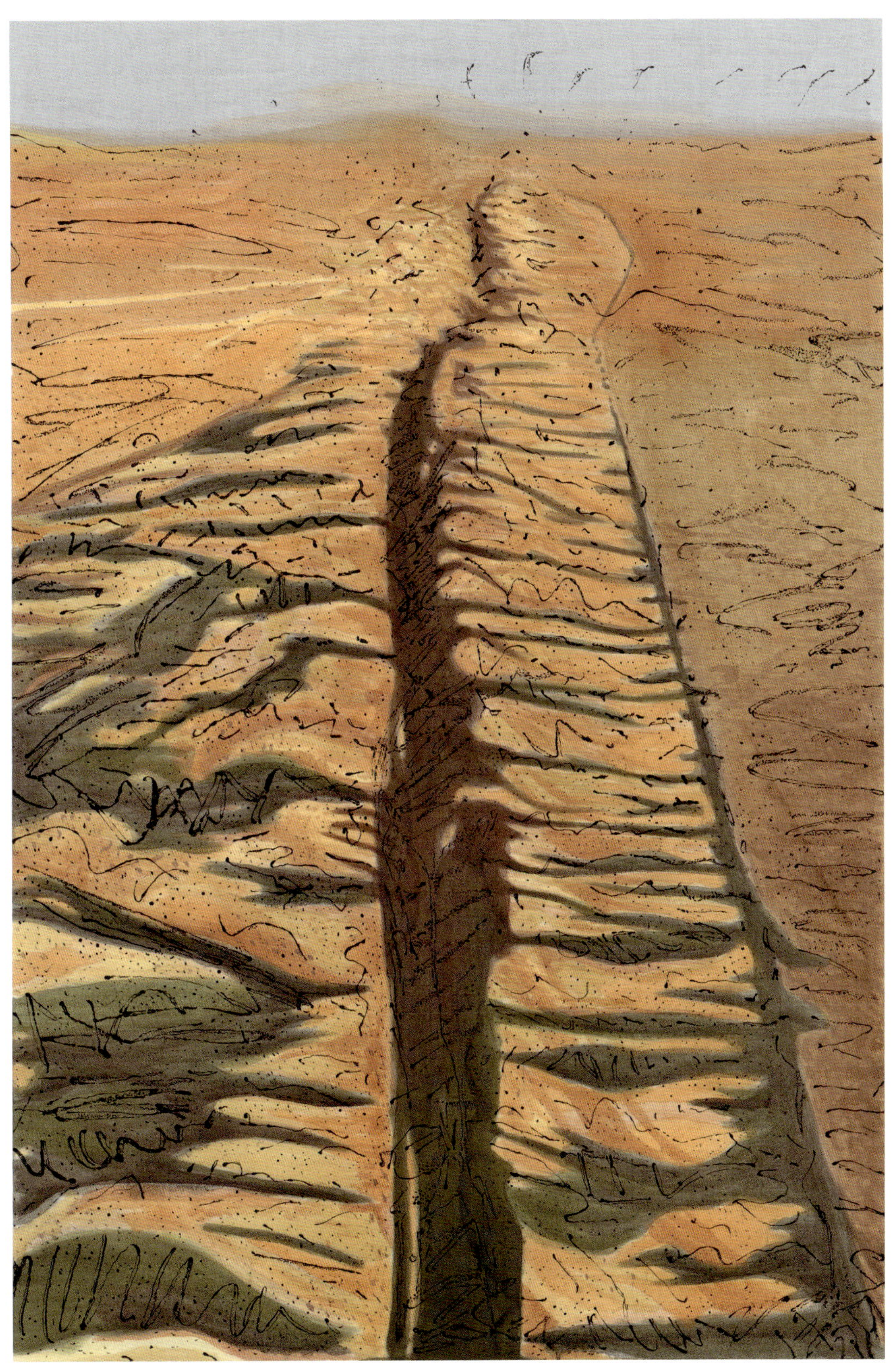

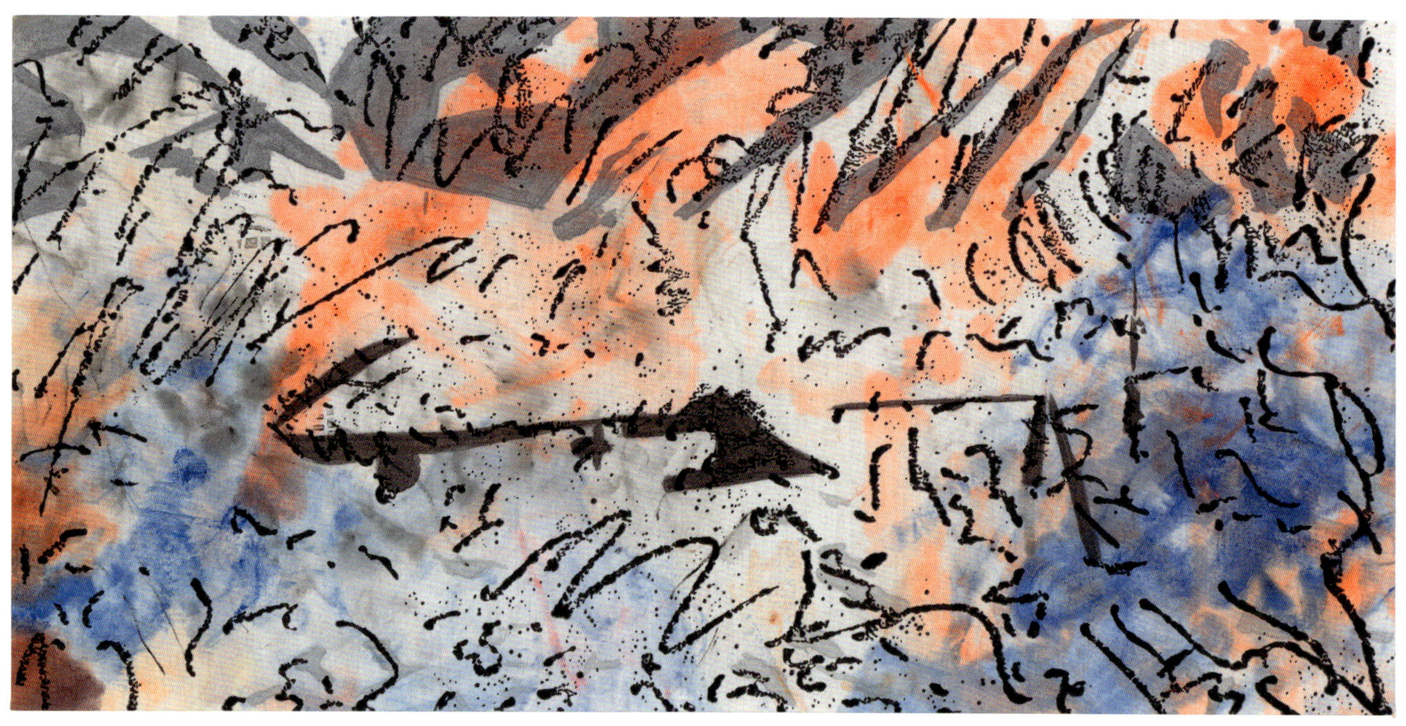

 ***Dropcloth Scribble Drone*, 2021** Oil and alkyd on linen, 24 ⅝ × 50 ⅝ inches | 62.5 × 128.6 cm

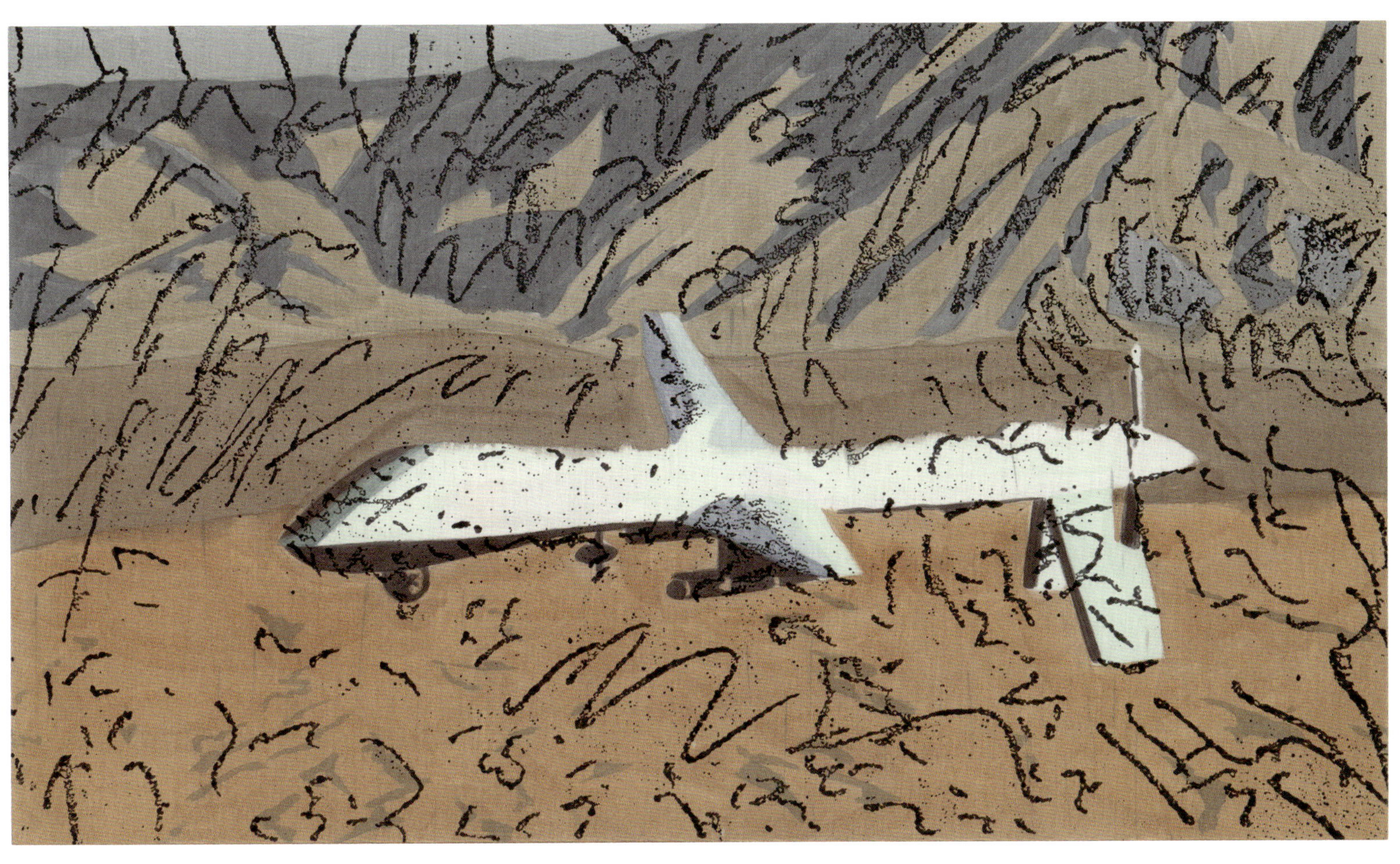

***Remote Control (Scribble)*, 2021** Oil and alkyd on linen, 48 × 84 inches | 121.9 × 213.4 cm

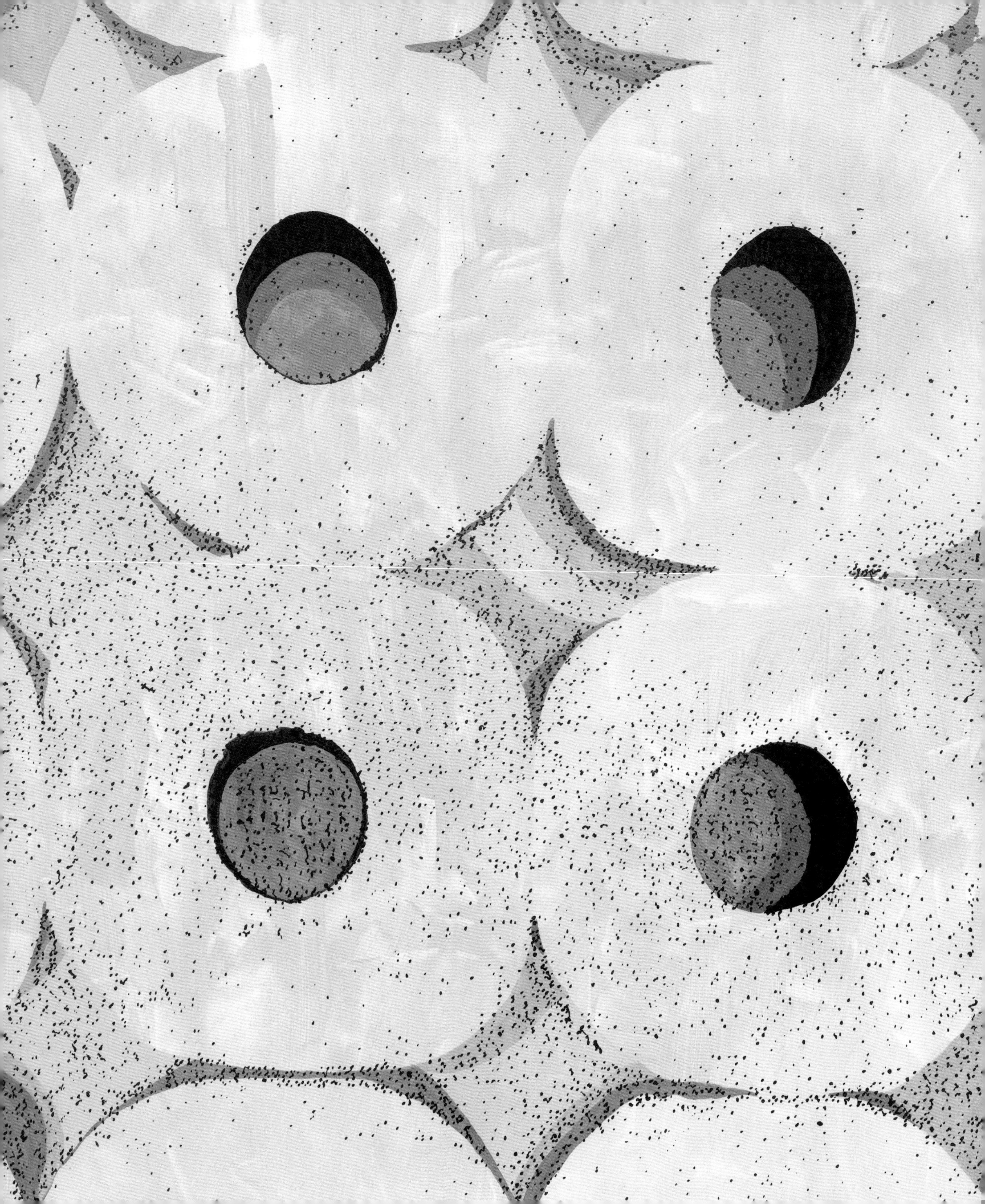

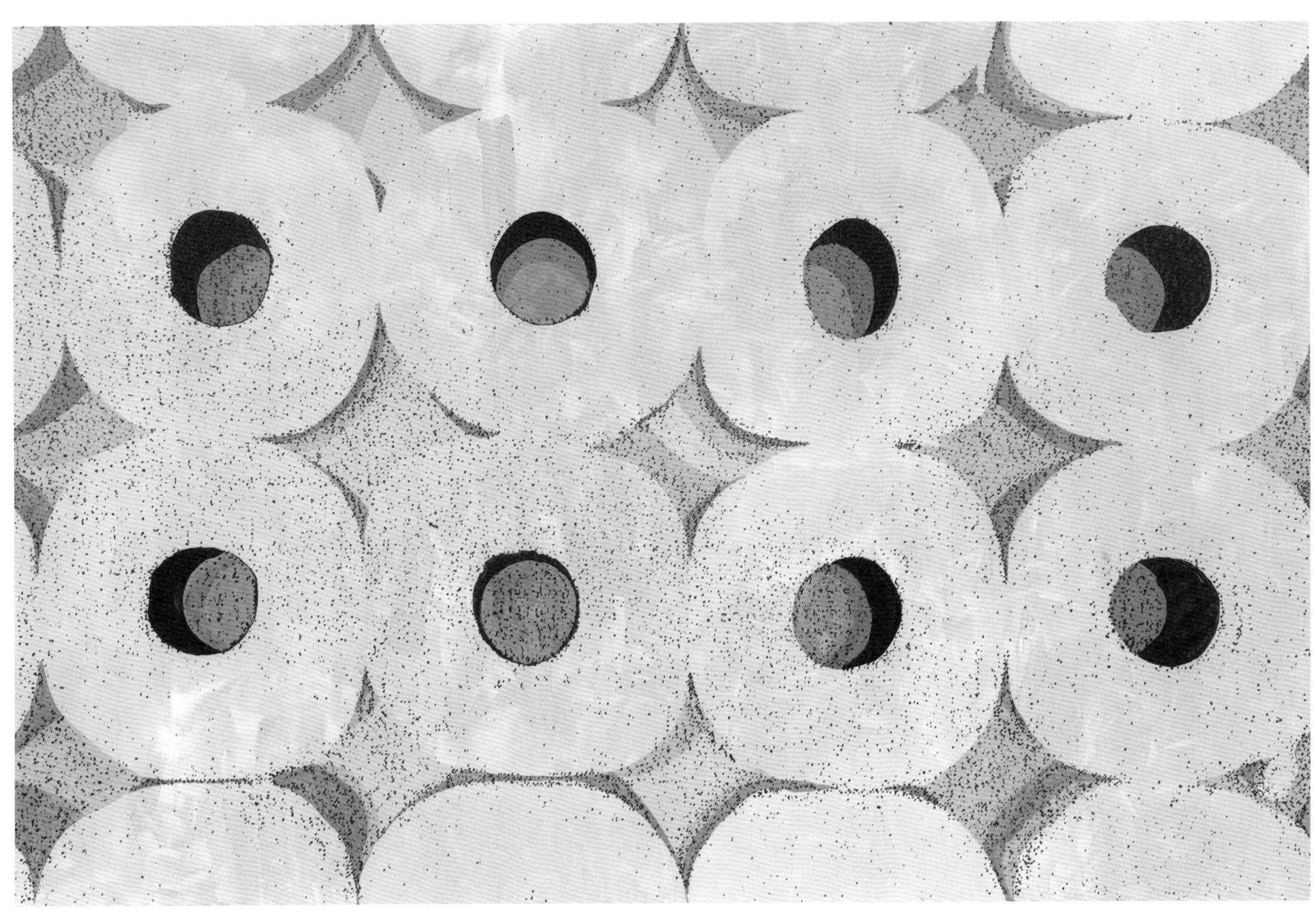

***Big Stash*, 2020** Oil on linen, 77⅛ × 117 inches | 195.9 × 297.2 cm

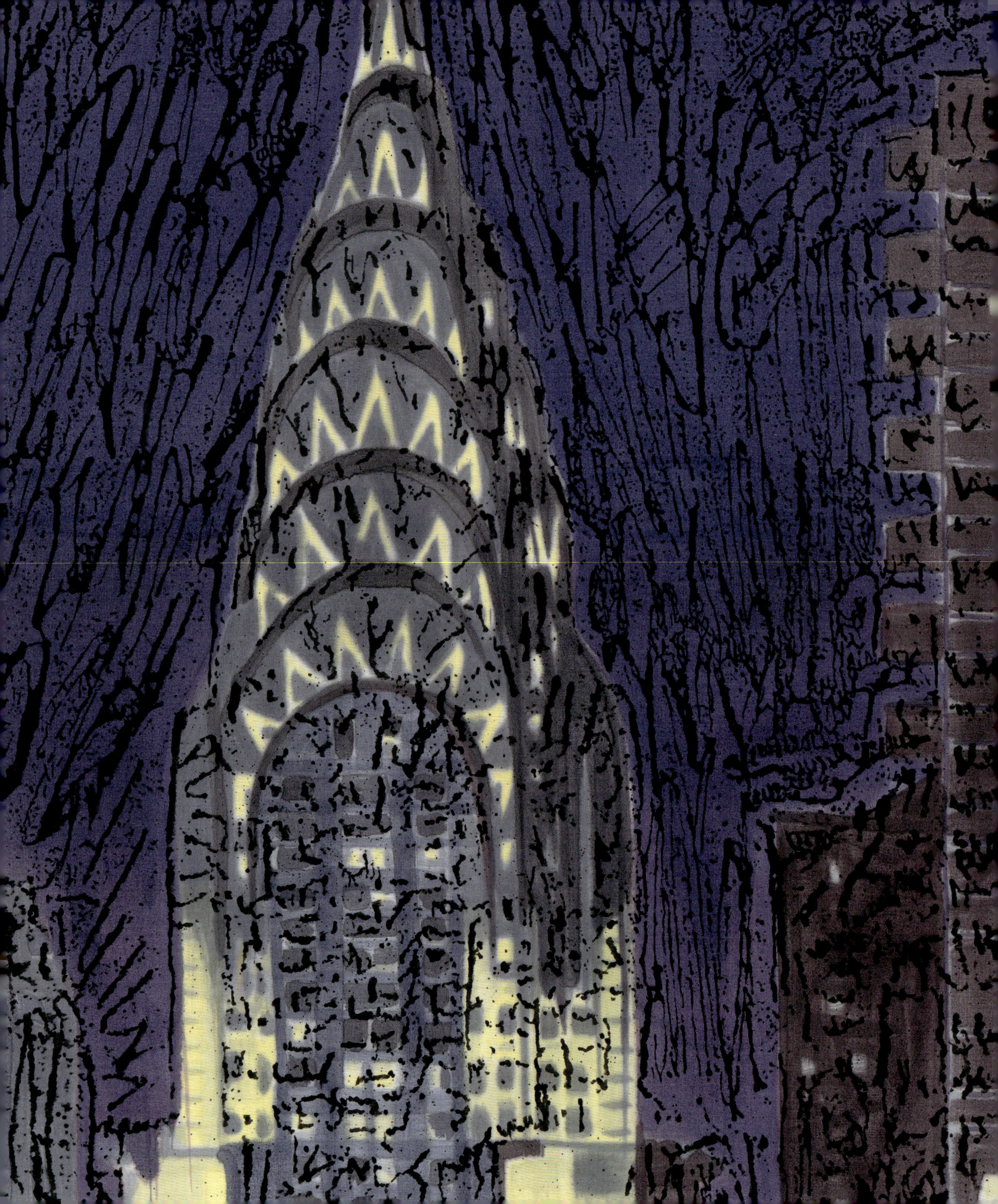

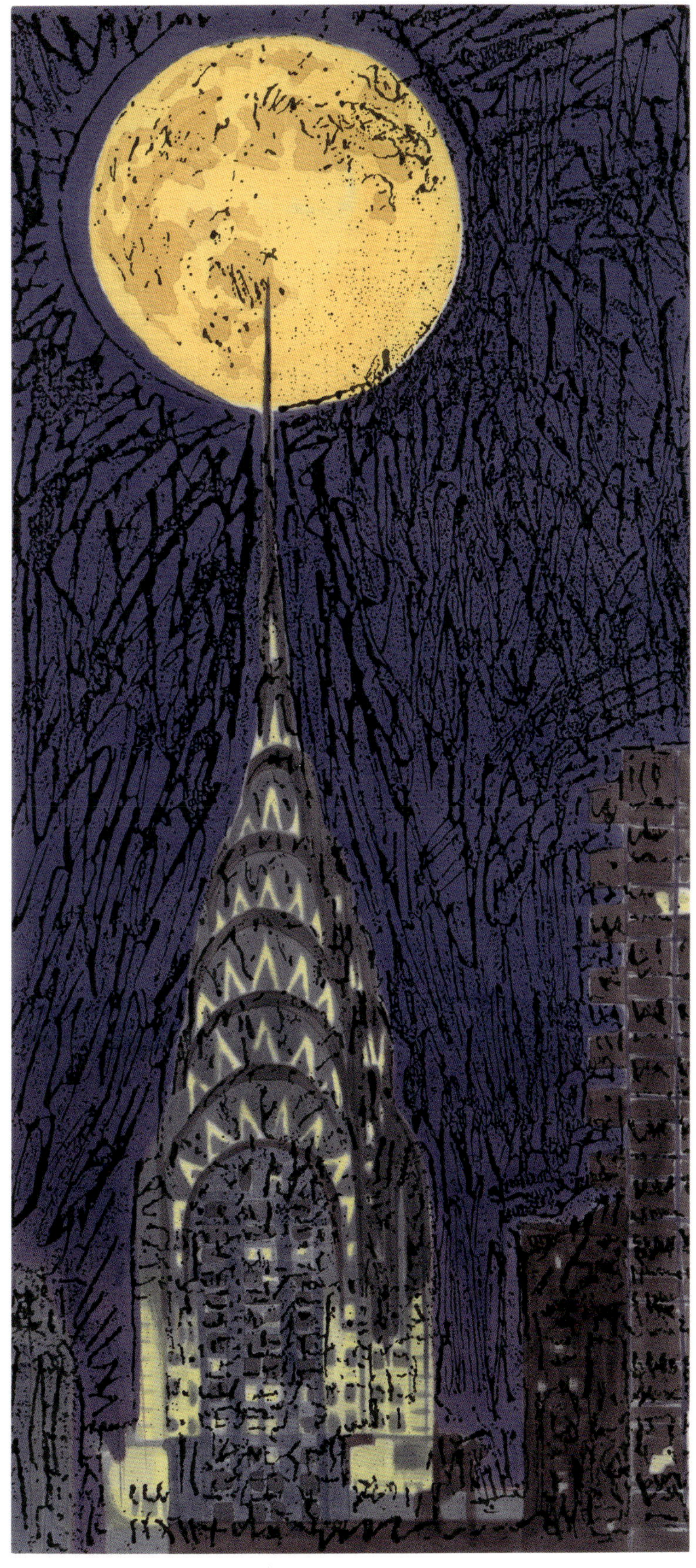

***Night Watch*, 2021** Oil and alkyd on linen, 86⅛ × 39⅛ inches | 218.8 × 99.4 cm

***Don't Forget to Howl at the Moon*, 2021** Oil, alkyd, and gesso on linen, 50 ¼ × 24 ⅝ inches | 127.6 × 62.5 cm

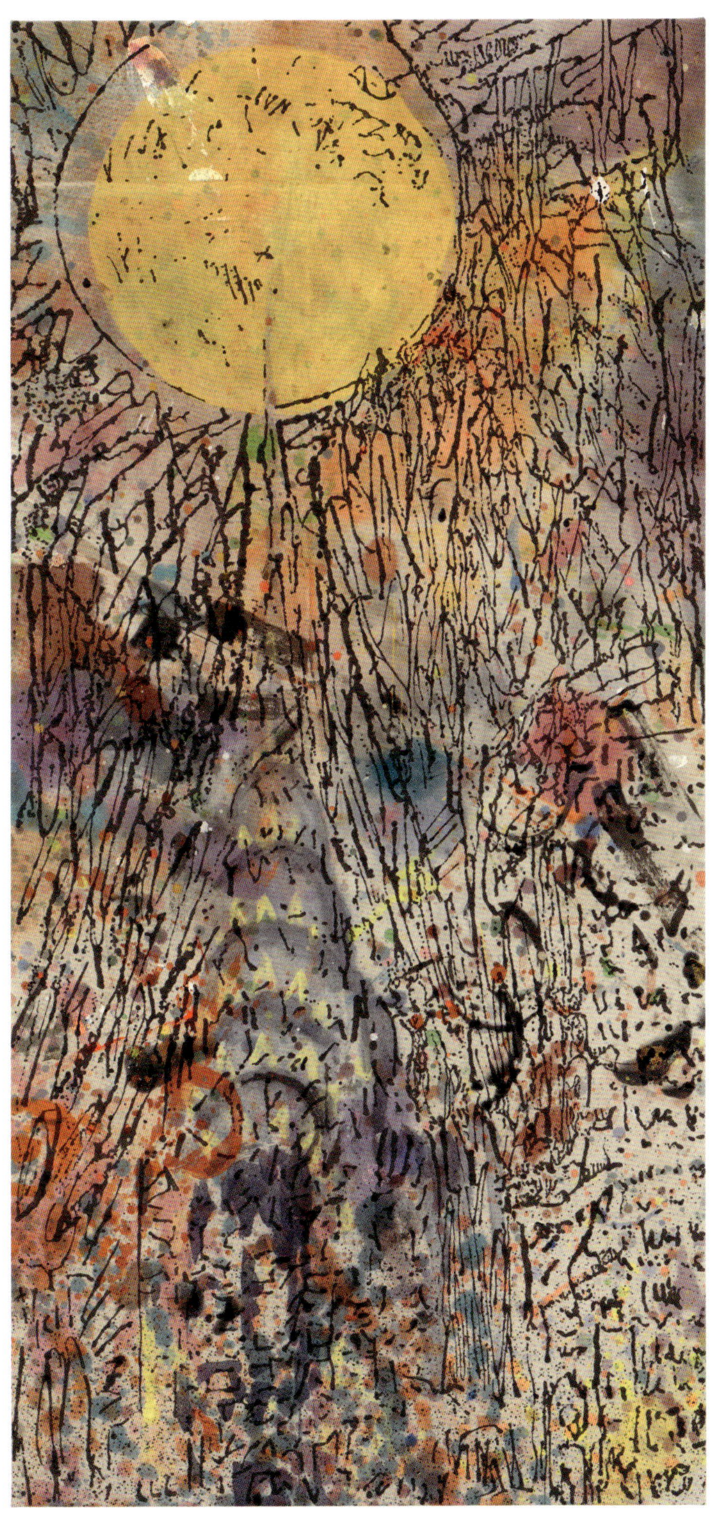

***Before During After (Caffi)*, 2021** Oil and alkyd on linen, 66⅛ × 42⅛ inches | 168 × 107 cm

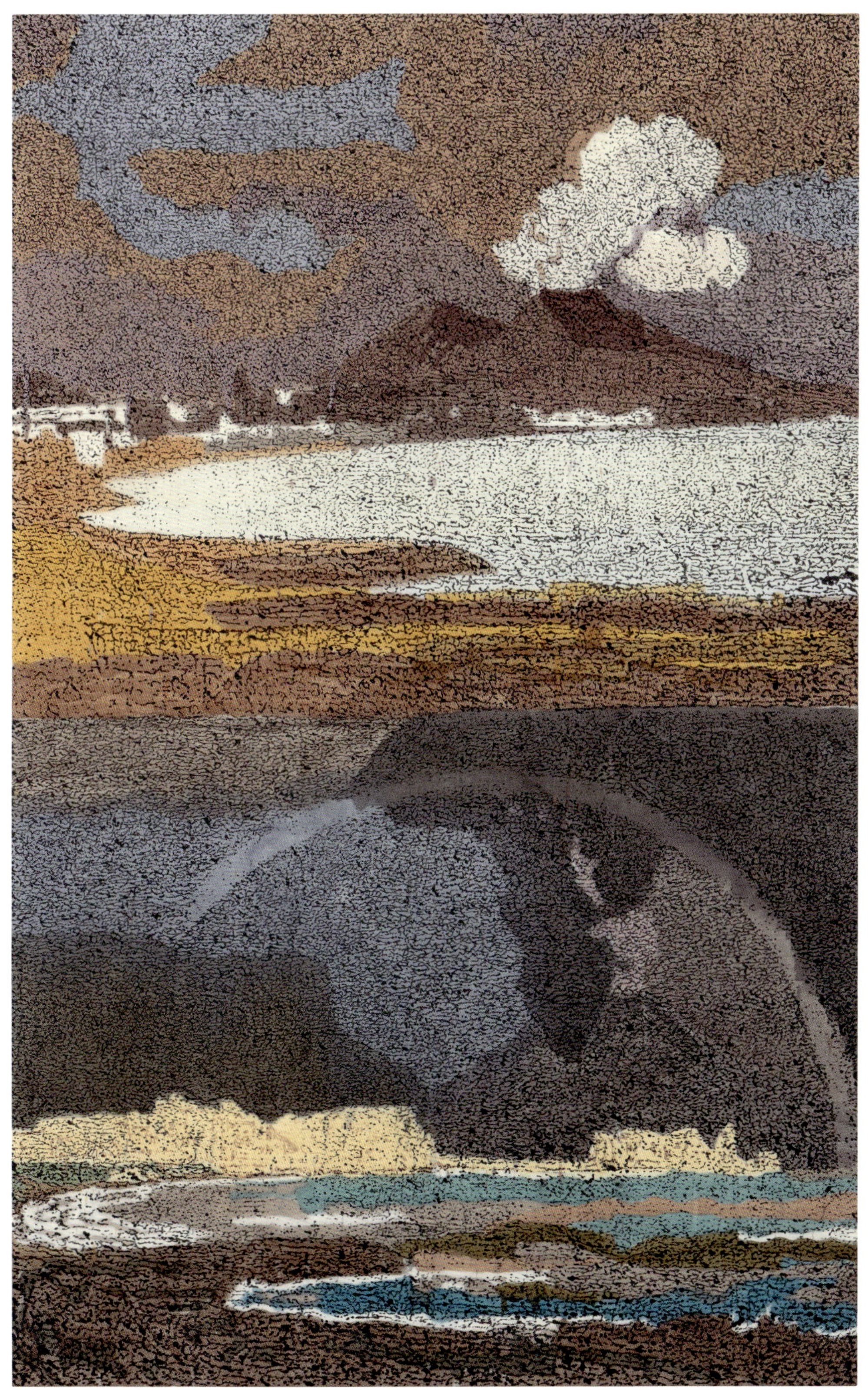

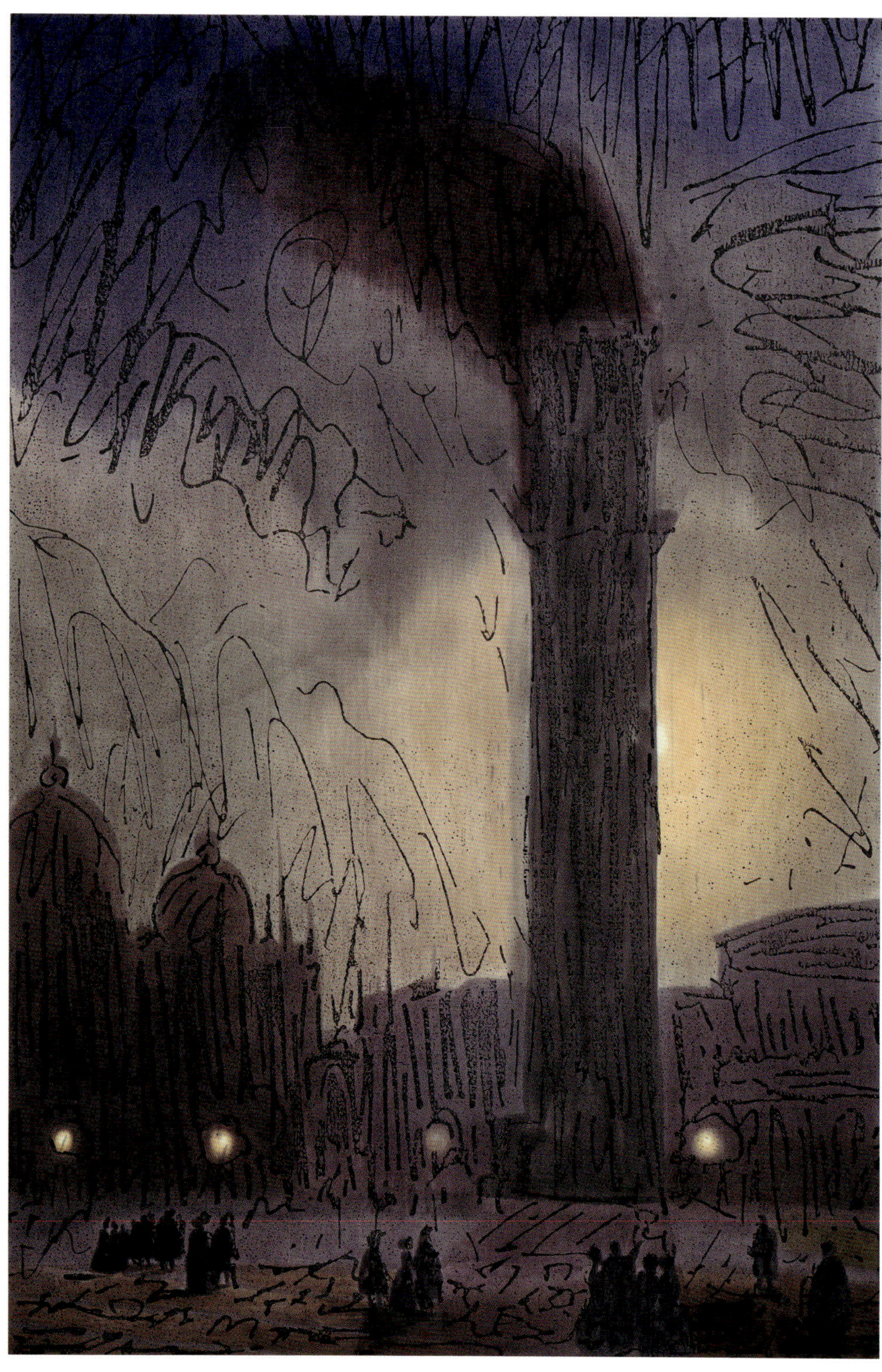

 ***Ciao Venezia (Ippolito Caffi)*, 2021** Oil and alkyd on linen, 137 × 92 inches | 348 × 233.7 cm

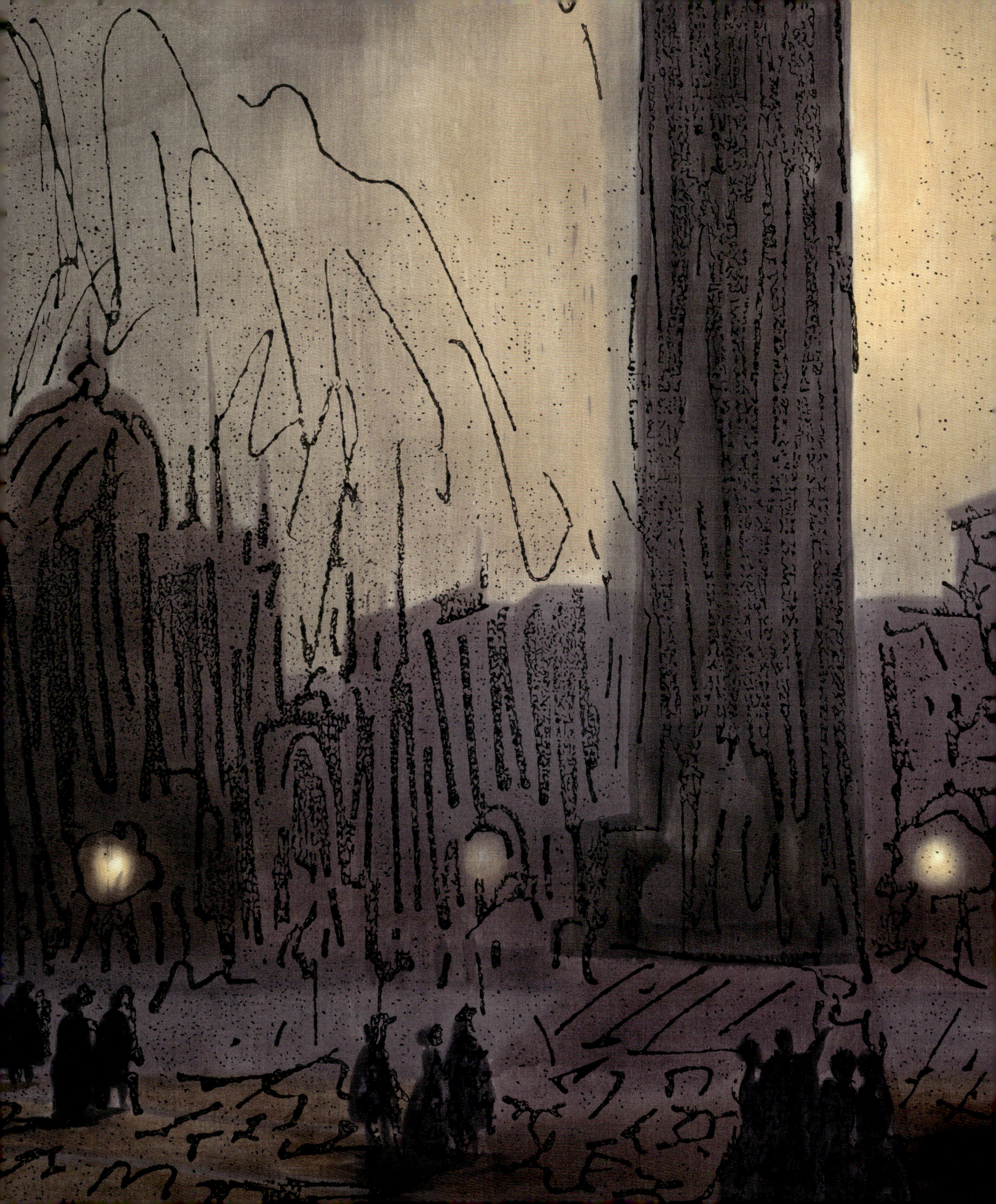

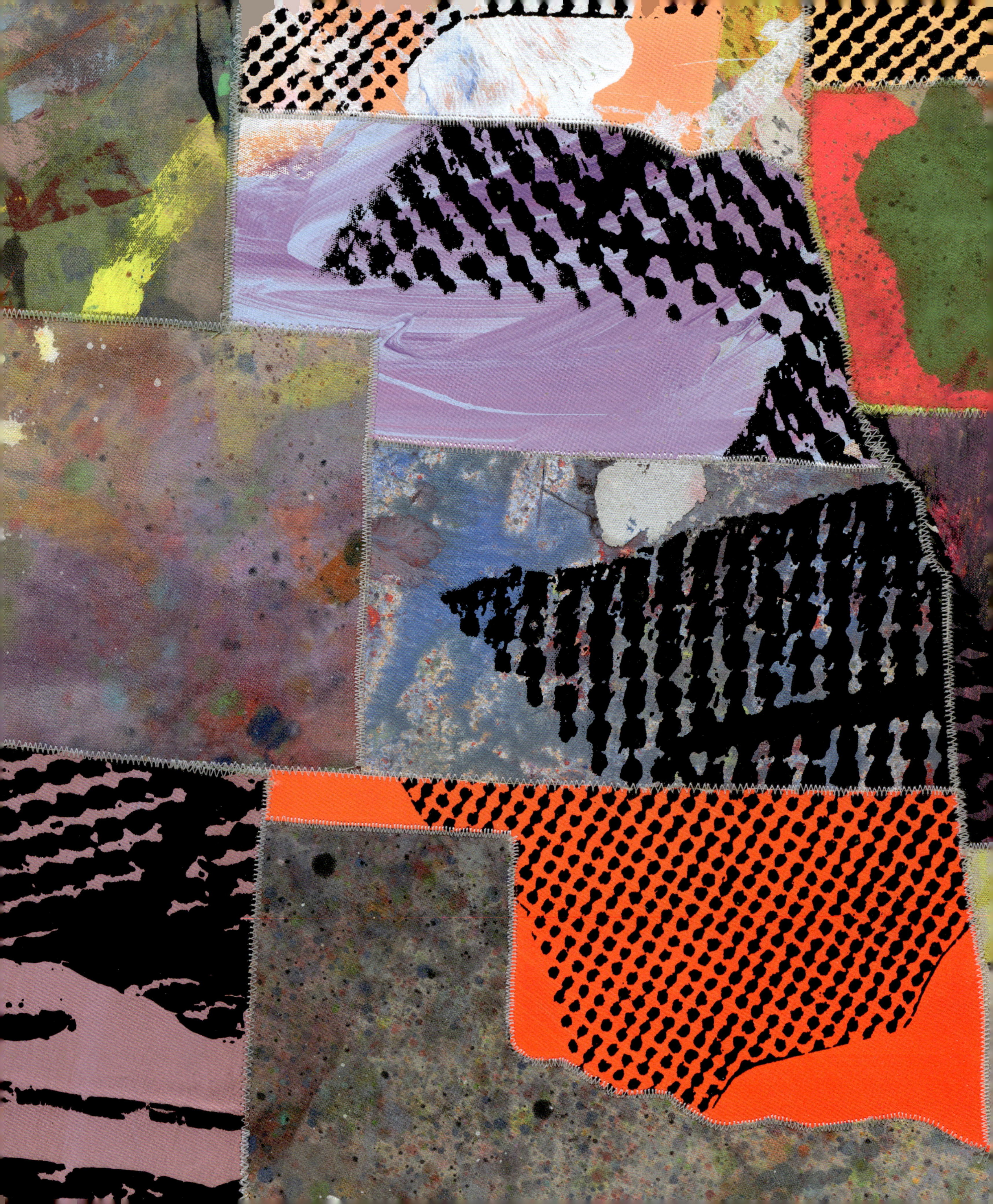

It's So American

Lynne Tillman

Nate Lowman pictures how Americans live now—what fascinates them, what hurts them, and what they love, which might be the same as what hurts them. Like him, an American, I grew up watching Westerns on TV and in movie theaters, where fierce-looking "red Indians" were demonized. I saw war films in which only the other side, the enemy, killed prisoners of war. I thought I knew who the bad guys were.

As Franz Kafka wrote, "My education has done me great harm in some respects."[1]

In 1994, I was writer-in-residence at the University of Sussex in Brighton, England. The PhD students were usually poor and drank a pint of Guinness for their dinner. I took my workshop to see *Pulp Fiction*, a kind of treat, I thought.

I laughed at the assassins' ironic Big Mac conversation and was amused by the famous John Travolta/Uma Thurman dance scene. But the students told me they were disturbed by the casual violence to which I had been indifferent. On the old Brighton boardwalk, I heard them, and remembered thinking, whimsically, I am so American. Even now, I know I have been desensitized to violence.

Yes, many white Europeans sought freedom from religious persecution, but in the so-called "New World" they stole land and freedom from Native Americans and used enslaved African labor. Historical aberrations live in a nation's DNA, its psyche, society, politics, and culture. Diverse and contradictory histories are written about any period in the past; there's never one story about events and people. Historiographies detail the ways that historians have performed their jobs—accurately, or with small or great distortions, with purposeful, fact-based revisions, with prejudice or lies, to recover truths, to damn or exculpate actors and actions. American history is under severe and serious examination, of its untruths about its beginnings, the myths, and ignored realities.

Looking at Nate Lowman's oeuvre, I see his response to this indifference. I perceive an "American family" art album. It's all here: national headlines, trivia, kitsch, military weapons, guns, mass murders, and domestic and foreign terrorism. Events can be sources, backgrounds, and subtexts in his work. The love of guns, Americans' desire to possess and use them, figures in his paintings of bedrooms, where all kinds of weapons lie on beds waiting to be taken up and used (see pp. 78, 79).

> My great-grandmother was a crazy quilter, and I have most of the quilts that got left behind. I'm sure that's where I got the idea to use all these errant scraps.
>
> —Nate Lowman[2]

The errant scraps come from drop cloths Lowman saved over the years, after having used them to protect the floors as he painted. He cuts them up and collages pieces into multicolored paintings of maps of the United States (fig. 11). From a distance, the maps are beautiful—they might be water lilies or funny Hans Hofmanns.

Cobble Hustle Weave, 2022 (detail)

Moving in closer and seeing the accidental and random drips and blobs, I think about the paintings' homely origin: each map is made from a crazy quilt, and now it represents these disunited states. Each state is distinct, and, like abstract art, there are swathes of color without figures. Abstraction beckons interpretation and projection, and I will see what I think about America now. The surface may be beautiful, but it's not a pretty picture.

In Lowman's painting *Drone* (2021; fig. 12), a military drone is in midair, in the center of the canvas, a massive whiteish-gray machine against a background of blue-gray hills or mountains. The ground is sand-colored, and may be sand. The drone is flying low.

Pilotless, drones fly missions to "eliminate" enemies without endangering Americans. They are meant to hit their targets "without collateral damage"—without civilians being hurt or killed. These unassuming, stealthy warplanes commit tragic errors; unintended deaths do happen. But these are "clean kills," metaphorically bloodless, not as dangerous as combat.

Here, the drone (Lowman has painted four, one of which is on paper) is undramatic, calm as drones are lethal. In a way, the work could be called "Portrait of a Drone." This way you have to face it.

One of America's horrific national tragedies especially captured Lowman's attention and led to a series based on an actual event:

> On October 1, 2017, Stephen Paddock, a 64-year-old man from Mesquite, Nevada, opened fire on the crowd attending the Route 91 Harvest music festival on the Las Vegas Strip in Nevada. From his 32nd-floor suites in the Mandalay Bay hotel, he fired more than 1,000 bullets, killing 60 people and wounding at least 413. . . . About an hour later, he was found dead in his room from a self-inflicted gunshot wound. . . . The incident is the deadliest mass shooting committed by an individual in United States history.[3]

The "deadliest mass shooting committed by an individual in United States history" hit home, figuratively and literally. Lowman was born in Las Vegas, a city whose image is indelibly linked with gambling and taking chances; its motto, "What Happens in Vegas Stays in Vegas," boasts of a Wild West for its hotel guests. But Vegas's wildness has been greatly overshadowed and overwhelmed by an irrational act much more "scandalous" and "shameful" than what happens in Vegas.

> This was the first mass murder I dealt with directly [in my work]. Six months after it, the Las Vegas Police Department released nearly thirty images from the crime scene. The images were provocative, because the event was; but [their] forensics' A-team wasn't documenting the shooting. I used oil paint to match the colors in the photos as accurately as possible, then painted a layer

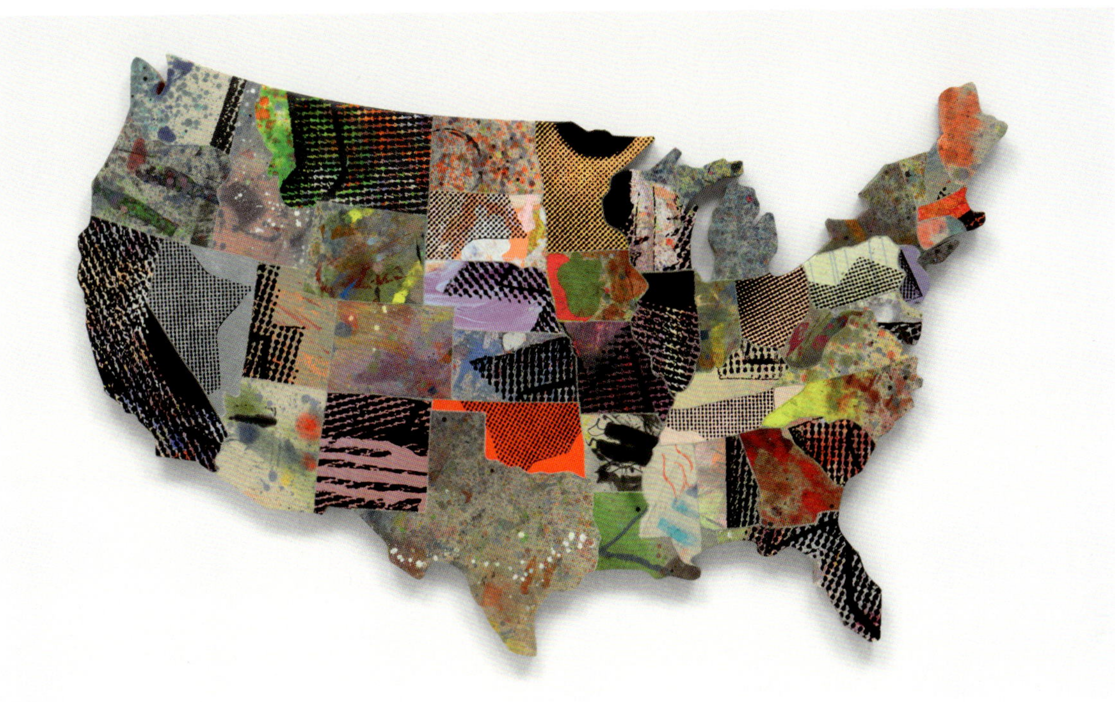

of black dots on top of the colors, like a black-and-white photocopy layered on top of a color picture, all done by hand, and blurring the lines. The rooms appear ordinary, not a place where such violence could have originated, where a homicidal man chose to destroy as many lives as he could. The clumsiness and badly lit dramatics of many of the photos seemed to tell an analogous story about the ways we will and will not understand this event for years to come.
—Nate Lowman[4]

The mass murder may have affected Lowman viscerally and psychologically—the killings happened in his hometown, also attacking his childhood and early memories. Whatever his initial motivations, Lowman responded with art.

The Vegas series is somber, bizarrely quiet, the antithesis of the noise, in all senses, of its subject matter. The deliberateness rests in the subdued and rather bland rooms, and his blurring the lines, I think instantly, between sanity and insanity.

Lowman's approach emphasizes the incident's ordinariness, there have been many massacres here. The grays, he told me, represent fogginess. The grays, and even the blurs, in a descriptive stretch, did bring to mind the fog of this ongoing domestic war, in which Americans kill each other every day.

What interrupts the calm and quiet are the "scribbles," which is how Lowman refers to the hand-painted, random-seeming streaks on the paintings' surface. They create a pictorial tension or dynamic, like a sudden turbulence in the room. Mark-making is a kind of writing, and in this horror chamber, it is writing on the wall, portending more chaos. And insinuating uncertainty.

Uncertainty is a facet in some of Lowman's work. That is, uncertainty in the way that Ludwig Wittgenstein argued about it in the use of the verb "to know." What does it mean to say, "I know." Where is doubt? And what do you know when you look at these pictures, the rooms from which a mass murderer shot off a thousand rounds of ammo. What does anyone know about these bullet holes. What meaning is to be ascribed to these objects

11. *Cobble Hustle Weave*, 2022. Oil, acrylic, alkyd, latex, dirt, and nylon thread on canvas on wood panel, 48¾ × 77¼ inches | 123.8 × 196.2 cm

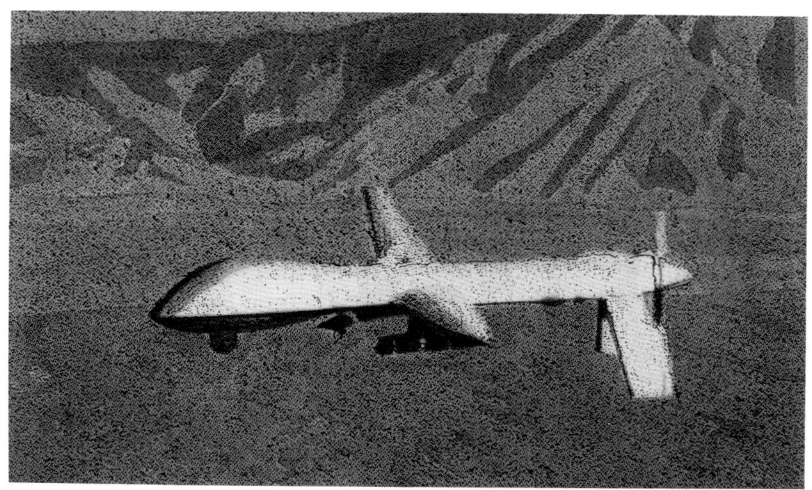

other than, I propose, that they represent slices of American life, portraits of the contemporary moment and its attributes and accessories.

Mass shootings are, supposedly, unnatural. People don't "naturally" turn into mass killers, or they do. Early humans were predators; predation exists, usually in other forms than mass killings—rape, kidnappings, domestic violence, and other forms of abuse and brutality. The scale and enormity of violence here seems "inhuman," even if human behavior includes every kind of good and grotesque act.

Lowman's paintings mark various meanings of a natural order. There is human-made aggression, such as mass killings, which might now be second nature. While the hurricanes, storms, fires, and floods he depicts, usually considered natural events—that is, beyond human control—have become more uncontrollable and devastating because of people's mismanagement and corruption of the earth's resources.

> I dread hurricane season.
>
> —Nate Lowman[5]

Recently, Lowman painted the eye of various hurricanes. Their fury and rage have beaten down and extinguished cities and homes, bridges and seawalls, causing huge floods. The canvases are large and dramatic: each eye stuns with ferocity. The storms are painted with especially garish colors that, Lowman explains, do not exist in reality (they are from meteorologists' graphics). The paintings are unique, each based on a specific hurricane's shape, and are named for that hurricane: Andrew (1992), Katrina (2005), Irene (2011), Sandy (2012), Harvey (2017), Irma (2017), Maria (2017), Florence (2018), Ida (2021).

Unlikely and "unnatural" colors match these hurricanes' increasingly unnatural state, that is, the storms have become more destructive and more numerous than ever before recorded. Human interference has caused the worsening climate. The concepts of nature and natural, since people are part of nature, will need new descriptions.

In response to Hurricane Ida, which had flooded his studio, Lowman executed *Yonkers, Sept. 1, 2021* (2022; pp. 132–133, detail p. 111).[6] *Yonkers* foregrounds two cars floating in water, submerged by Ida's massive flood. The storm water, which is the painting's ground, is murky, mauve, a purply gray, a fusion of colors. The effect reminded me of how, when mixing paint, the resulting color becomes so diffuse it is hard to define.

12. *Drone*, 2021. Oil and alkyd on linen, 36 × 63 inches | 91.4 × 160 cm

13. *Burning Farm*, 2022. Oil and alkyd on linen, 37 × 95 inches | 94 × 241.3 cm

A flood drags and carries everything in its wake, the water filthy with bacteria, poisons, muck, unhealthy even to the touch. The flood transforms water into a dangerous killer, a "natural" terminator.

I am drawn to this particular painting, it is beautiful and deadly. It feels intimate, and for readers to understand my attraction better, here is a closer description of it:

In the bottom left foreground, a car is submerged, immobilized. A second car is also; it is also toward the left of the work, but veers toward the center of the canvas, and is nearer to the top of the painting. Both cars are silver or silvery white—they are different models, lined up, as if drowned together at the same time. Their headlights reflect on the murky water, and bursts of red light, like small fires, appear in front of both cars.

In this context—against the murky purplish gray background—the hand-painted slashes seem like unformed words, they might be about struggling. It's a stretch, I know, to suggest this interpretation, but I can imagine it here, some sort of intimacy. Now Lowman's mark-making is about human gestures, and so represents human loss. Where are the drivers and the passengers?

It is a particularly tender work, heartbreaking and curiously romantic. Maybe because of the cars. Because Americans love their cars, or because driving can make people feel free. They can escape, or just get away, ZOOM. But not here.

Cars let people move from place to place, that's a freedom, or just as likely a necessity, a lost job, a need to find work elsewhere. For people without a place to live, cars can become their home. While abandoned or junked cars look sad, they were once attached to people. Cars are attachments. People love their cars, are identified, even judged by them. People identify with them. Cars 'r' us.

In *Yonkers* cars are metonymic, they are lost or dead people. They can't move. They have lost the freedom they promise, and to Americans, freedom is about being able to move, just as flight to the Futurists meant freedom and progress into the future.

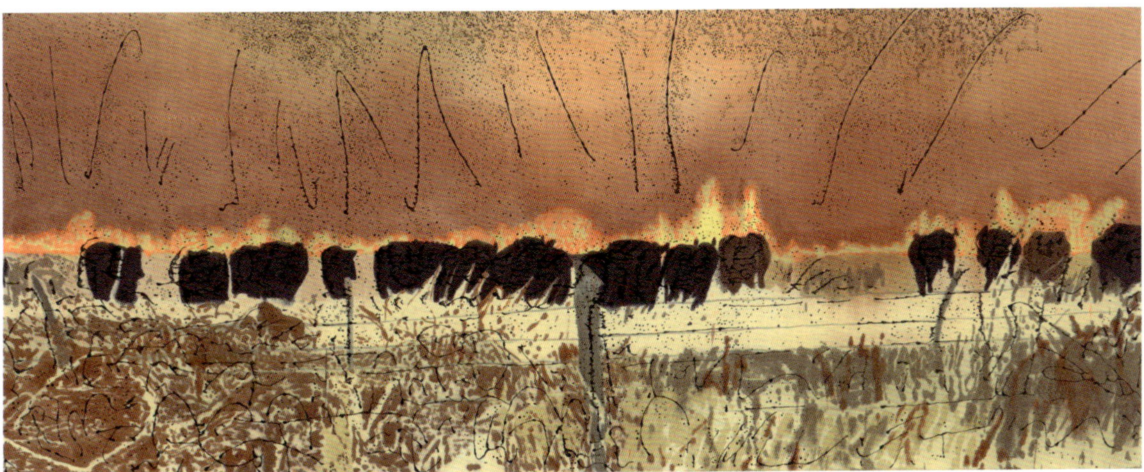

At age 18, an American can expect to move another 9.1 times in their remaining lifetime, but by age 45, the expected number of moves is only 2.7.[7]

In comparison:

Recent research indicates that, on average, Britons move once every 23 years.[8]

Movement also is in the American DNA. Early settlers pushed west, leaving one place for a better one, they hoped. But they stole land and decimated Native American tribes. In Frederick Turner's Frontier thesis, which has been thoroughly discredited, he proposed that, when Americans traveled west to the Pacific, the arduous crossing separated them from Europe and transformed them into a new people and nation. They would have left their past behind.

That myth of the making of Americans valorized movement as progress; it was an American virtue and was used to excuse genocide. Still, the idea was sutured into the American imagination, where the invention of cars encouraged that idea of movement being an American's essential liberty. It's why advertisements for SUVs show huge cars gliding up mountains and traveling on rough roads—this is the American way of life—while actually SUVs mostly clog highways and city streets.

Lowman's work represents a troubled, contentious, and contradictory America. It wonders how come guns and AR-15s have been assimilated here, how come military-grade weapons wind up on beds, how come so many schoolchildren are dying in school shootings—how did this happen. His art is not didactic and doesn't tell anyone what to think. He sometimes renders offbeat, funny objects, like painted air fresheners, and regularly depicts disturbing scenes and difficult events. Then the work stands on its own, confounding a viewer who wants to know what it all means.

To many of us Americans, this country is perplexing and vexing, and its future seems very uncertain. America becomes more disturbing with every bullet shot. An inescapable and essential aspect of Nate Lowman's work is an engagement with this America. He challenges himself to render unwanted realities as he challenges viewers to see them with their eyes wide open.

1. Franz Kafka, *The Diaries of Franz Kafka, 1910–1923*, ed. Max Brod (New York: Schocken Books, 1976), p. 15.

2. Nate Lowman, in conversation with the author, New York, October 6, 2022.

3. Wikipedia, s.vv. "2017 Las Vegas shooting" (accessed online).

4. Lowman, in conversation with the author.

5. Lowman, in conversation with the author.

6. The painting exists in two sizes. The larger version is shown on pages 132–133. The smaller version is *Yonkers Sept. 1, 2021 (Second Version)*, oil and alkyd on linen, 55 × 98 inches (139.7 × 248.9 cm).

7. "Calculating Migration Expectancy Using ACS Data," United States Census Bureau, last revised December 3, 2021 (accessed online).

8. "How often do Brits move in their lifetime?" *Open Access Government*, March 13, 2019 (accessed online).

Yonkers Sept. 1, 2021, 2022 (detail)

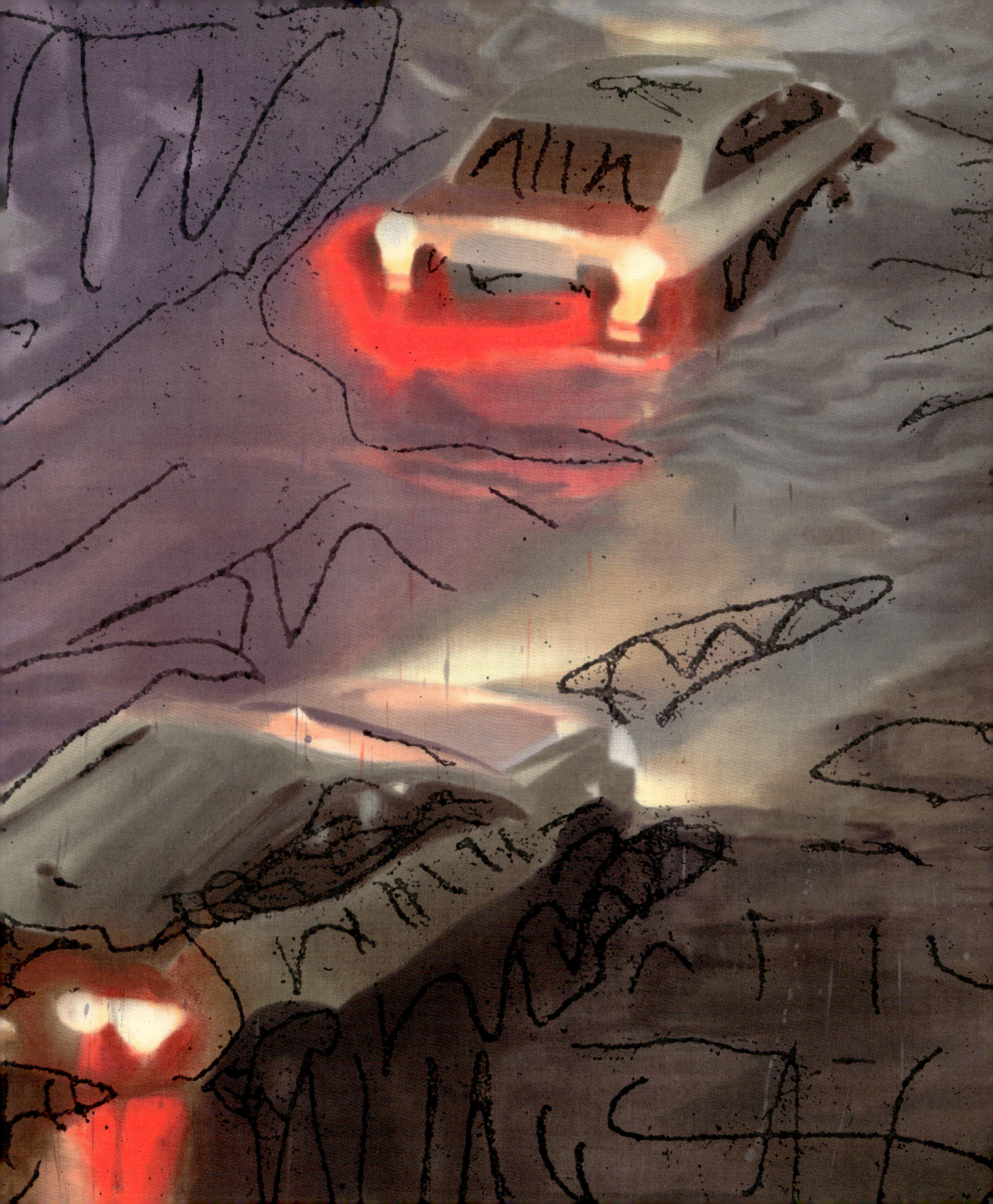

Hurricanes

***We Are Seeing People We Didn't Know Exist*, 2011** Oil and alkyd on linen, 62 × 75 inches | 157.5 × 190.5 cm

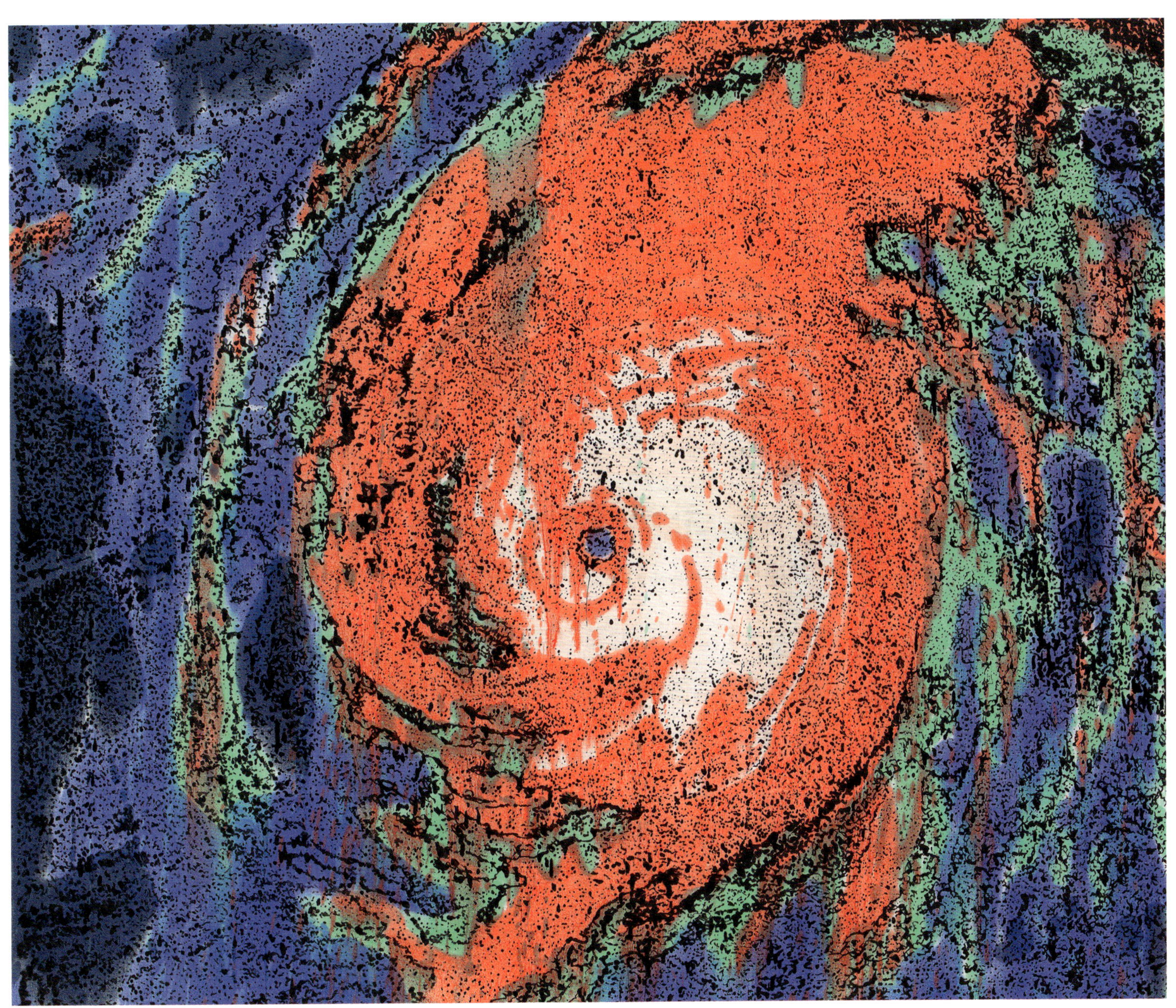

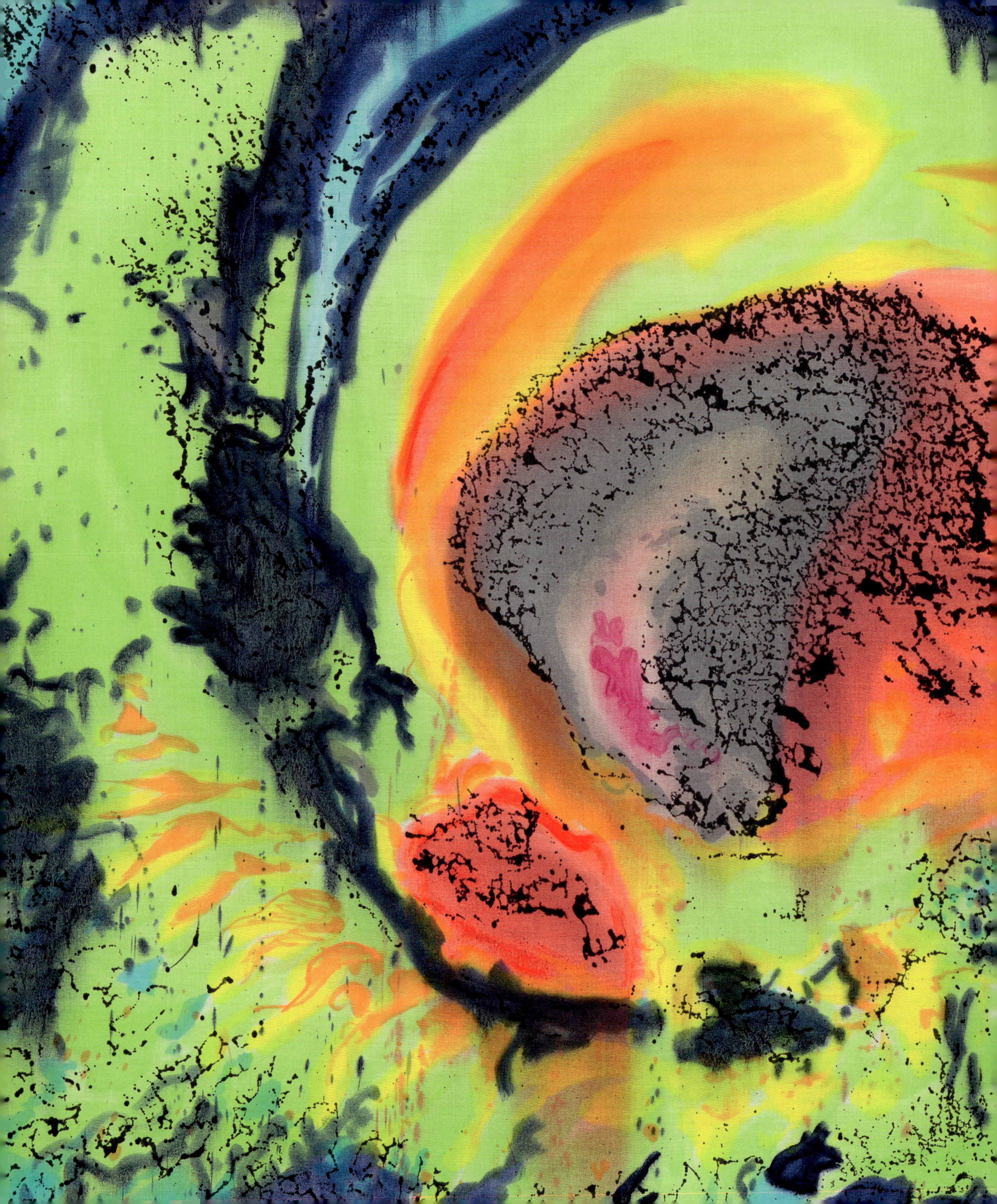

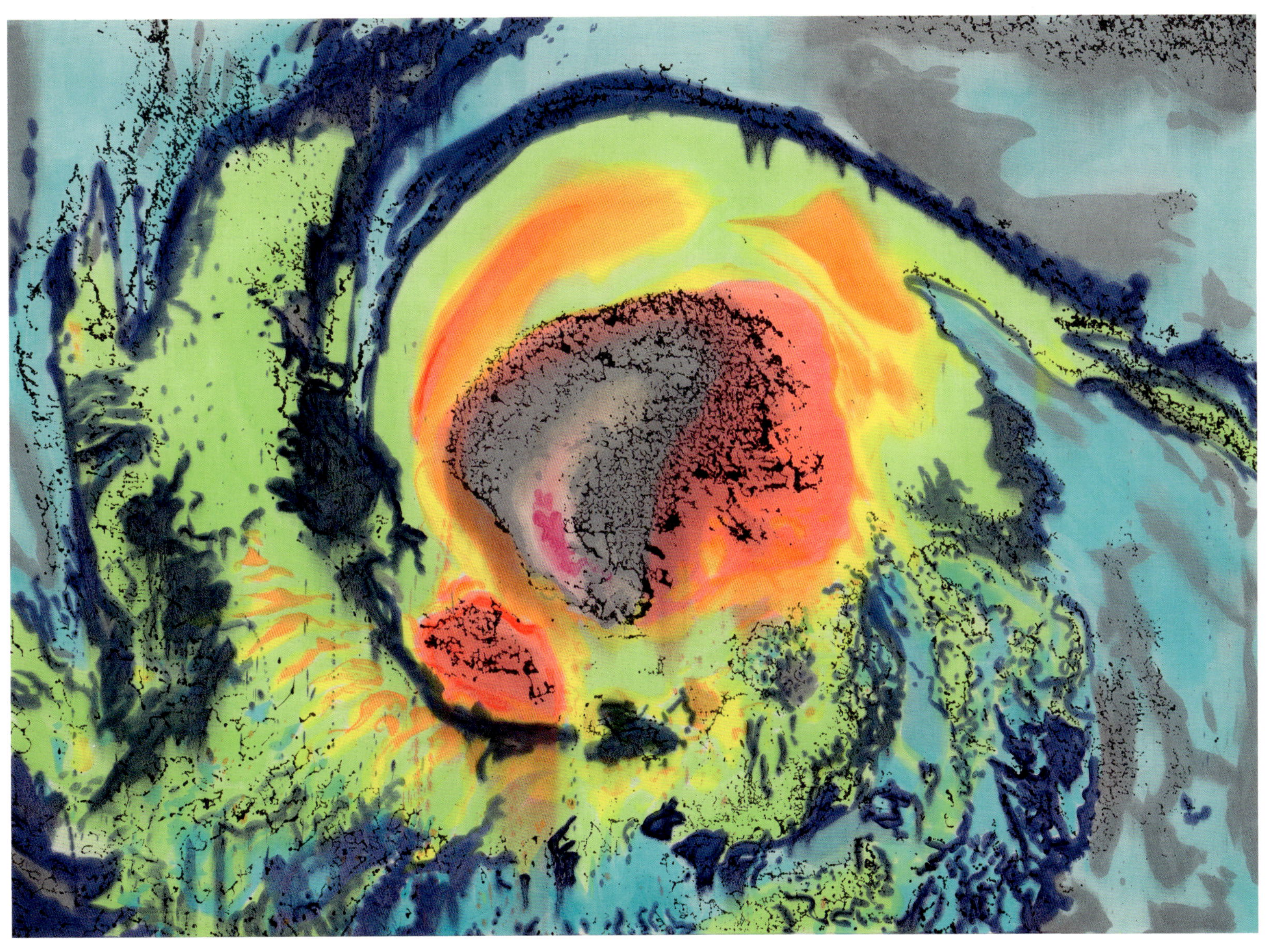

***Irma*, 2017** Oil and alkyd on linen, 90 × 126 inches | 228.6 × 320 cm

***Harvey*, 2017** Oil and alkyd on canvas, 90 × 126 inches | 228.6 × 320 cm

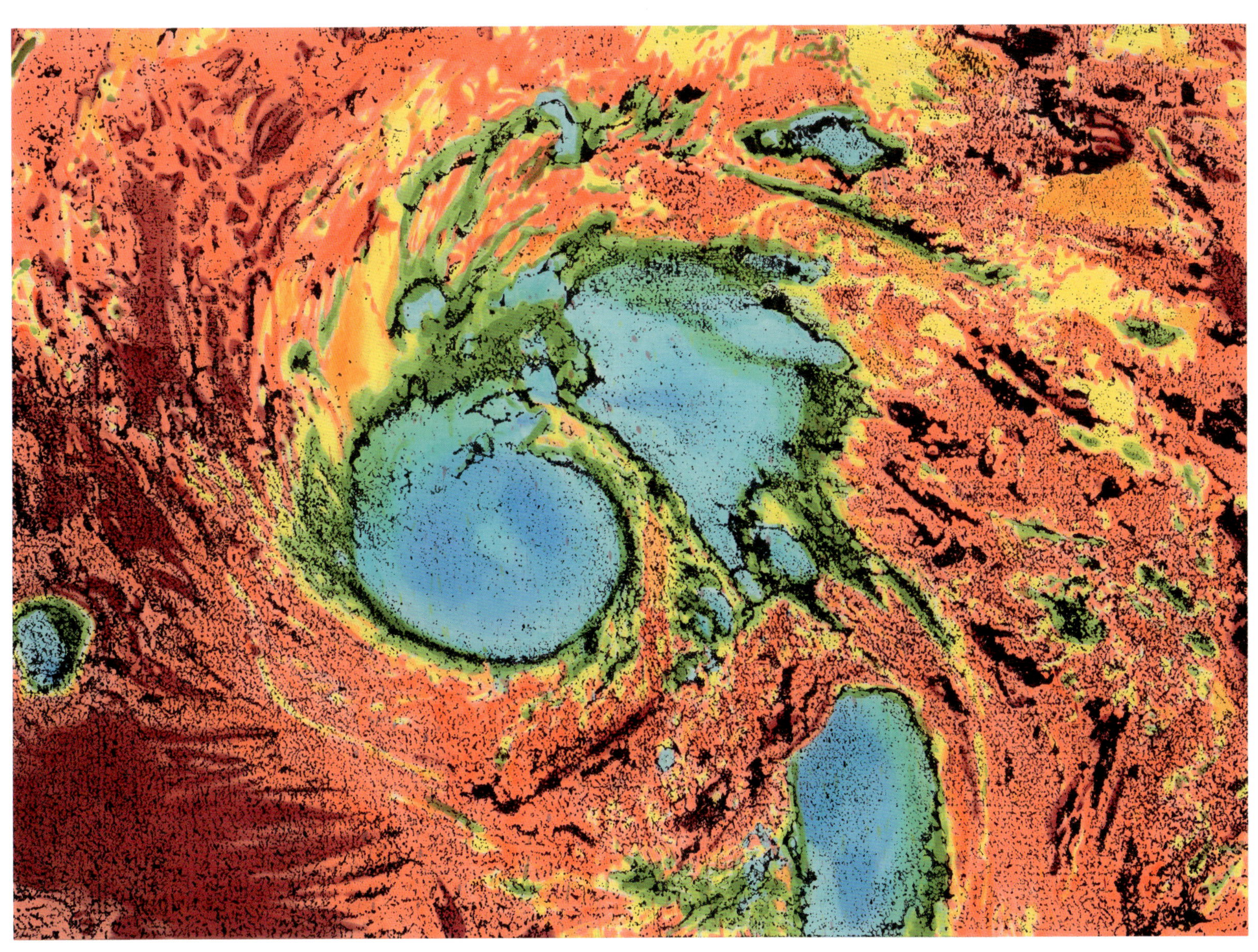

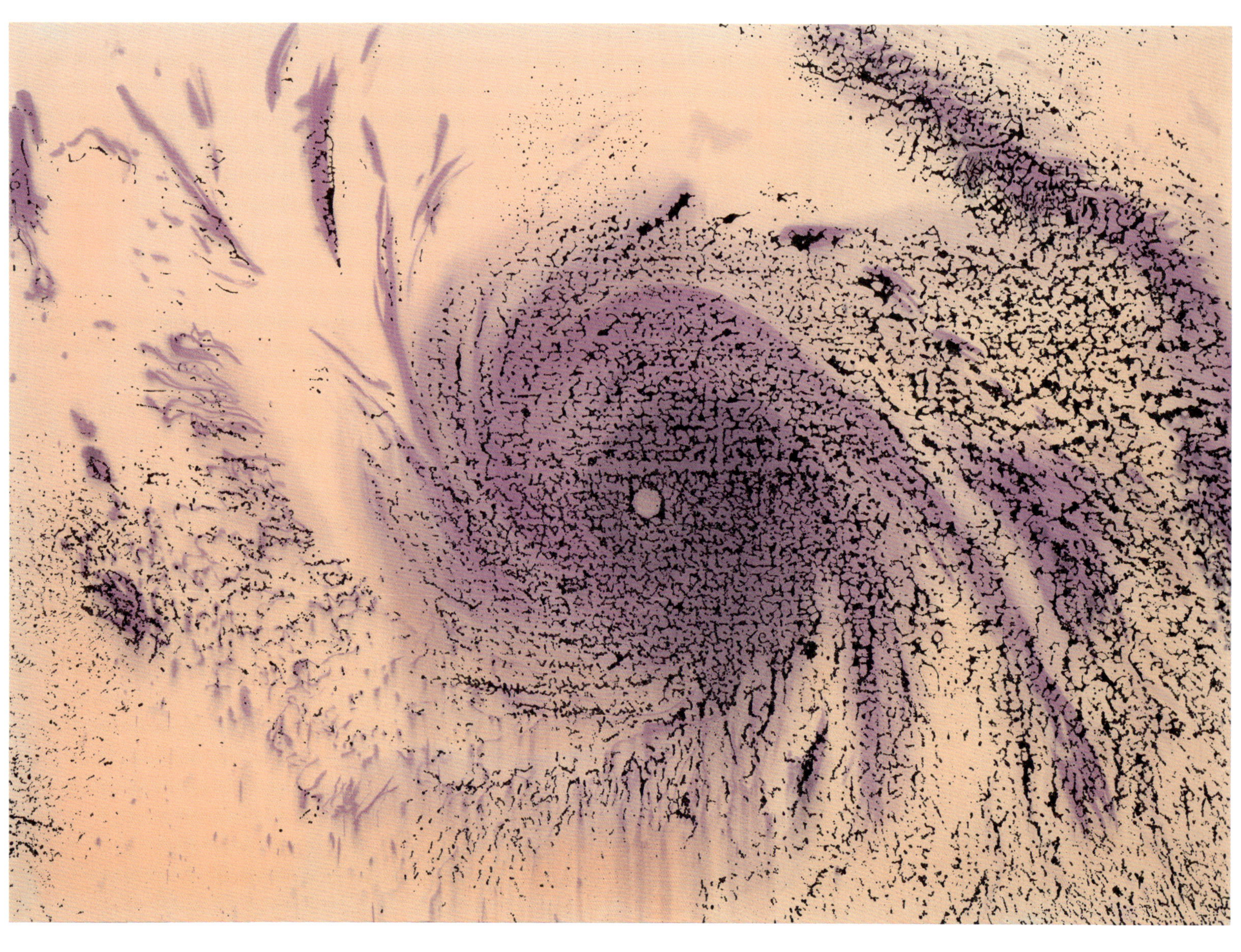

 ***Maria*, 2017** Oil and alkyd on linen, 90 × 126 inches | 228.6 × 320 cm

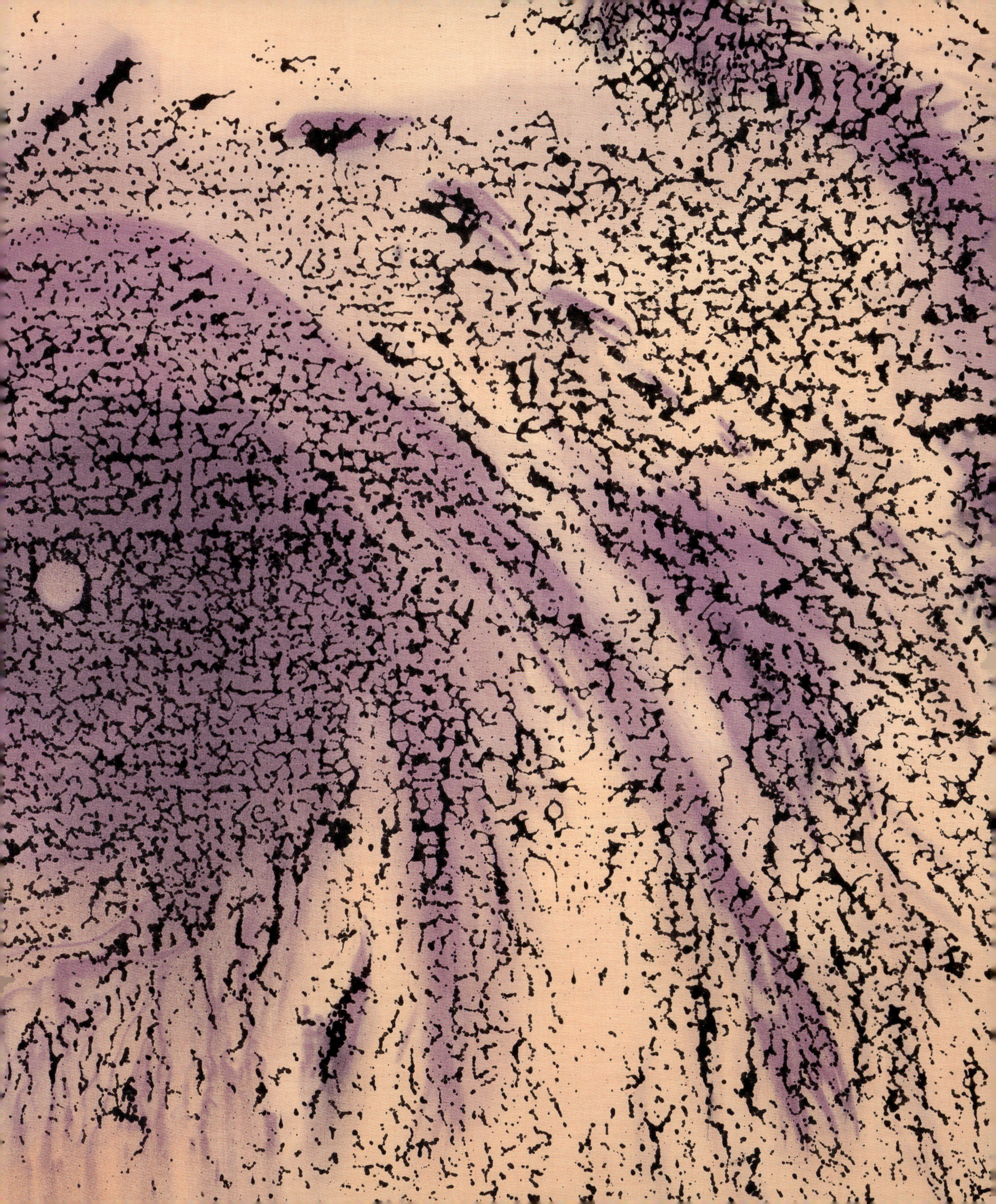

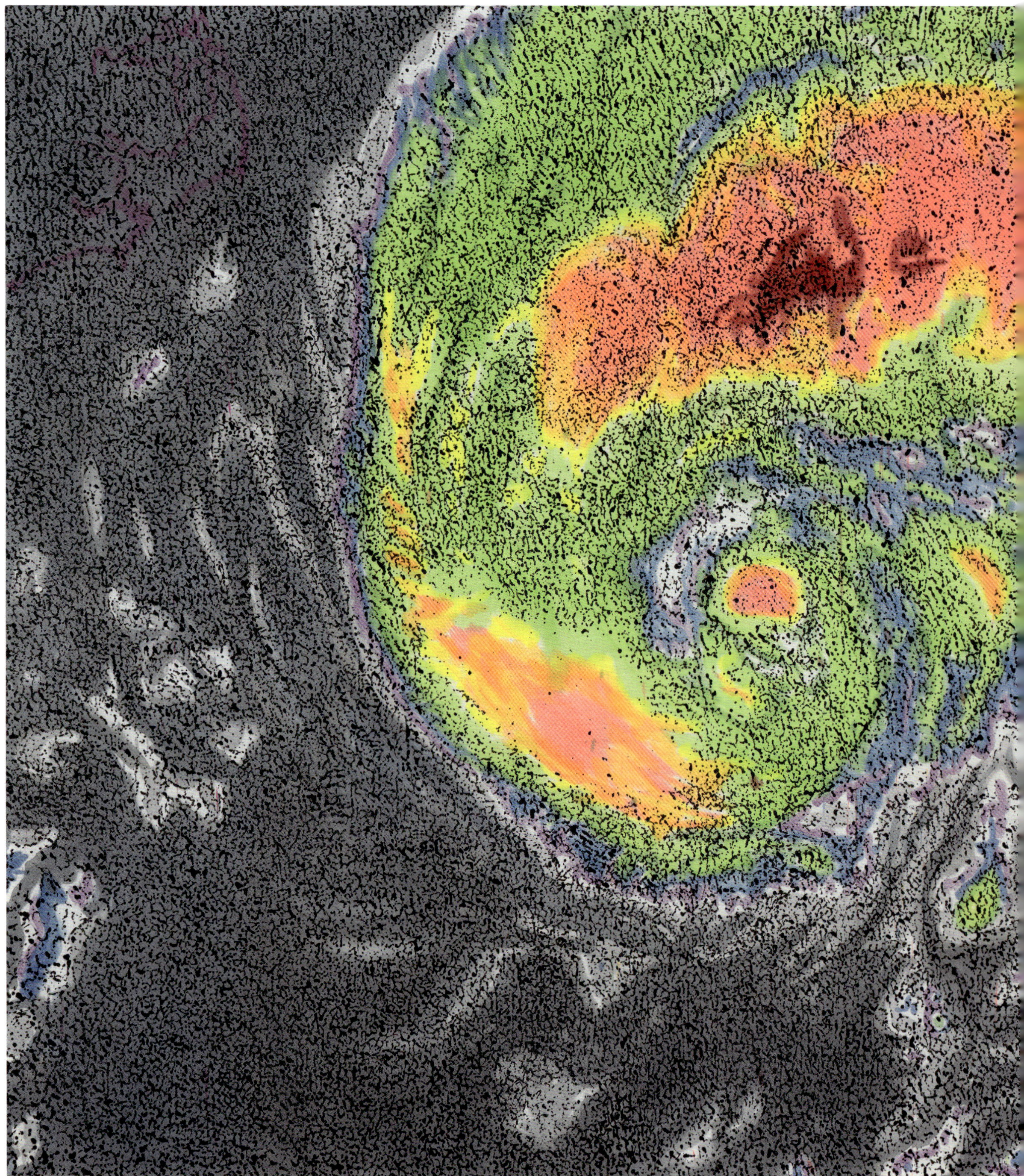

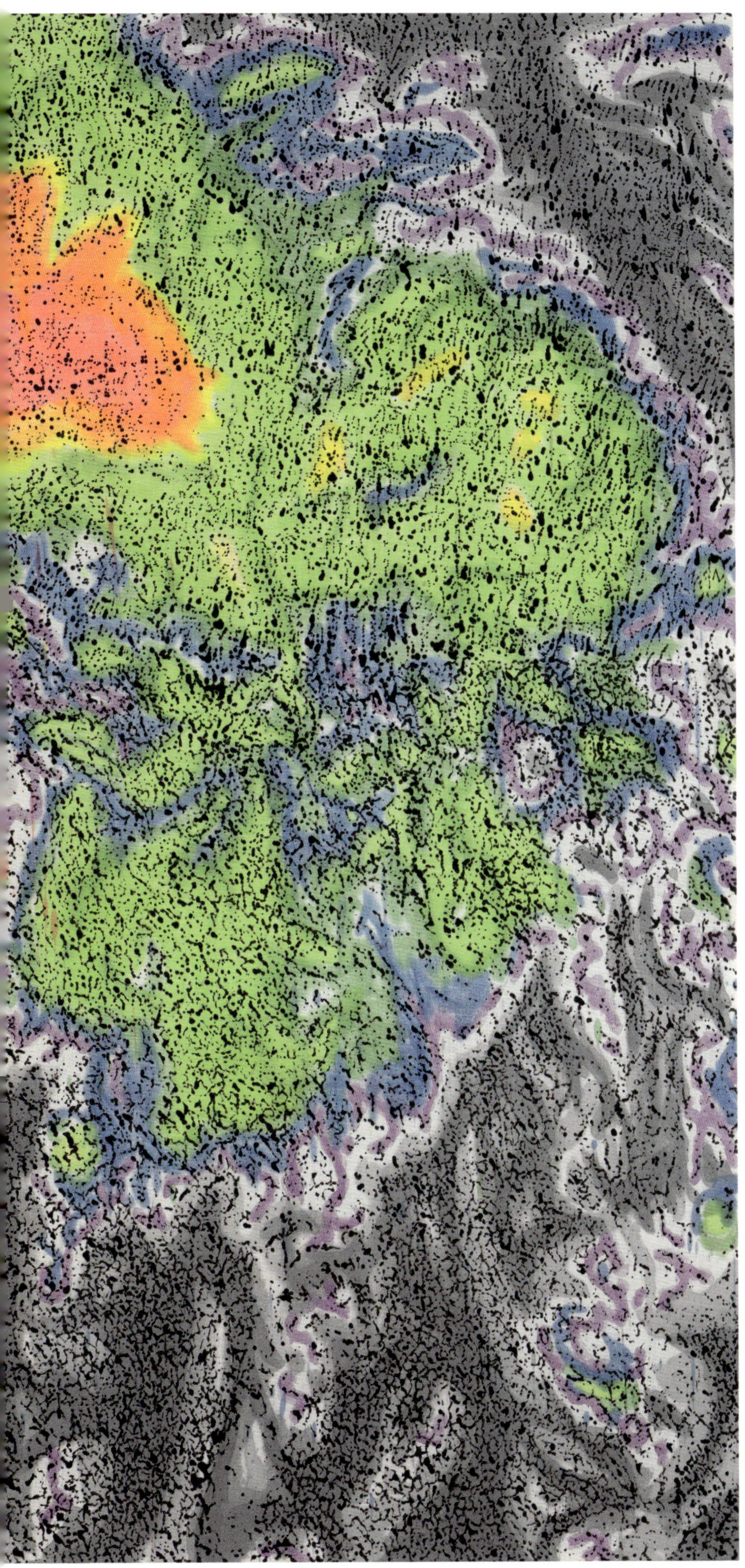

***Maria*, 2018** Oil and alkyd on linen, 84 × 120 inches | 213.4 × 304.8 cm

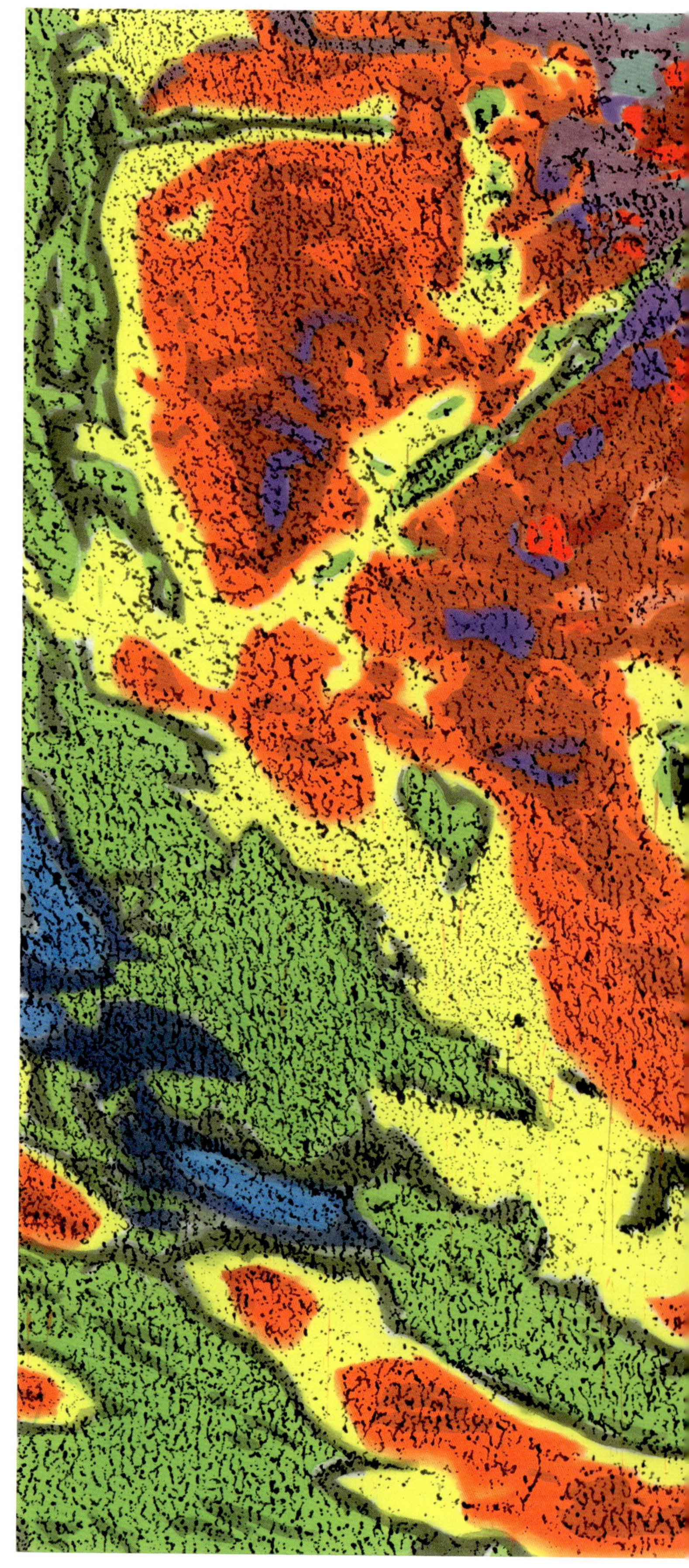

 ***Andrew*, 2020** Oil and alkyd on linen, 90 × 126¼ inches | 228.6 × 320.7 cm

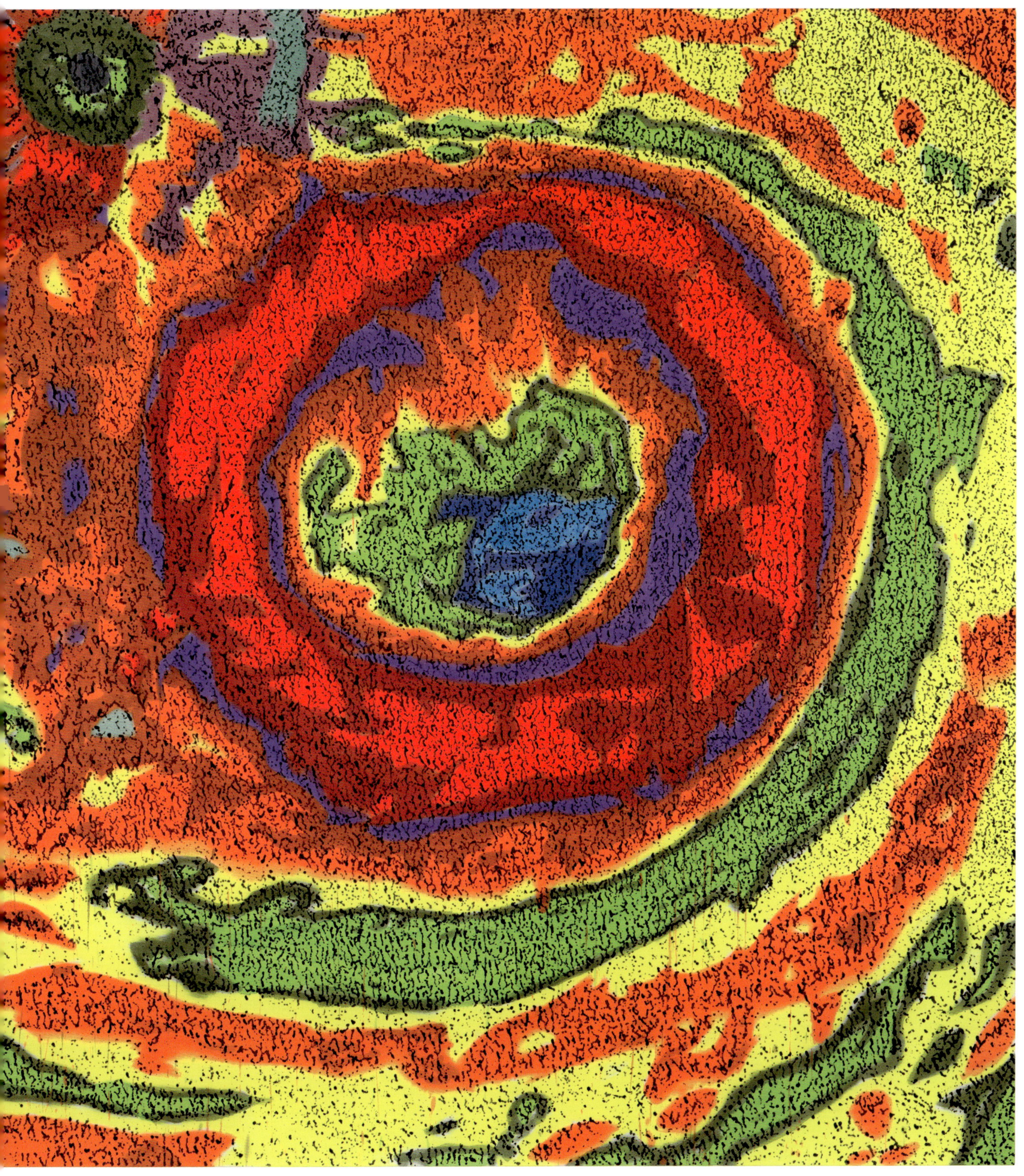

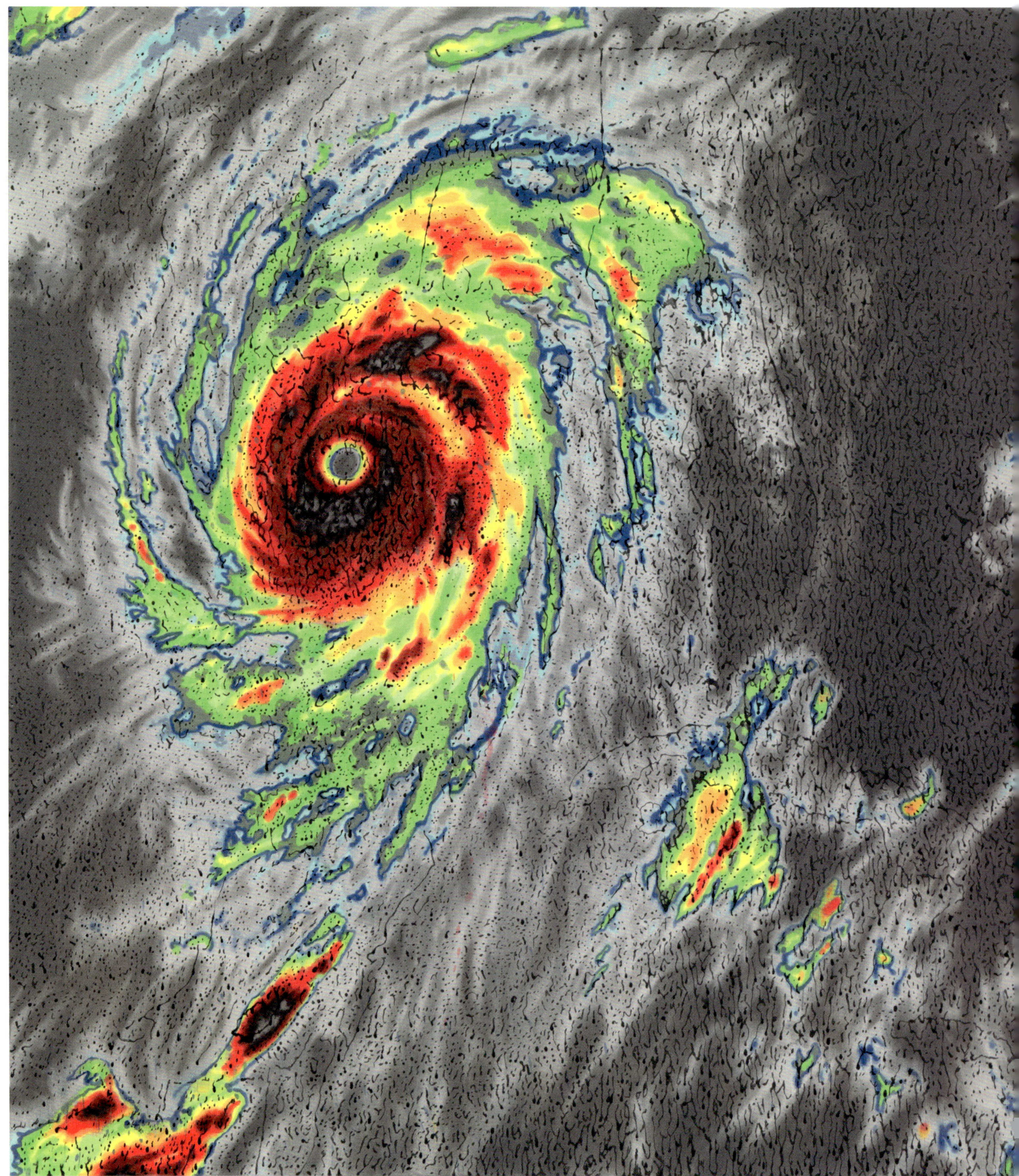

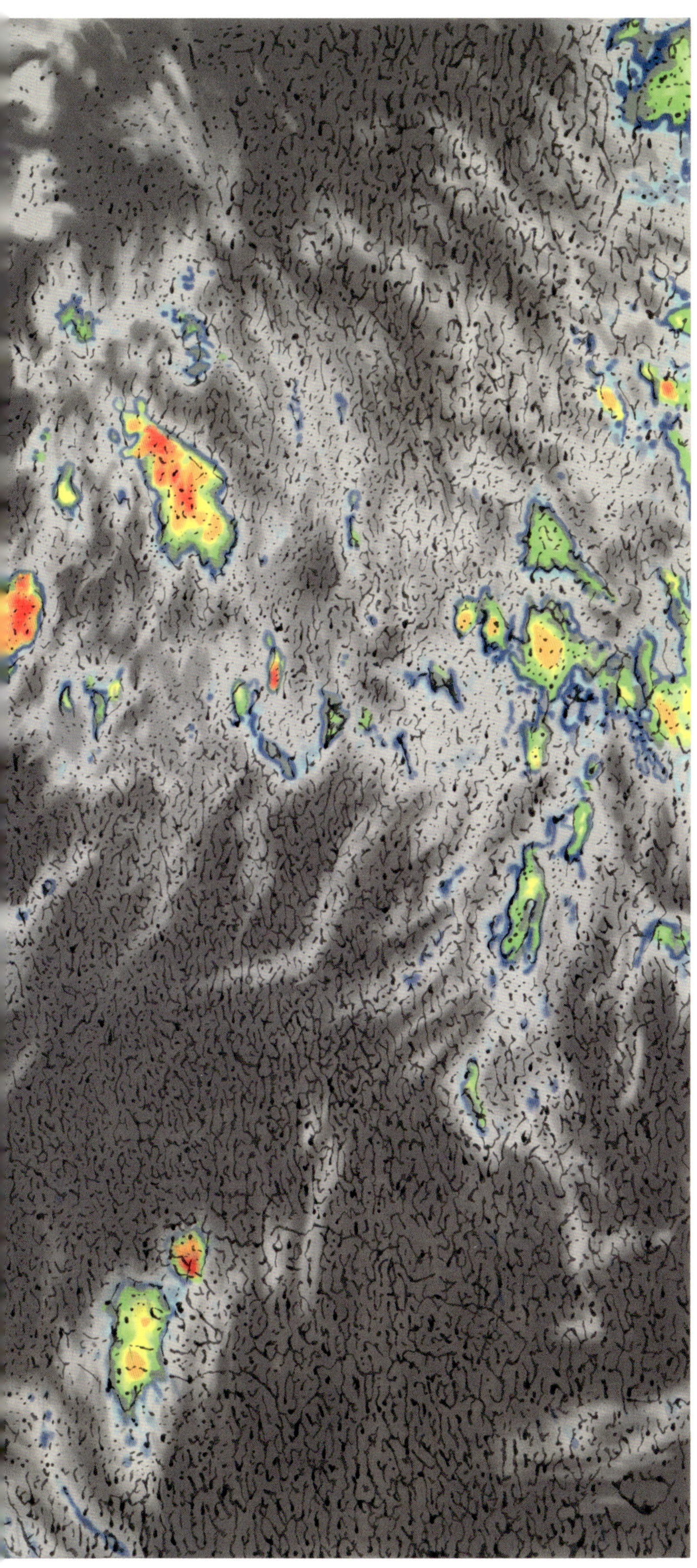

***Katrina*, 2022** Oil and alkyd on linen, 90 × 126 inches | 228.6 × 320 cm

***Florence*, 2022** Oil and alkyd on linen, 90 × 126 inches | 228.6 × 320 cm

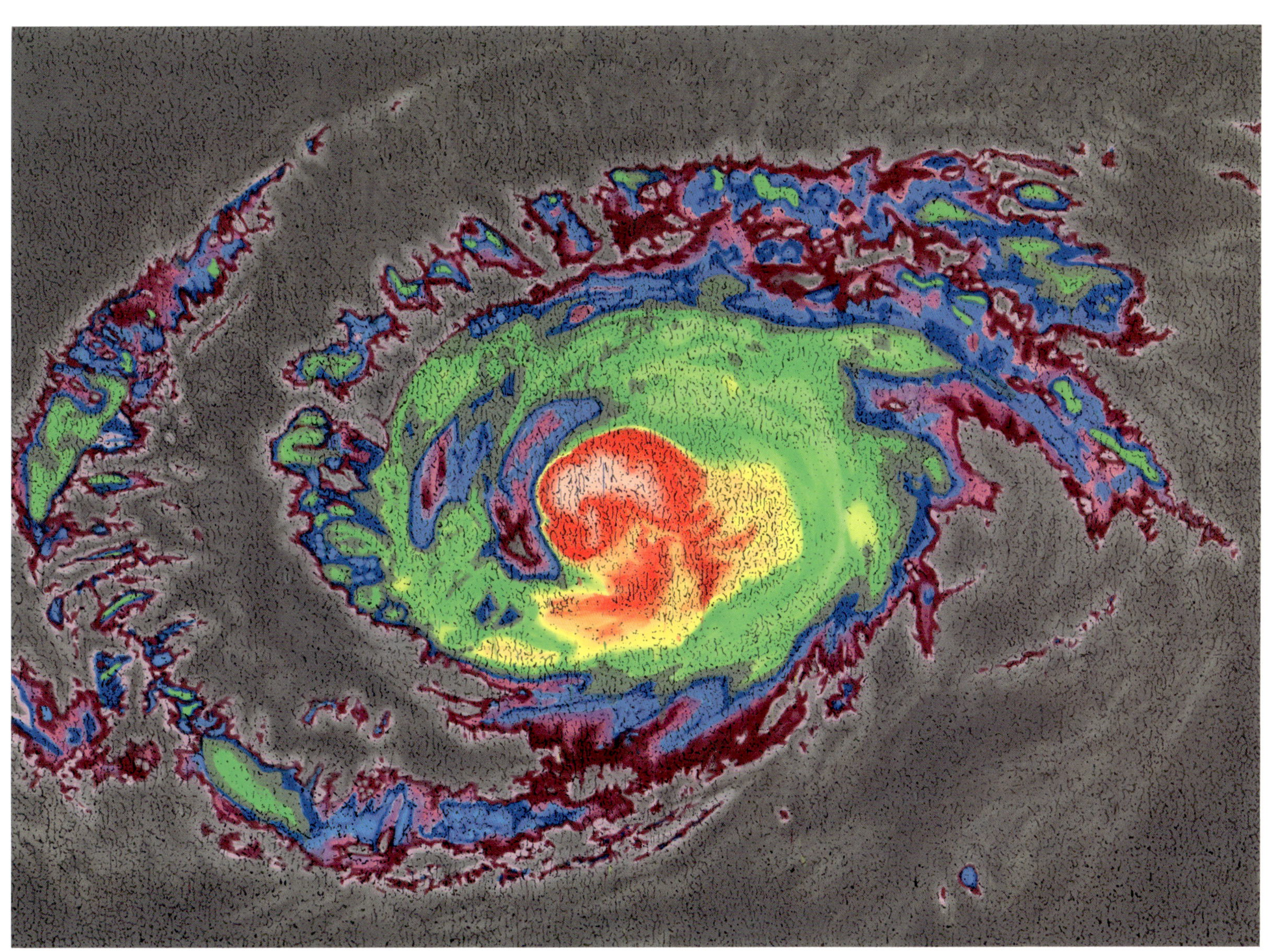

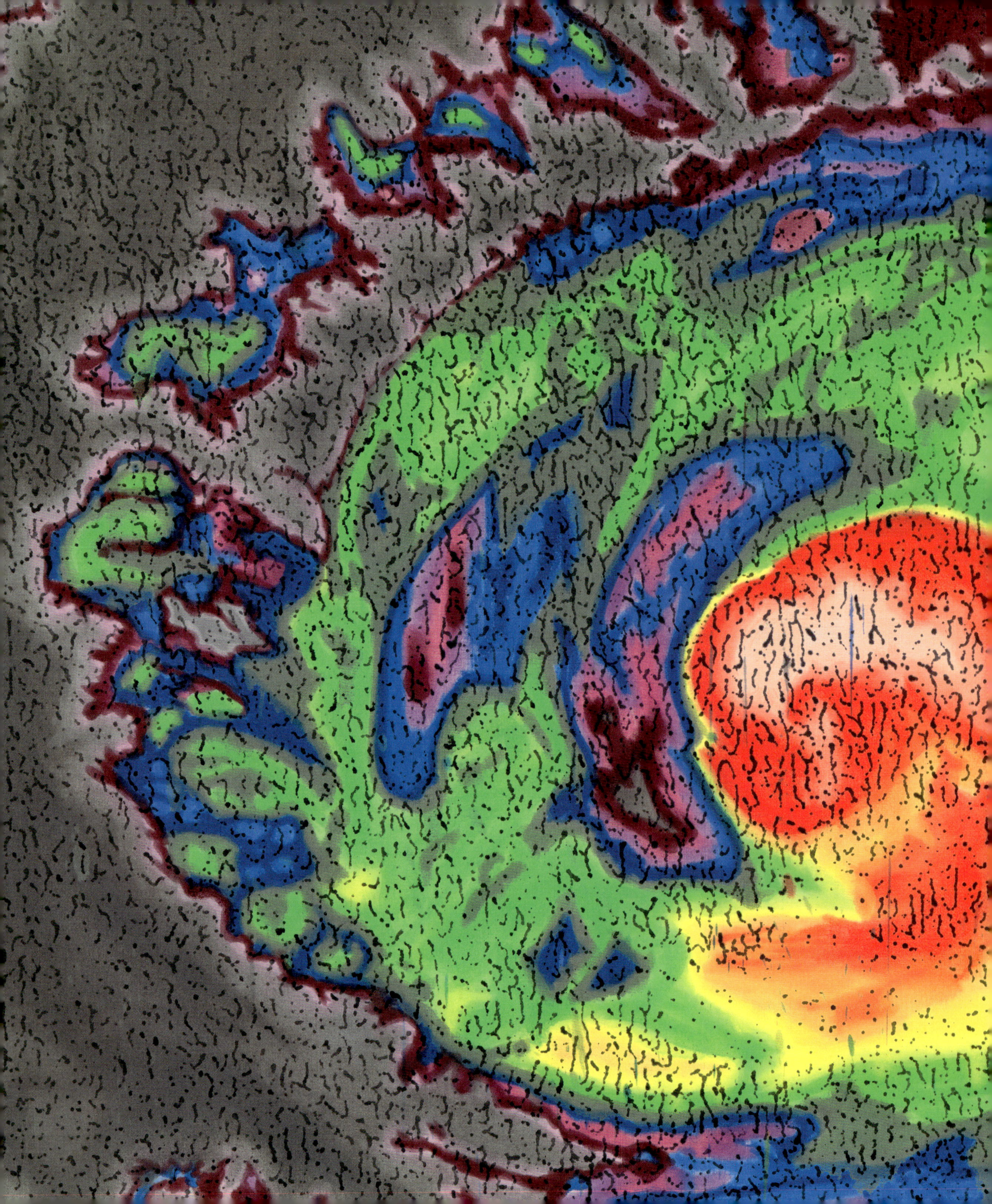

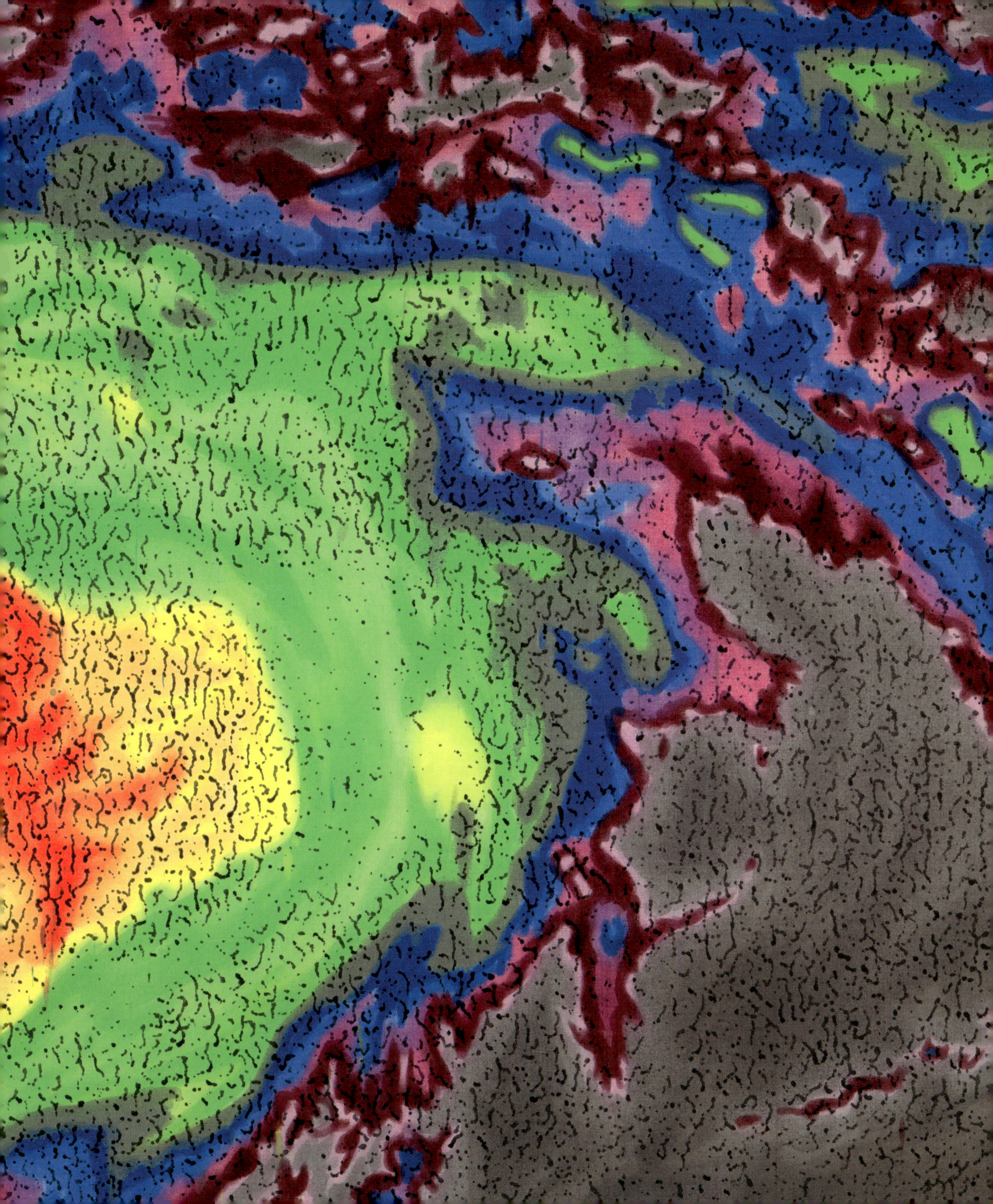

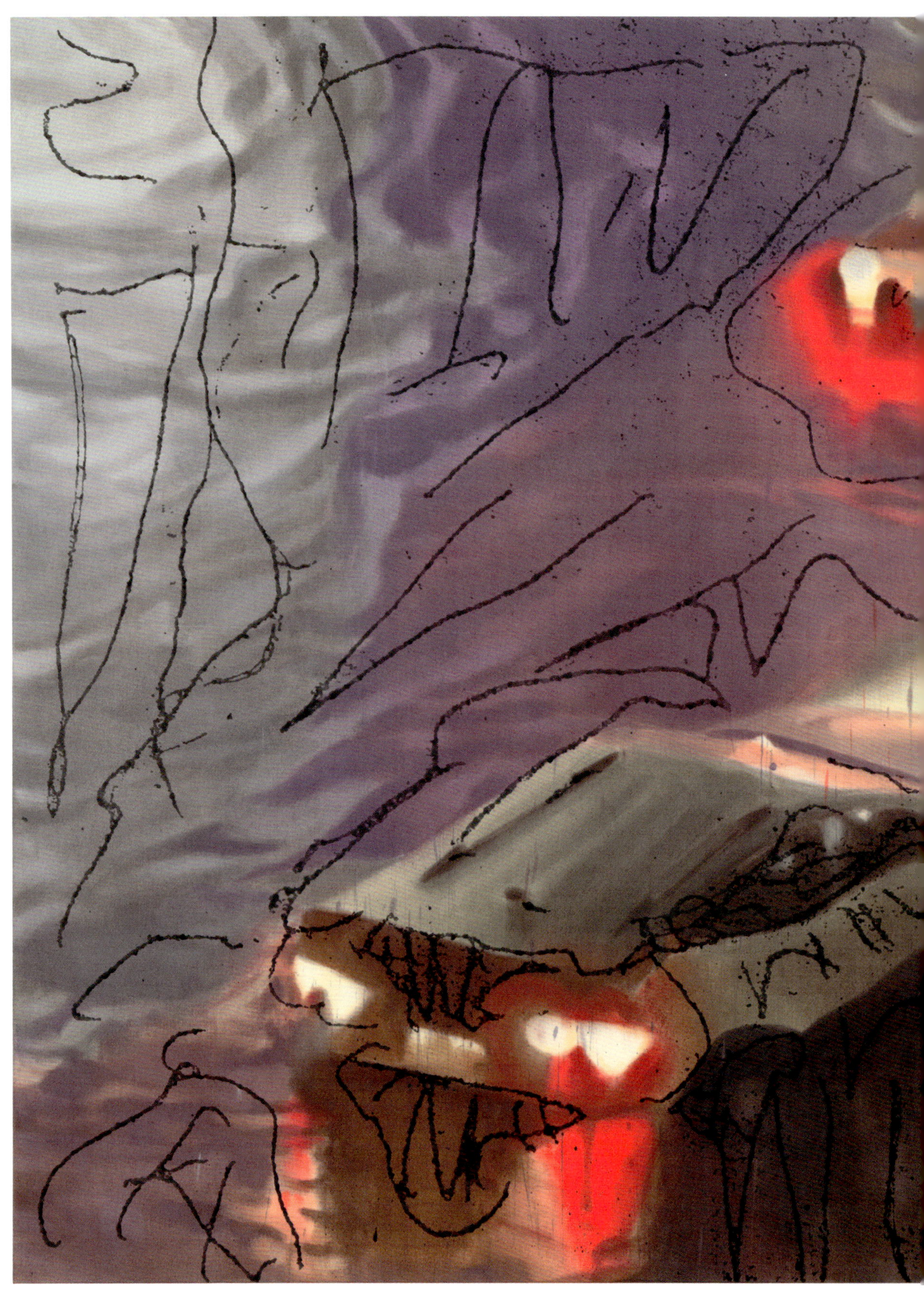

 ***Yonkers Sept. 1, 2021*, 2022** Oil and alkyd on linen, 82 ⅝ × 147 inches | 209.9 × 373.4 cm

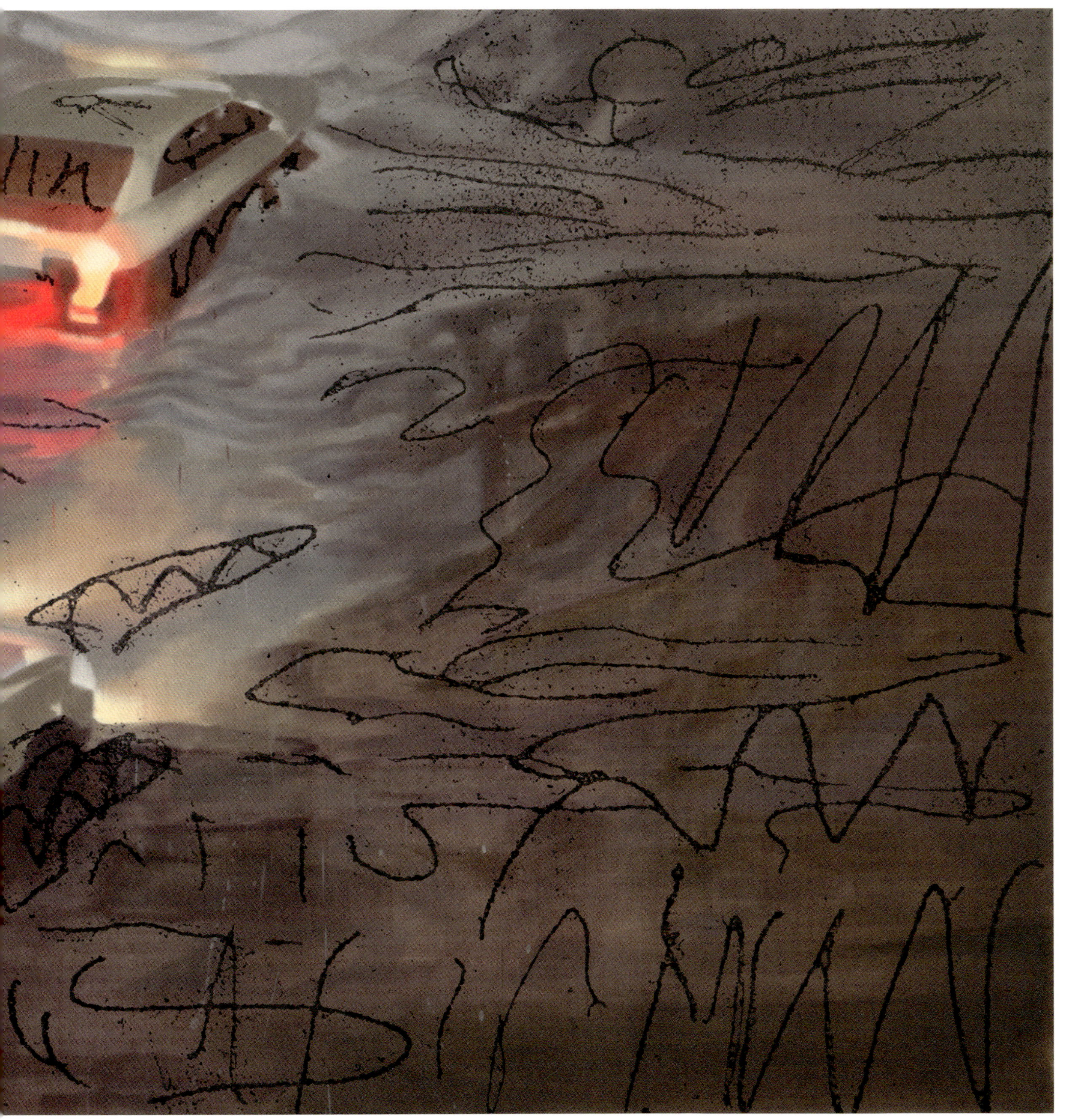

 ***Irma*, 2021** Oil and alkyd on linen, 90 × 126 inches | 228.6 × 320 cm

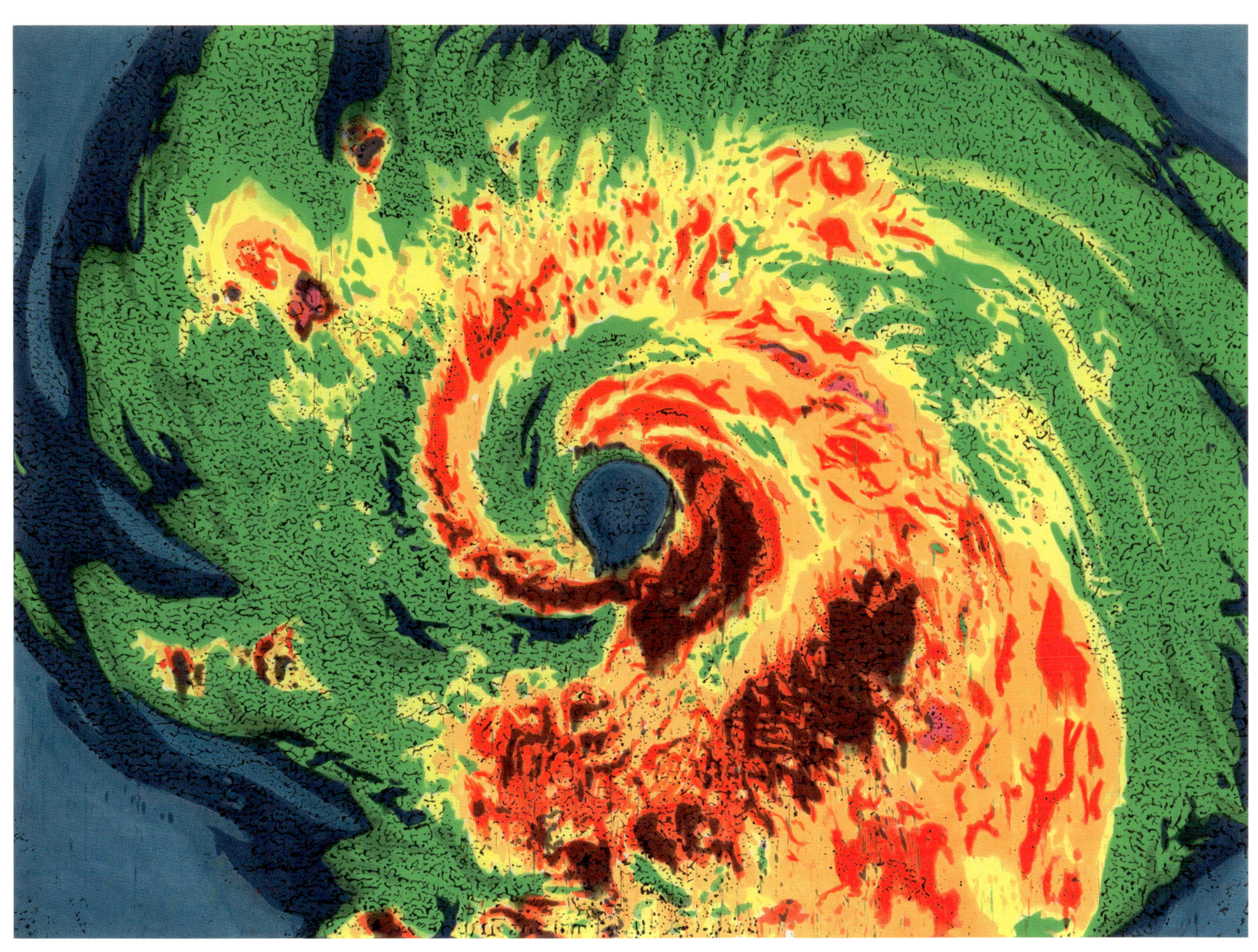

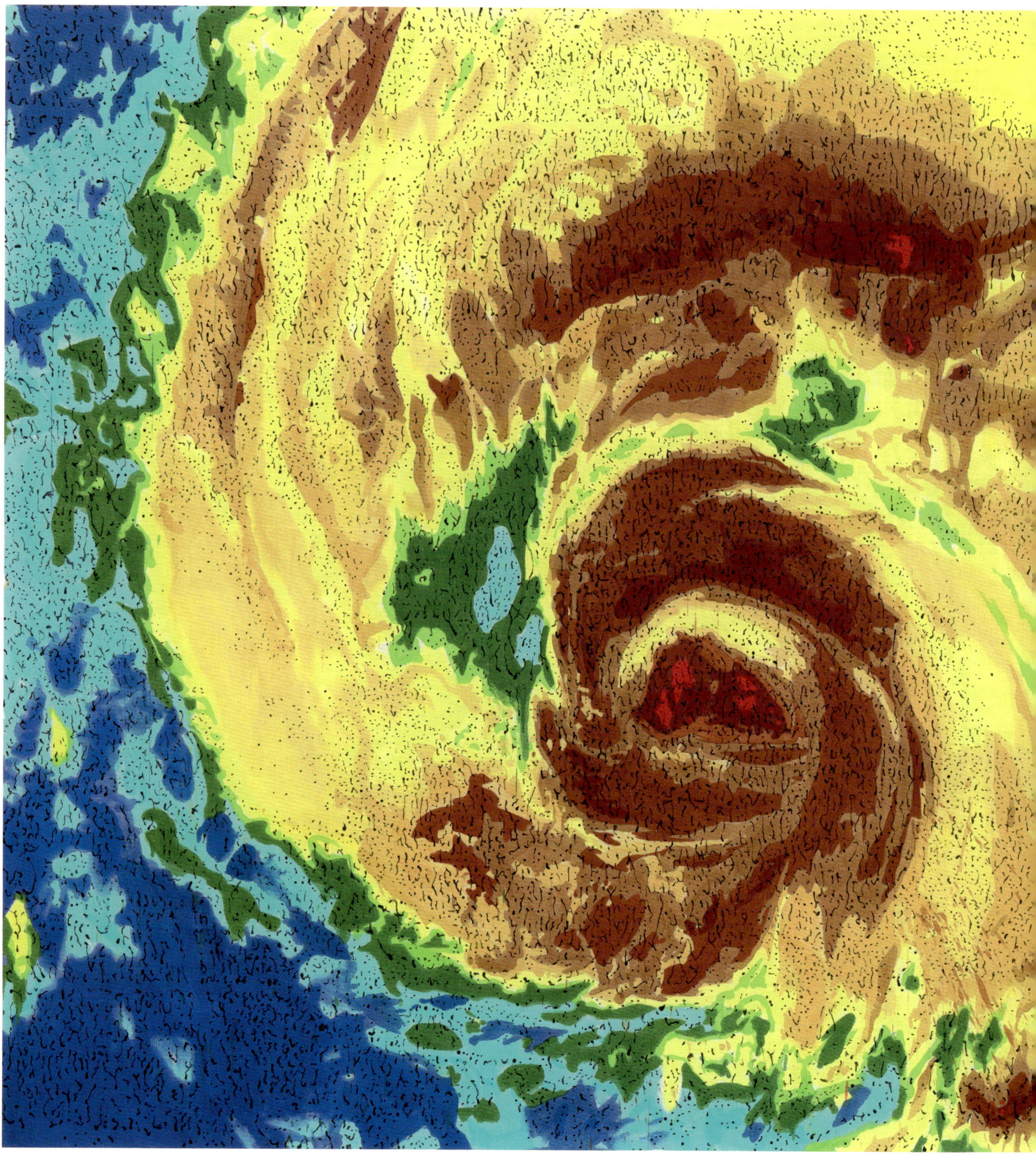

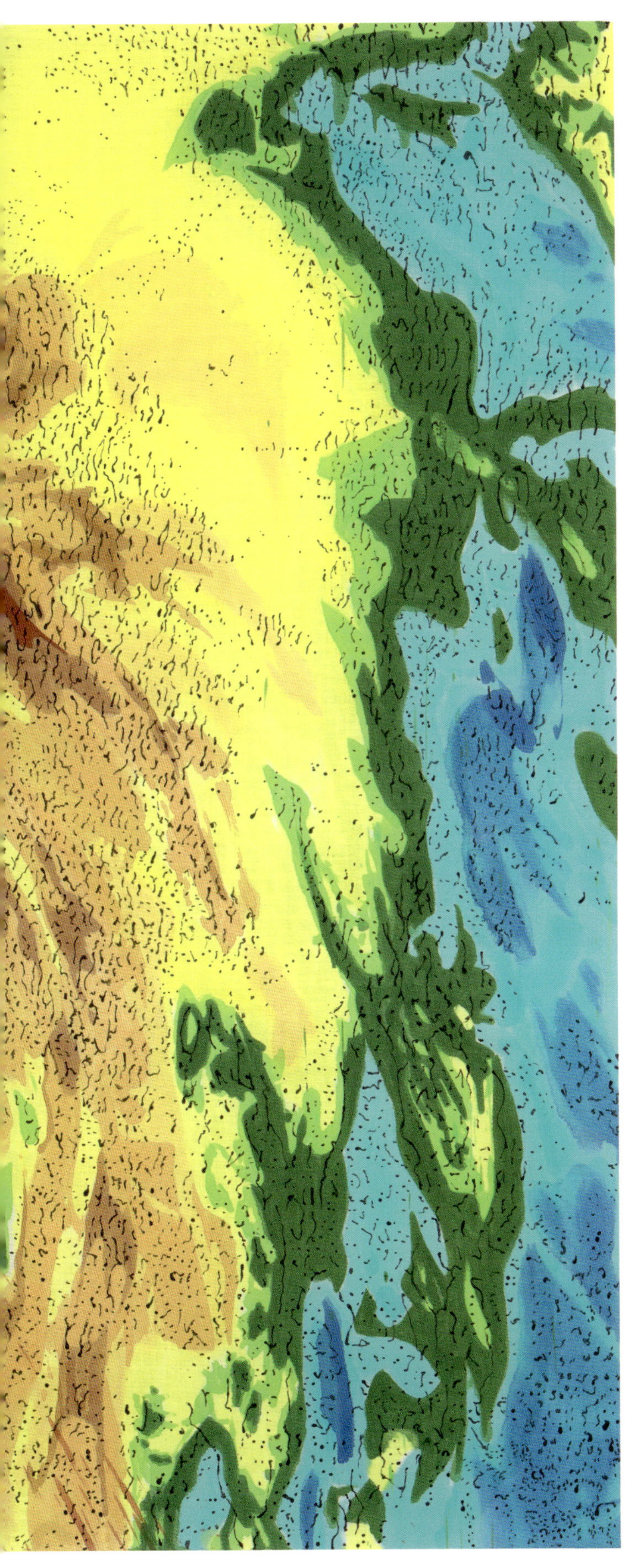

***Irene*, 2021** Oil and alkyd on linen, 90 × 126 inches | 228.6 × 320 cm

138 ***Irma*, 2022** Oil and alkyd on linen, 90 × 126 inches | 228.6 × 320 cm

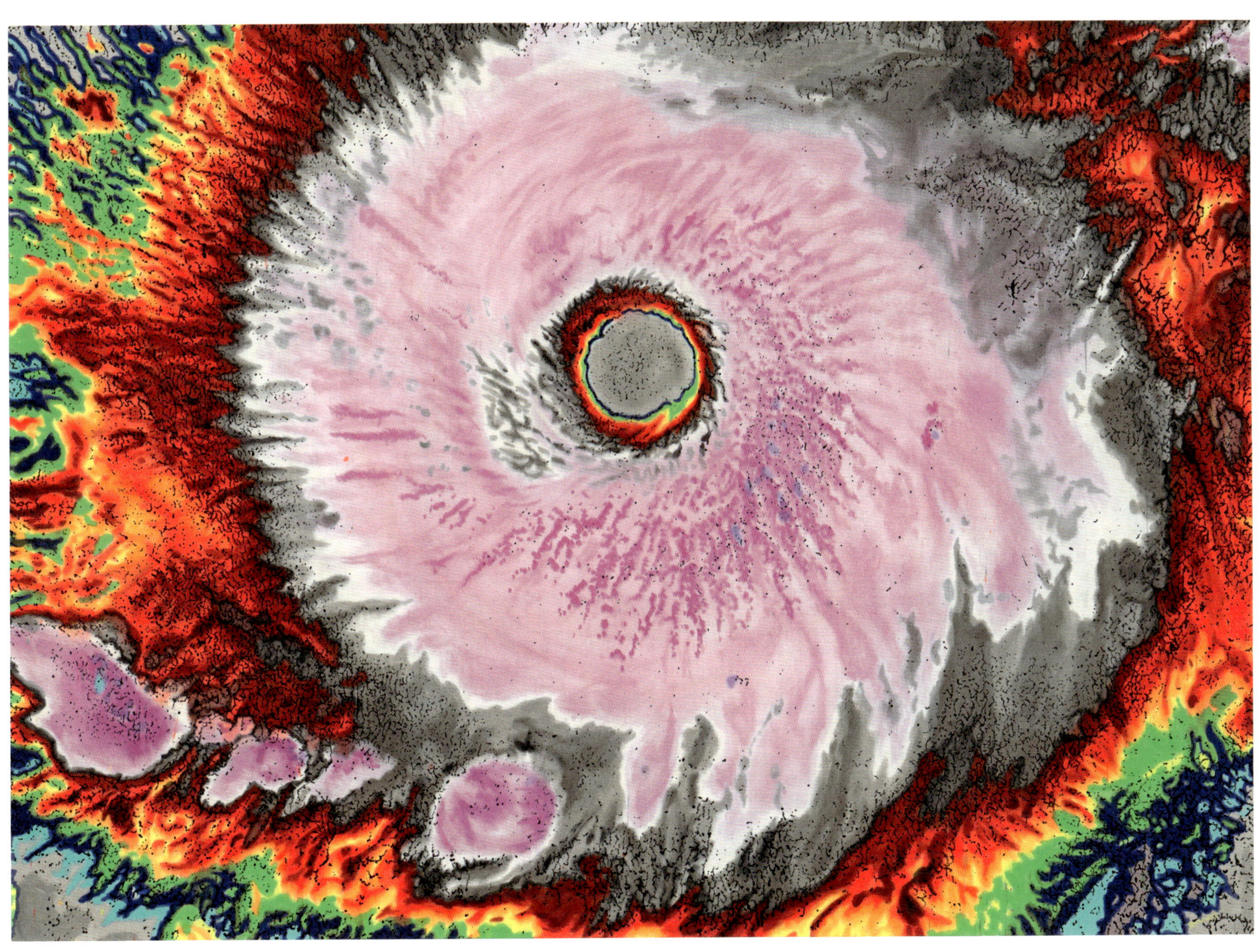

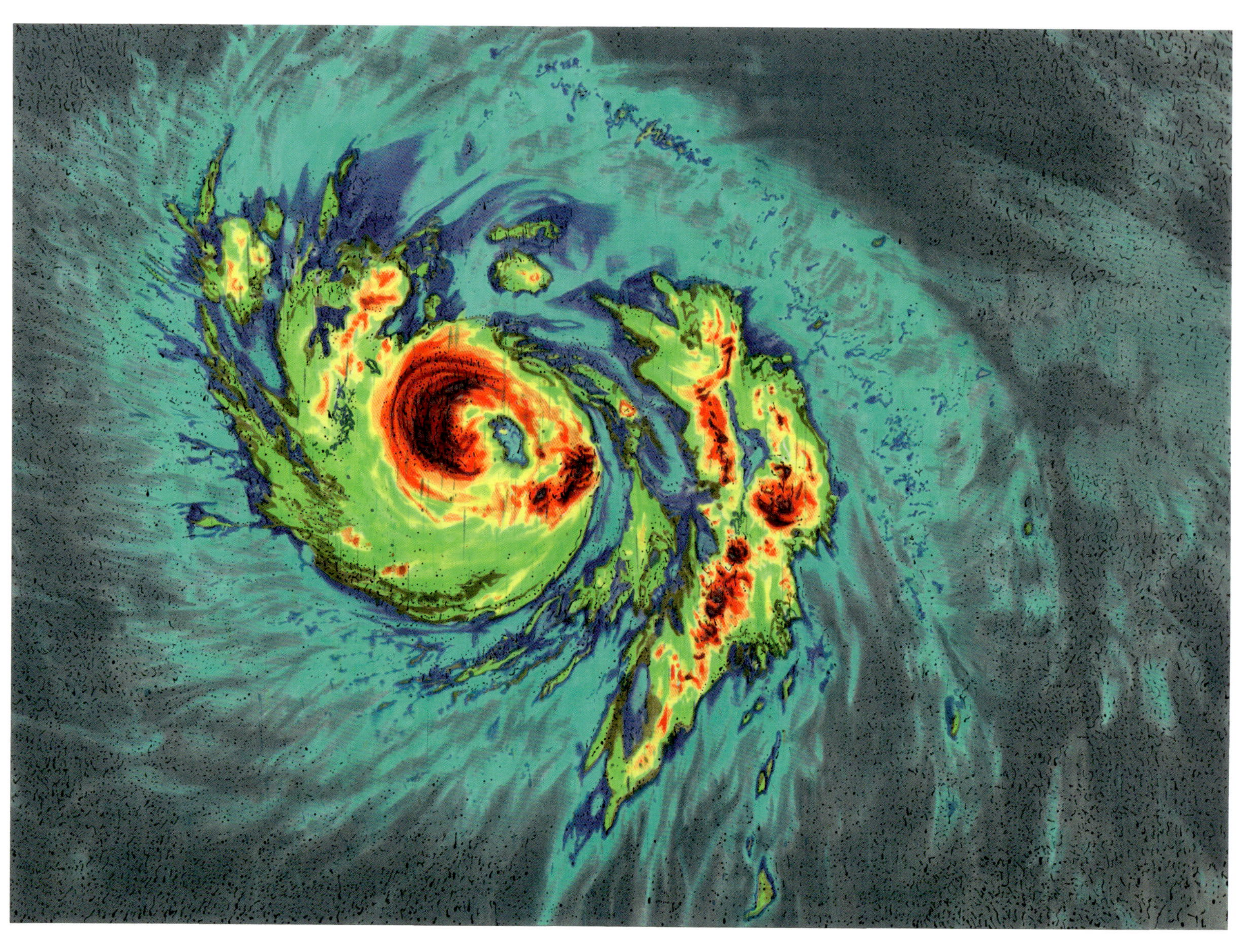

 ***Maria*, 2022** Oil and alkyd on linen, 90 × 126 inches | 228.6 × 320 cm

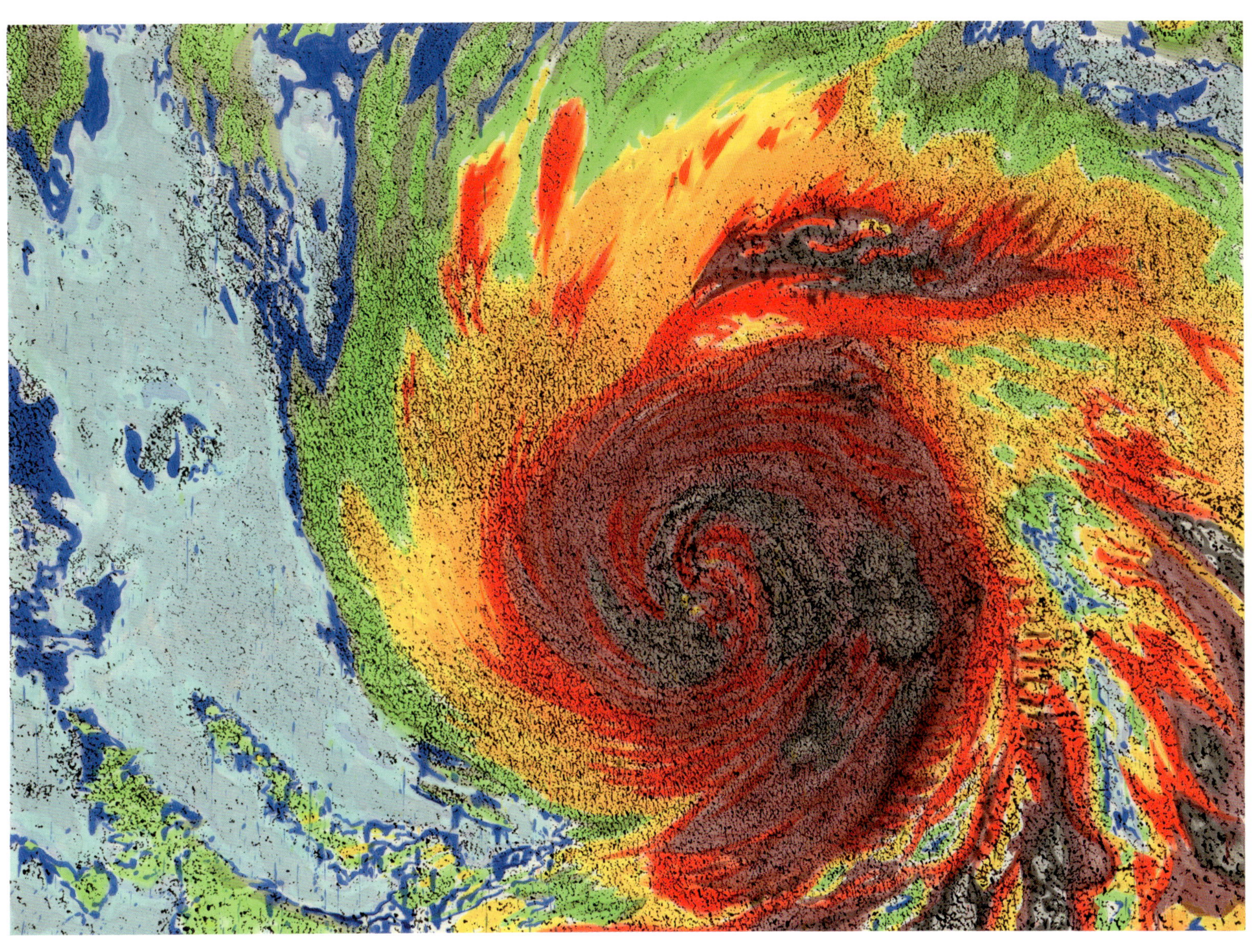

***Sandy*, 2020** Oil and alkyd on linen, 90 × 126 inches | 228.6 × 320 cm

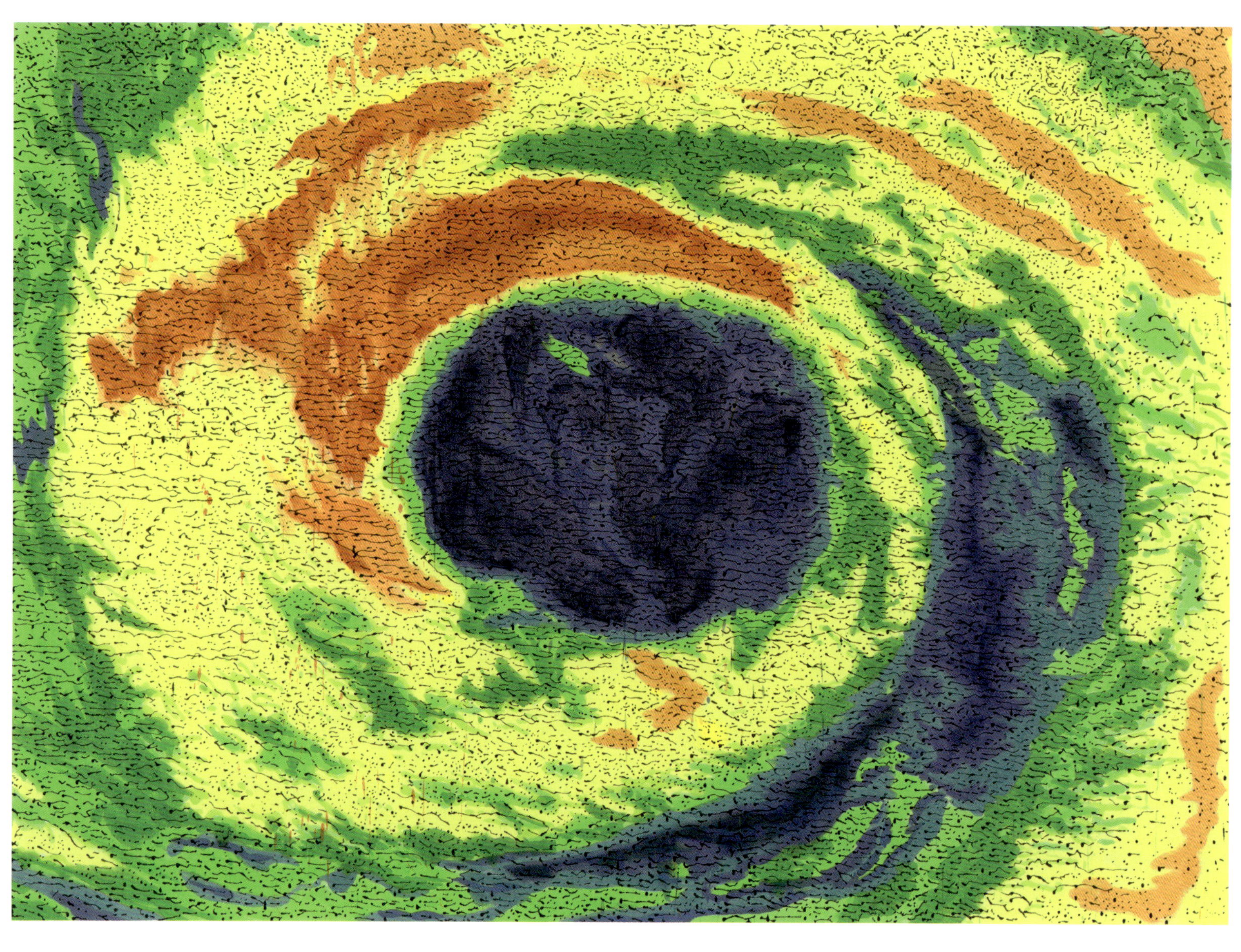

 ***Florence*, 2021** Oil and alkyd on linen, 90 × 126 inches | 228.6 × 320 cm

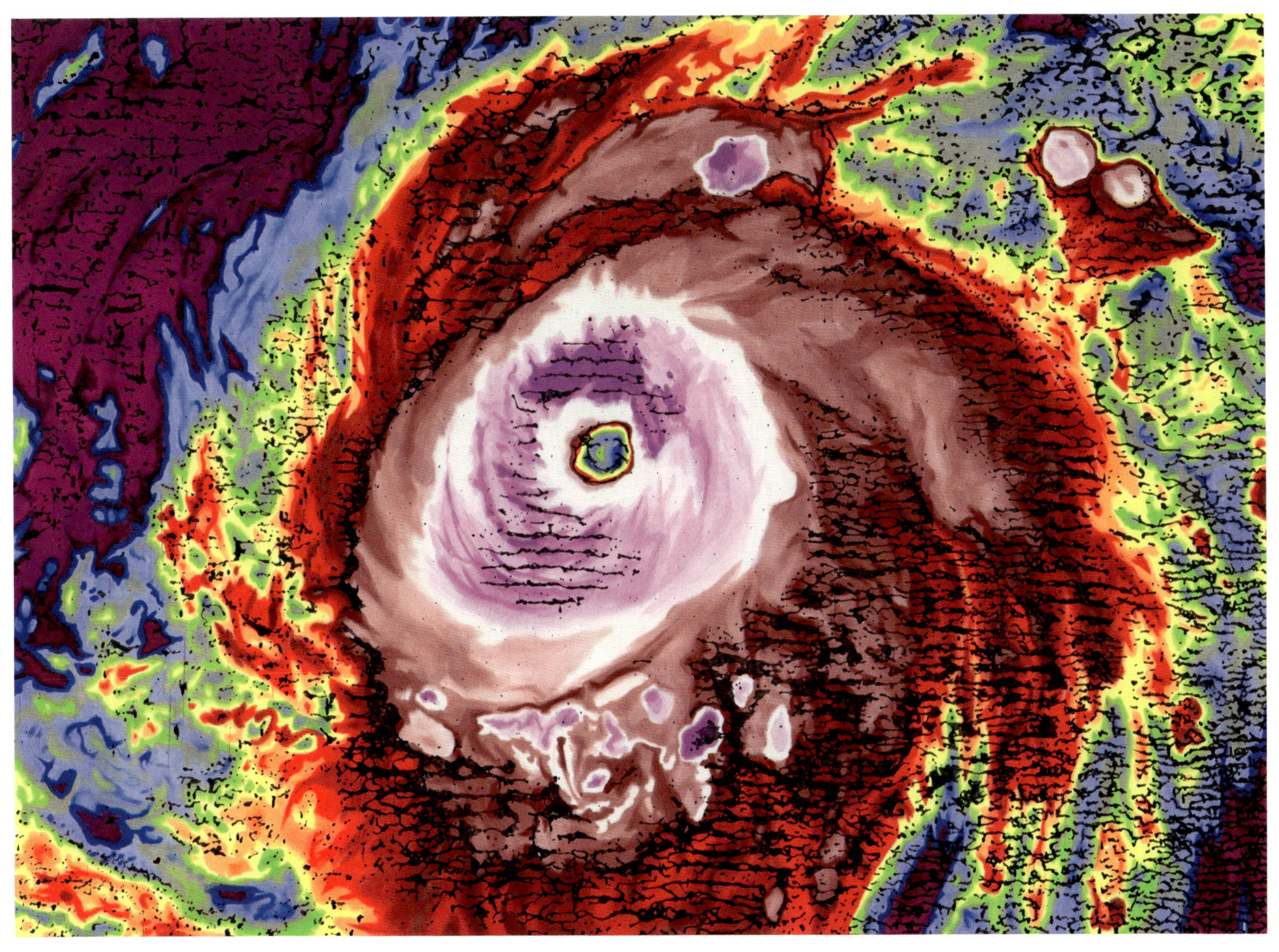

***Ida*, 2022** Oil and alkyd on linen, 90 × 126 inches | 228.6 × 320 cm

***Andrew*, 2022** Oil and alkyd on linen, 90 × 126 inches | 228.6 × 320 cm

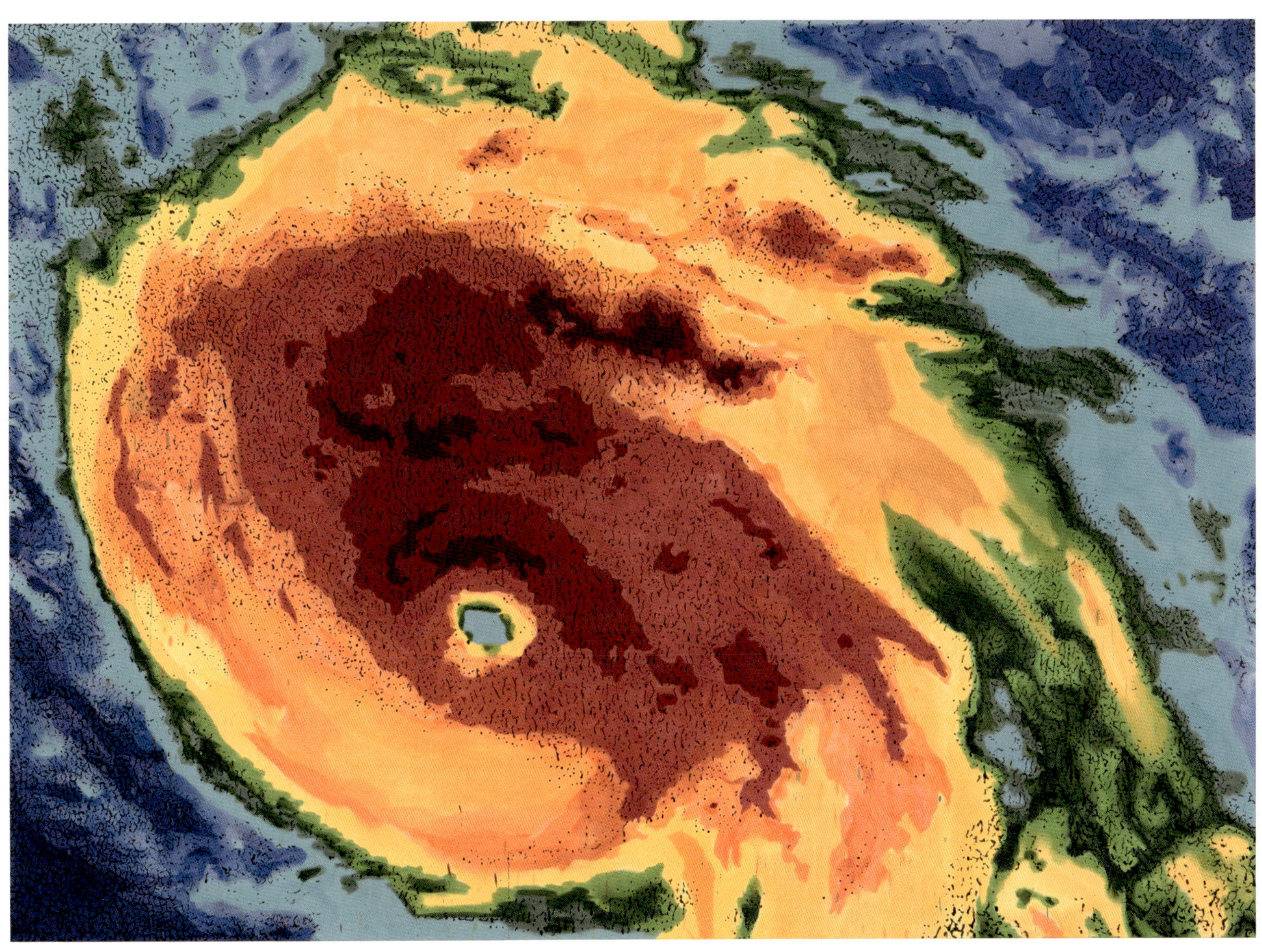

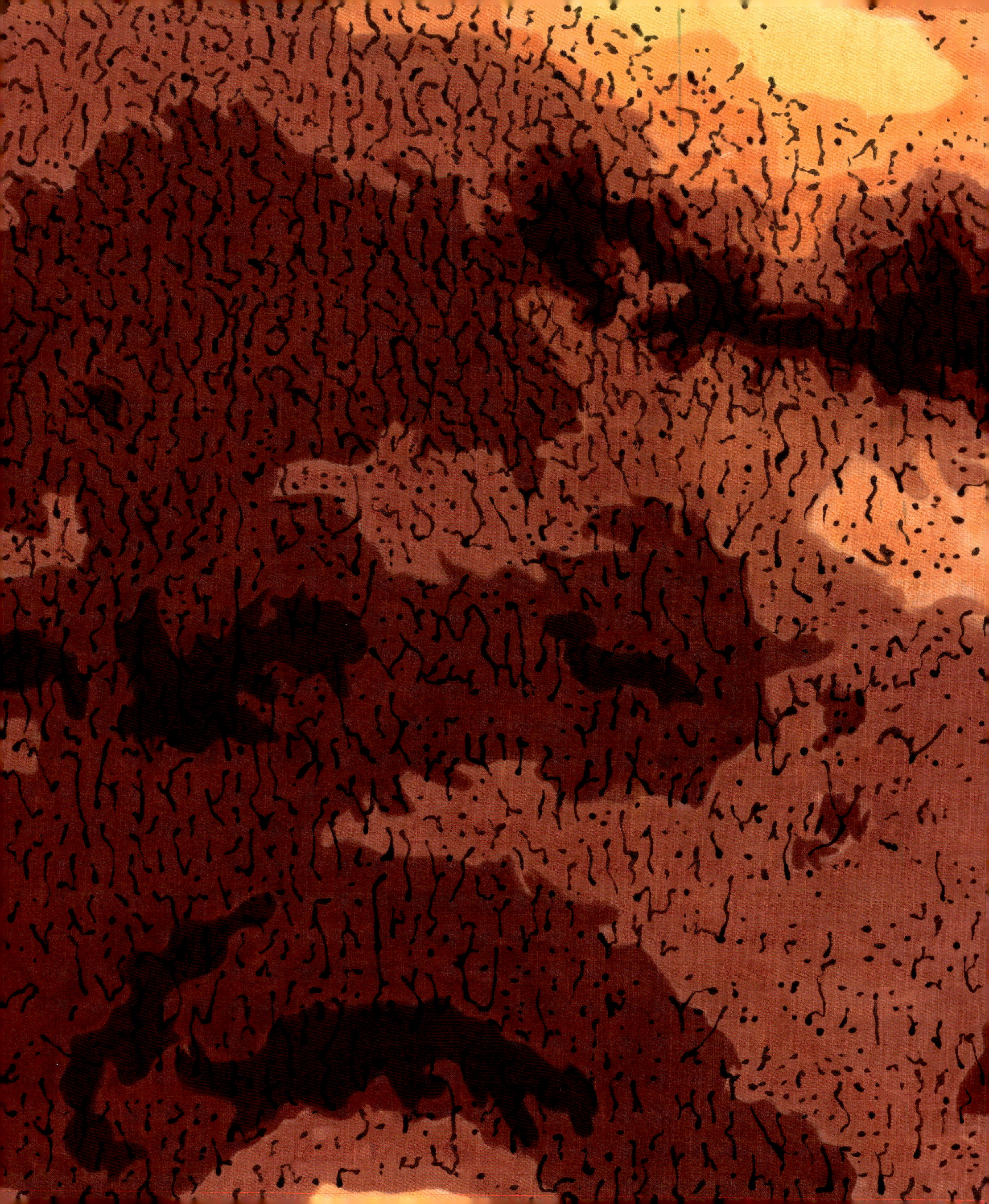

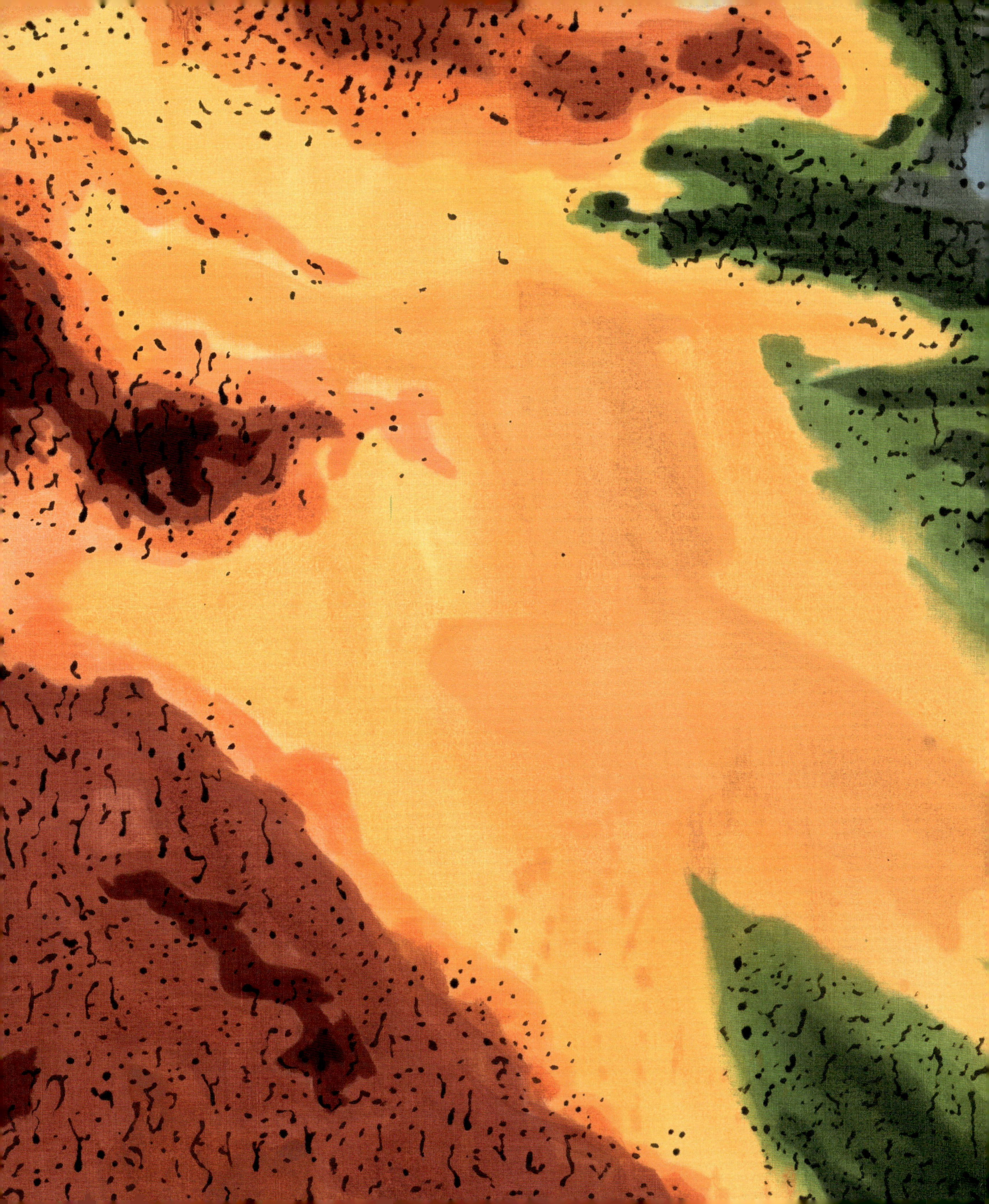

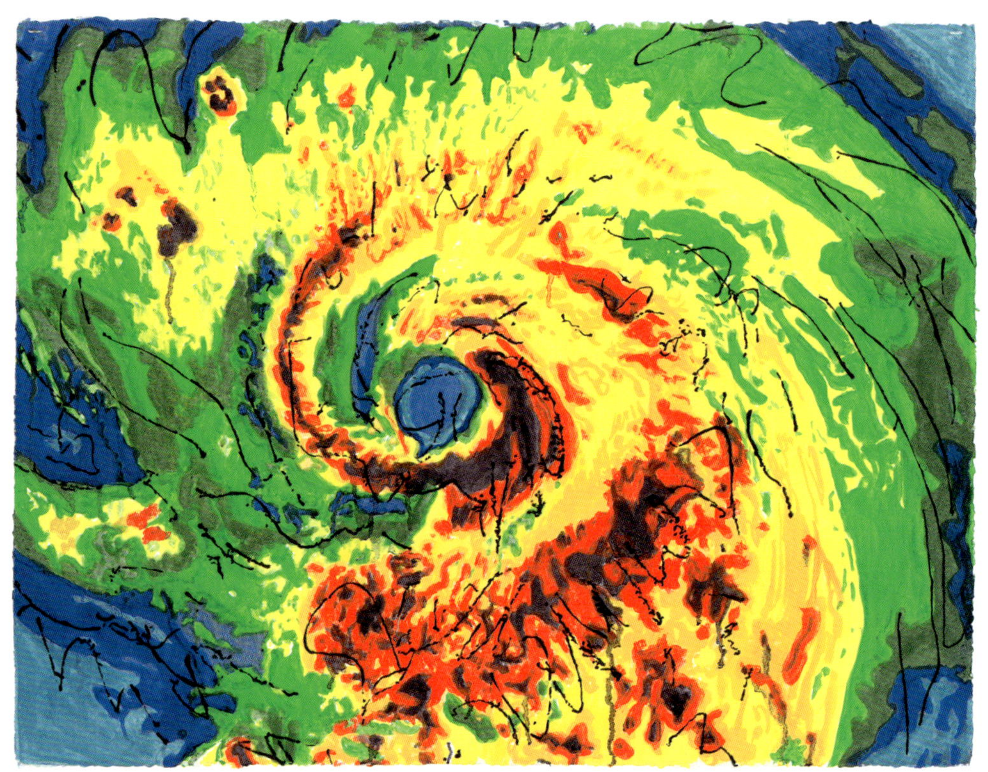

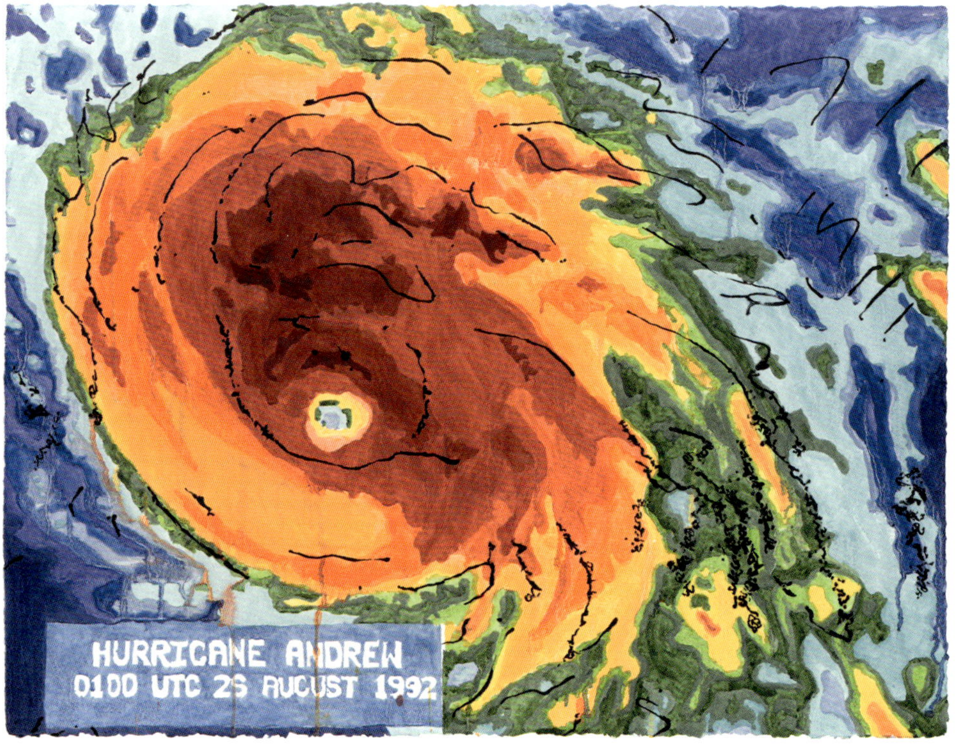

***Irma Paper*, 2022** Oil on paper, 22 ½ × 30 inches | 57.1 × 76.2 cm

***Andrew Paper*, 2022** Oil on paper, 22 ½ × 30 inches | 57.1 × 76.2 cm

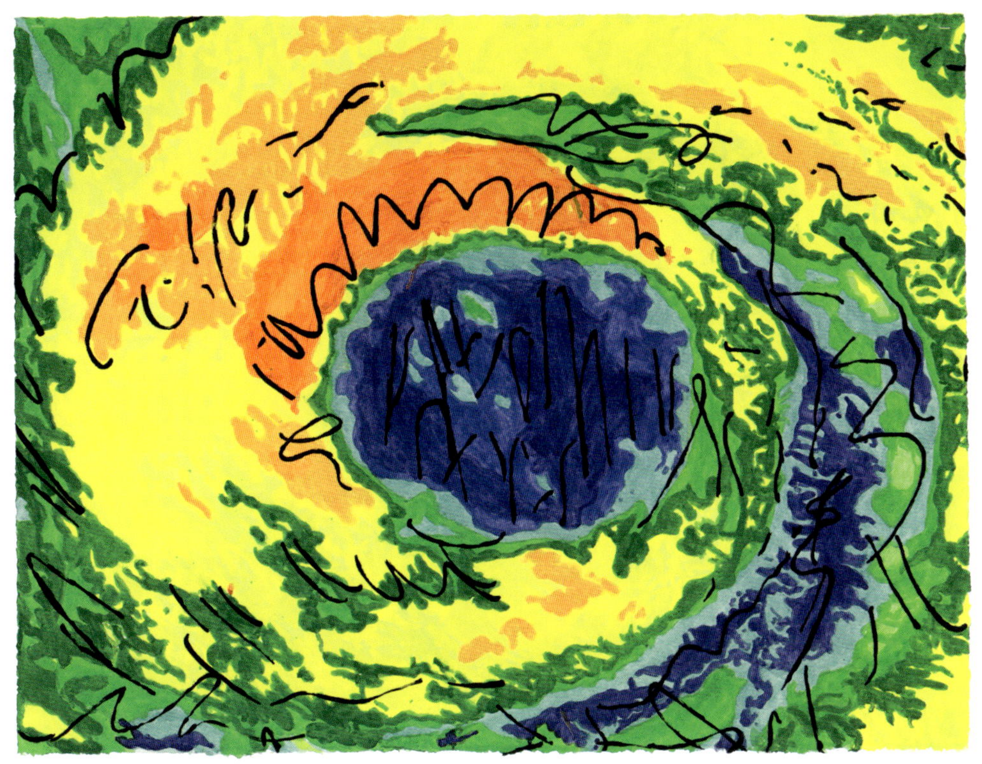

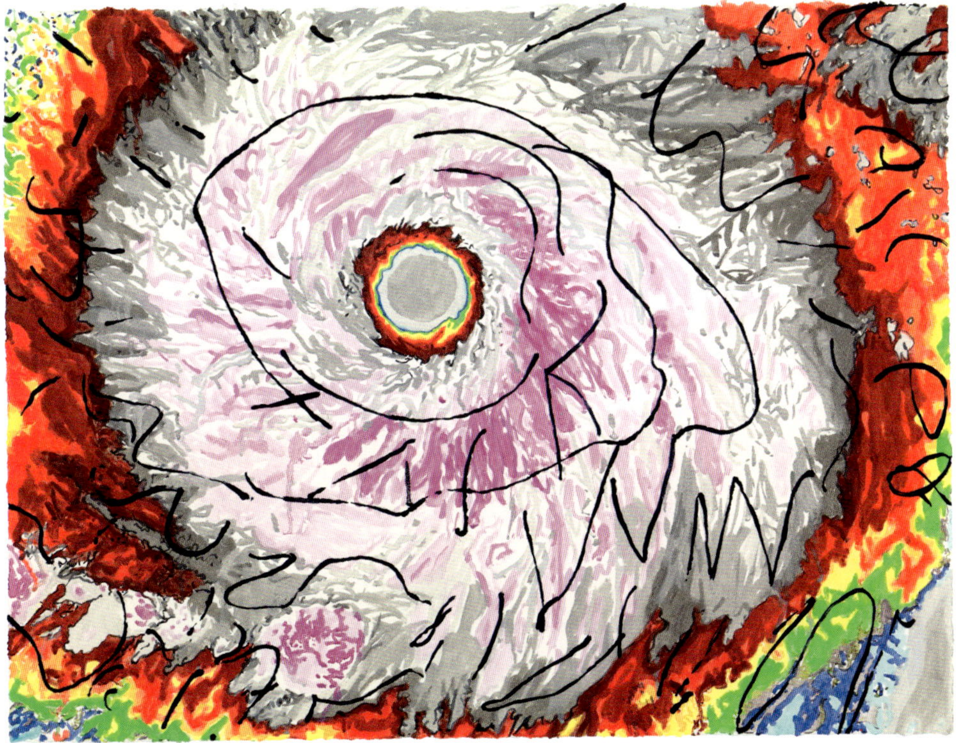

***Florence Paper*, 2022** Oil on paper, 22½ × 30 inches | 57.1 × 76.2 cm

***Irma Paper*, 2022** Oil on paper, 22½ × 30 inches | 57.1 × 76.2 cm

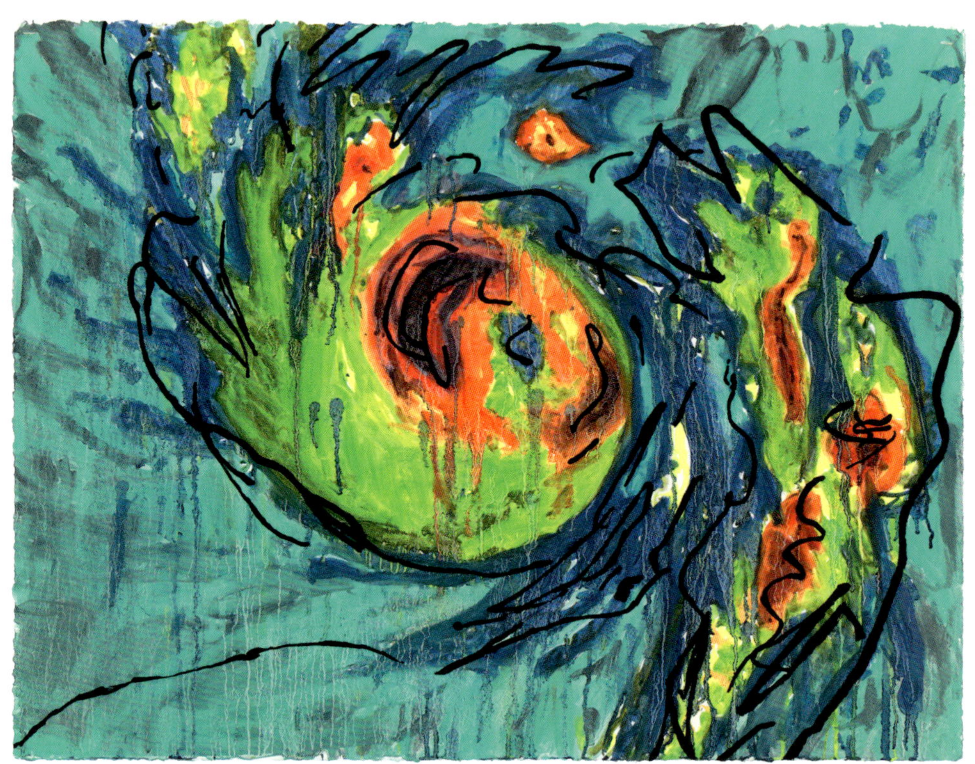

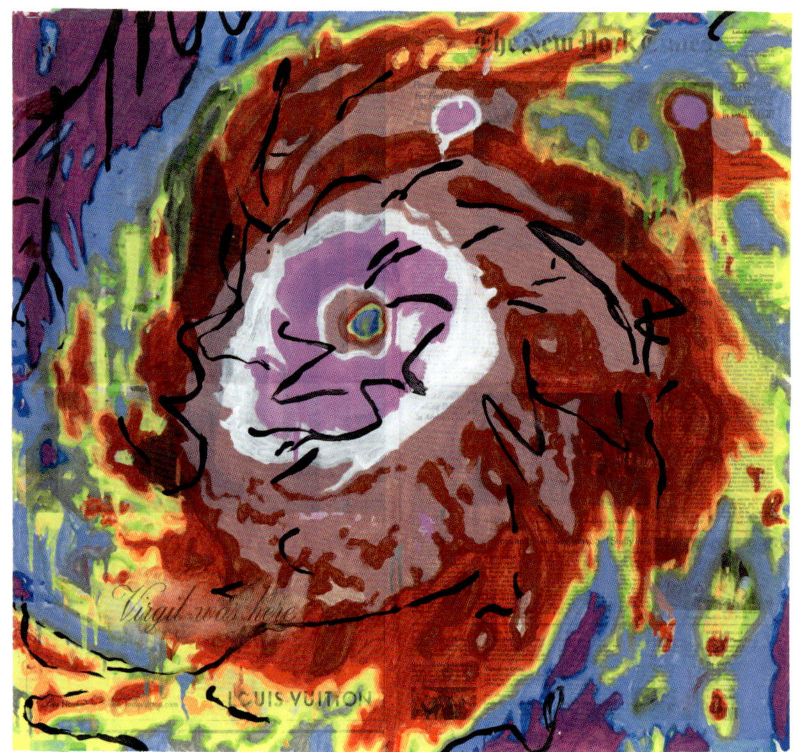

***Maria Paper*, 2022** Oil on paper, 22½ × 30 inches | 57.1 × 76.2 cm

***Last Day of Hurricane Season 2021 (NYT/V.A.)*, 2022** Oil on newspaper, 22 × 24 inches | 55.9 × 61 cm

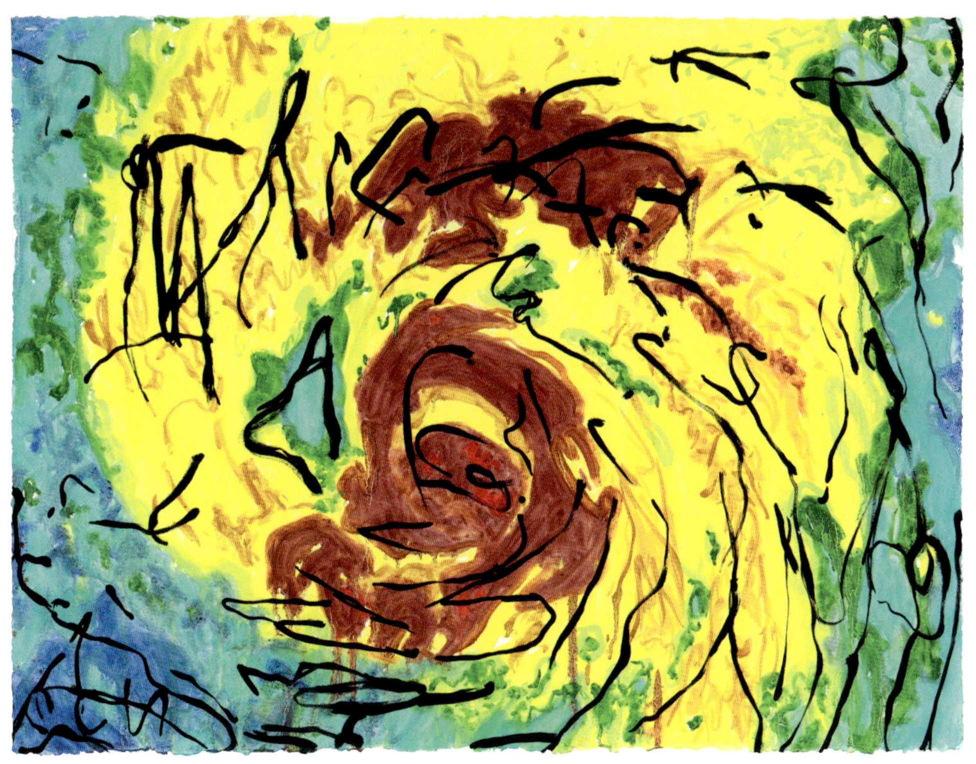

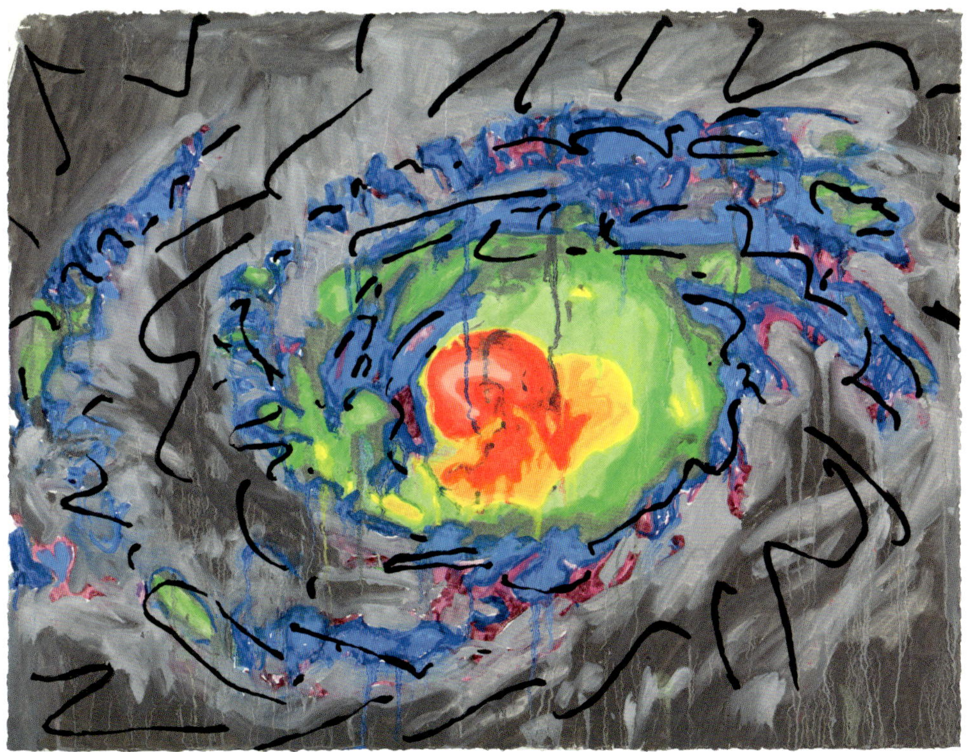

***Irene Paper*, 2022** Oil on paper, 22½ × 30 inches | 57.1 × 76.2 cm

***Florence Paper*, 2022** Oil on paper, 22½ × 30 inches | 57.1 × 76.2 cm

Following pages: Installation views, *Nate Lowman: Let's Go*, David Zwirner, New York, 2022

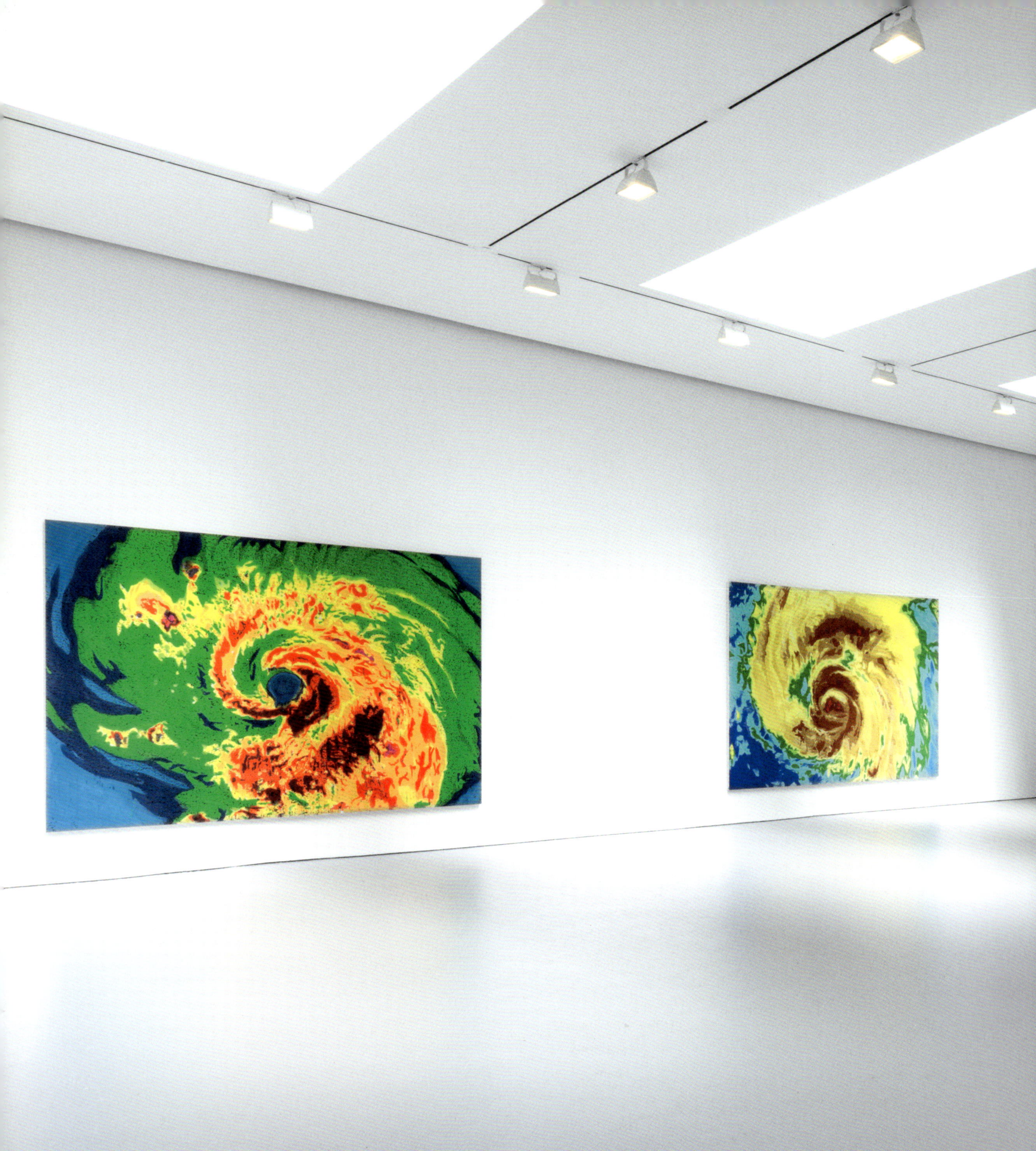

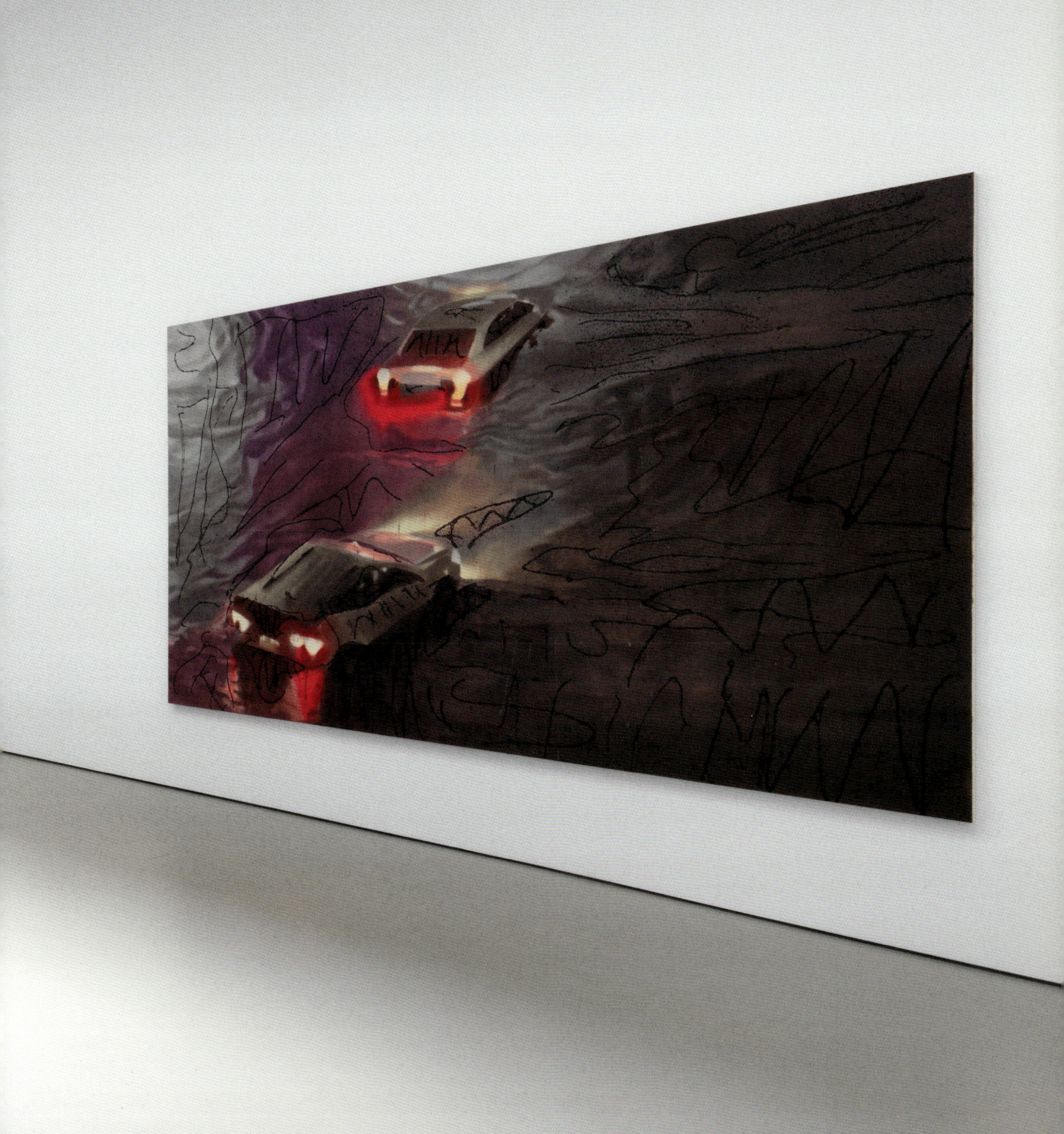

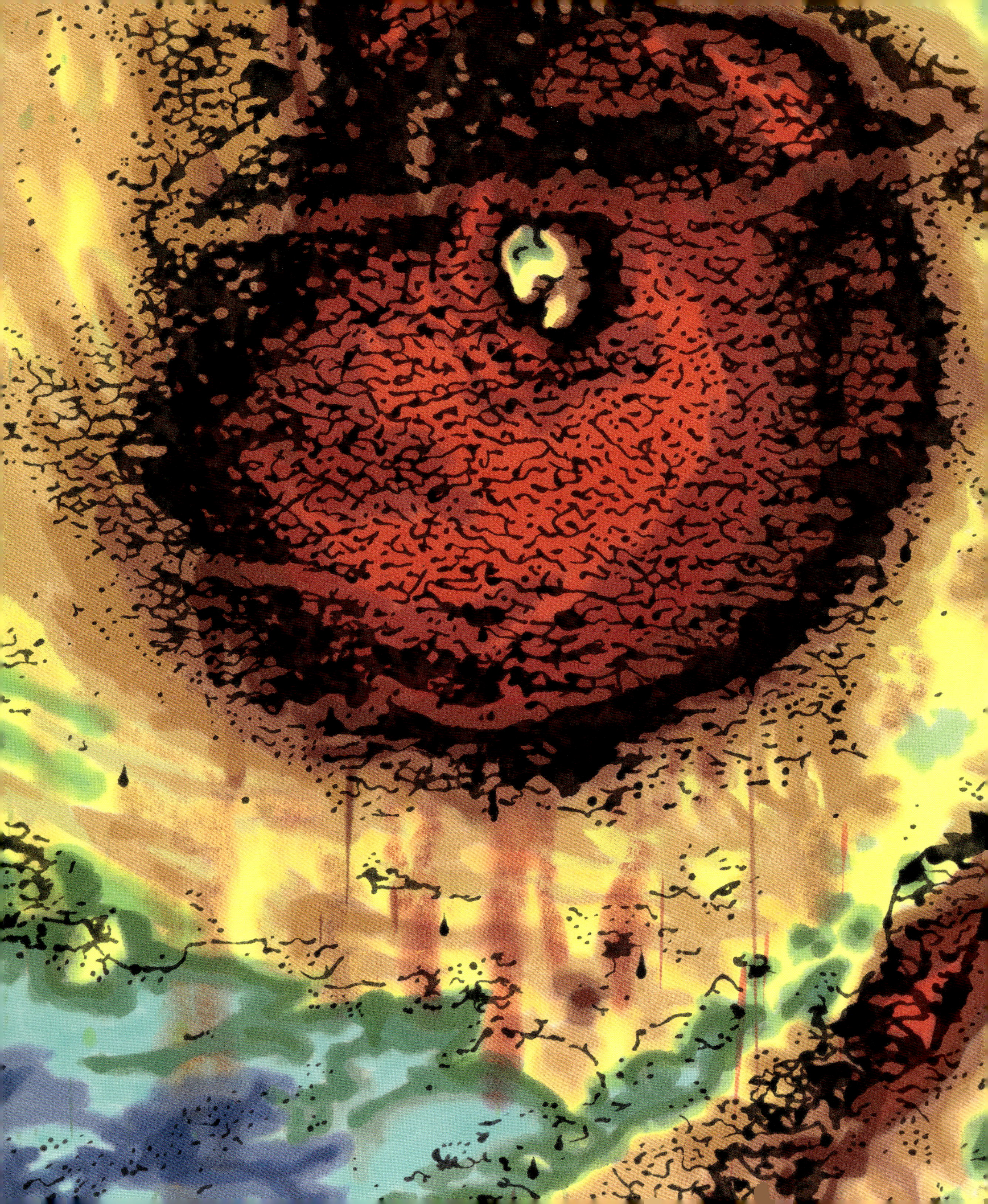

Here:

Jim Lewis

This is the world that we made (all of us): by turns banal and terrifying, slightly washed-out, reproduced and reproduced, shot, sometimes altered, printed, broadcast, uploaded, smothered by intervening memories, but always ember-radiant at its core. Of the chronicles of suffering and disaster, natural and man-made, there is no end. Story follows story, photo follows photo: here's the hospital room where the young woman lived on life support; here's footage of the tornado tearing the roof off a school building; here's a picture of the shooter from his high school yearbook; and so on, because there's always a so on.

A kind of fame accrues to these things, to the photographs, I mean, which sticks in the memory long after the people depicted have faded away. The tape from the police officer's dash cam, the rising waters seen from an upper floor, the canister spewing tear gas, the flyers put up by people who've lost their loved ones. Calamities happen every day, somewhere, to someone else. In the end it becomes a kind of celebrity, not of people but of events. We know the names Katrina and Sandy, Uvalde and Orlando and Sandy Hook, better than we know the names of anyone involved, be they aggressor or victim. The Las Vegas shooting of 2017 was the single largest massacre perpetrated by an individual in American history: sixty people died, more than four hundred were injured by gunfire, and another four hundred or so were hurt in the panic that followed. I'll wager that not one American out of a thousand can name the man who pulled the trigger.

To a great extent this is simply the result of a recent press convention, according to which the names of those who commit atrocities are mentioned as little as possible, in the hope of dissuading copycats. This is no doubt wise (though it doesn't seem to have stopped the killing), but it's also disorienting, since it tends to treat all disasters and deaths as given, as things that simply happened, rather than things that someone specific did or suffered (a notable exception: George Floyd). The true player, it appears, isn't the person caught up in a catastrophe, it's the catastrophe itself: tornadoes and mudslides, epidemics, wars and mass shootings, riots, bizarre accidents, suicides, crashes. When they make the news at all, we see them for a moment, and then perhaps a moment the day after, and then the next one takes its place. This is called news, and it's as constant as the rotation of the planet.

We may think of this as a failing of some sort, but it isn't. As I was writing this, the eight billionth living human was born, and a lot of things are bound to happen on a small planet with a large population. But good news isn't news. If it were, the morning's paper would be filled with lists of all the airliners that landed safely the day before, rather than an account of the one that crashed. But it's not like that. Somewhere Michael Herr, the great war reporter, writes, "Vietnam is what we had instead of happy childhoods." And by "we" he means all of us, civilians and soldiers, actors and observers. In much the same way, I think, news, and the recollection of news, is what we have instead of happy

Sandy Poppy, 2022 (detail)

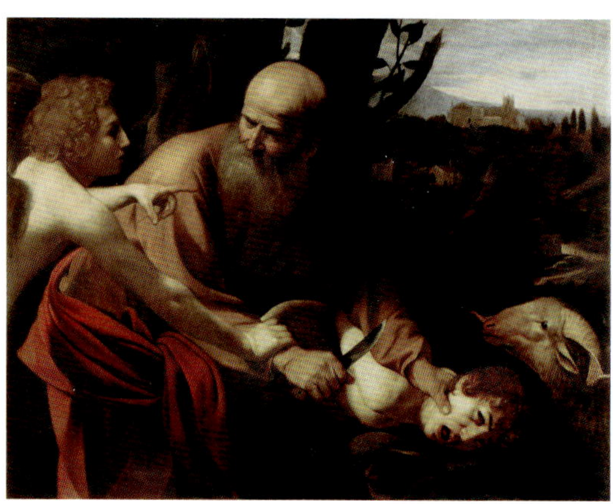

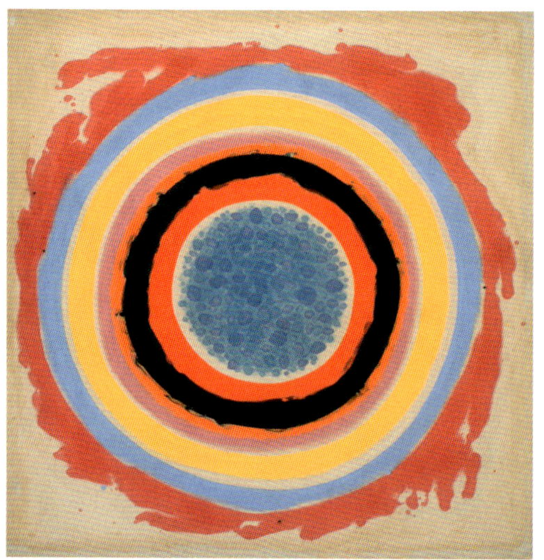

childhoods. It's where so many of our memories lie, how we mark the passing years, the naïve things we cared about, things the water has weakened and washed away, but not entirely effaced.

But we're not supposed to be talking about news here: we're supposed to be talking about painting, though the two of them can sometimes be hard to sunder. As Ezra Pound famously said, "Literature is news that STAYS news," and the same is true of art, whether it's a Caravaggio, a Cezanne, a cave painting at Lascaux, or a Robert Irwin. Every time you encounter it, you feel the shock of confrontation, the sense that, say, *The Sacrifice of Isaac* has happened just before you looked at it, that the world has been made new again by the process of remembering.

And of course art is made anew as well: one good image extends along a multitude of axes, just as an eight of hearts means one thing if you're drawing to a full house, quite another if you're going for a flush, and a third if you're trying to tell someone's fortune. When I look at Lowman's hurricane paintings and his Las Vegas series, I see a dozen different precursors, formal, theoretical, and emotional: Robert Smithson's *Spiral Jetty*, Kenneth Noland's targets, Mike Mandel and Larry Sultan's book *Evidence*, Robert Gober's memorial installations, Jack Goldstein's lightning paintings—and then, stretching back farther, the rococo masters: Giovanni Battista Tiepolo, Jean Honoré Fragonard, François Boucher (figs. 15–19). I have no idea which of these, if any, were in Lowman's mind when he was working. I've asked him, but like most good artists, he's demurred. So we can play this game forever, but I wonder sometimes what exactly it's for: a wholly unnecessary legitimation process, a way of explaining the unfamiliar by way of the familiar, a pointless demonstration of erudition.

Nevertheless, I feel compelled to add two more points of comparison, which I think are especially relevant to us as spectators, if not to Lowman as a painter. First, Gerhard Richter's documentary paintings of the Baader-Meinhof Gang, his work *Eight Student Nurses* (1966), and so on; and then Andy Warhol's *Death and Disaster* series (figs. 20, 21). There, too, enormous weight is balanced on a series of paintings fashioned from plain

14. Caravaggio, *Sacrifice of Isaac*, c. 1603. Oil on canvas, 40⅞ × 53⅛ inches | 104 × 135 cm

15. Kenneth Noland, *Inside*, 1958. Magna on canvas, 68¼ × 67¼ inches | 173.4 × 170.7 cm

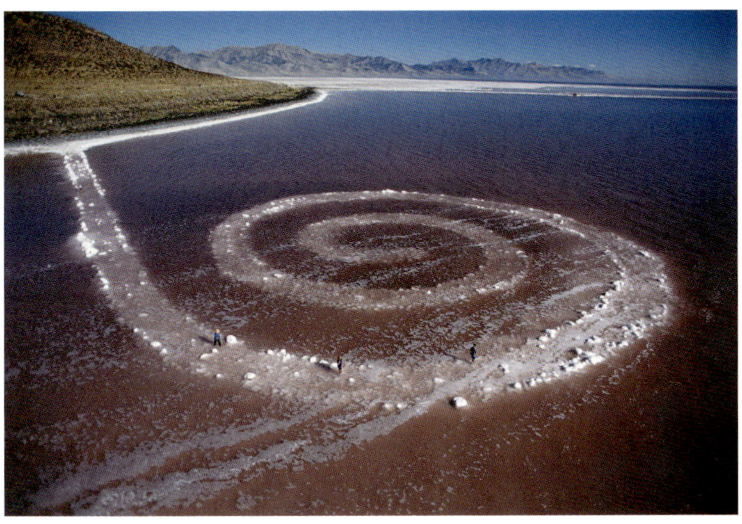

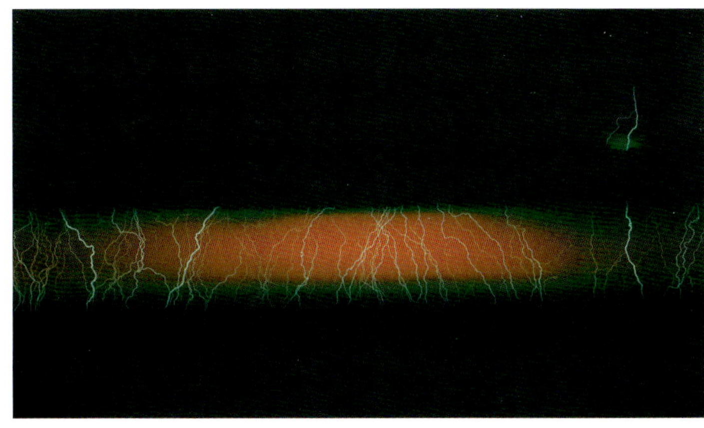

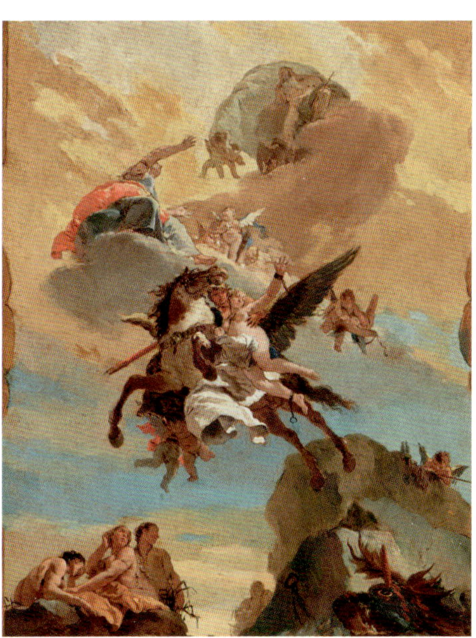

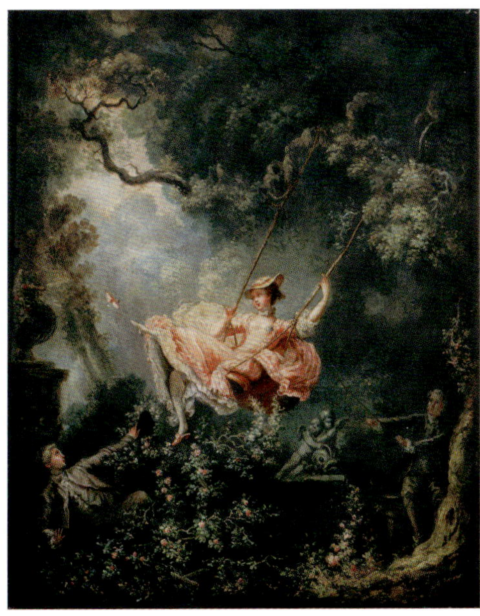

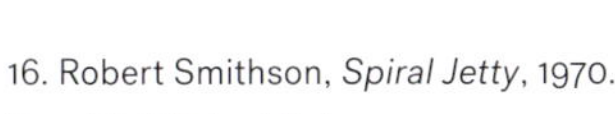

16. Robert Smithson, *Spiral Jetty*, 1970. Great Salt Lake, Utah

17. Jack Goldstein, *Untitled*, 1983. Acrylic on canvas, 96 × 168⅛ inches | 243.7 × 427 cm

18. Giovanni Battista Tiepolo, painted sketch for *Perseus and Andromeda*, c. 1730–1731. Oil on canvas, 20⅜ × 16 inches | 51.8 × 40.6 cm

19. Jean Honoré Fragonard, *The Swing*, c. 1767–1768. Oil on canvas, 31⅞ × 25¼ inches | 81 × 64.2 cm

but loaded photographs. But Richter had a didactic impulse to contend with, even if none of us—including Richter himself—knew quite what it was; and Lowman is one of the least didactic artists I know. What he's after is something more elusive, more private but less personal. One hurricane, another, another: these are disasters, but not ones that I would think he bears close to his heart. Why, then, did he choose them? Why does anyone choose anything.

As for the Warhols, they explore the same sort of material, but I've long held that Warhol's work—not just the *Disaster* series, but the rest of it, too—is motivated by his fear of death. "People die," he seems to be saying. "Do you see them all, dying out there? But I won't die, because celebrity is immortal" (he was wrong about that), "and besides, I'm a machine" (he was wrong about that, too). And this, too, is far beyond anything Lowman would say for himself.

I love these paintings, especially the hurricanes. Have I mentioned that? As a general rule, a writer in my position isn't supposed to say such things: a more Apollonian stance is usually more appropriate. But I do, and one of the things I love about them is how indisputably ugly they are. They're spectacular, confident, complex, mysterious, and minatory. They're also hideous: when Lowman first sent me images of them two years ago, attached to text messages, I laughed out loud. Who on earth came up with those god-awful colors, who decided, for example, that brown was going to be so prominent? No doubt someone at NOAA, the federal agency that creates and distributes the maps, someone who apparently somehow thought it would be readable, though it clearly isn't. Do the brown parts represent faster winds and heavier rains, or just the opposite? They say that colors in nature never clash—an odd point, largely because it's true. But someone employed by the federal government did their damnedest to prove otherwise, by knocking all the tones out of whack. Josef Albers would have had a stroke.

Well, art isn't about beauty: not always anyway, not exactly. Mostly, it's about ugliness, about demonstrating that there's some new, deep structure to the world that doesn't fit, but which nevertheless makes sense, hence what appears to be ugly is actually beautiful, first in an ugly sort of way, and then simply so. Thus we chip off another fragment of visual norms. John Ruskin famously accused James McNeill Whistler—Whistler!—of "flinging a pot of paint in the public's face." And Ruskin was famously wrong, as are almost all accusations of homeliness against an artist's work. The risk, you see, in making such work is not that it'll stay ugly, because that almost never happens. The risk is that it'll become beautiful too quickly and too easily, and I've seen that happen many times. The longest holdout I can think of is Mike Kelley, some of whose work still looks gloriously wretched twenty or thirty years after he made it. I hope these Lowman paintings stay ugly for at least that long, because there's a great advantage to their very disharmony.

First, they remind us how artificial the whole image is, how compromised; because they're not pictures at all, really, the originals I mean. They're more like pictograms,

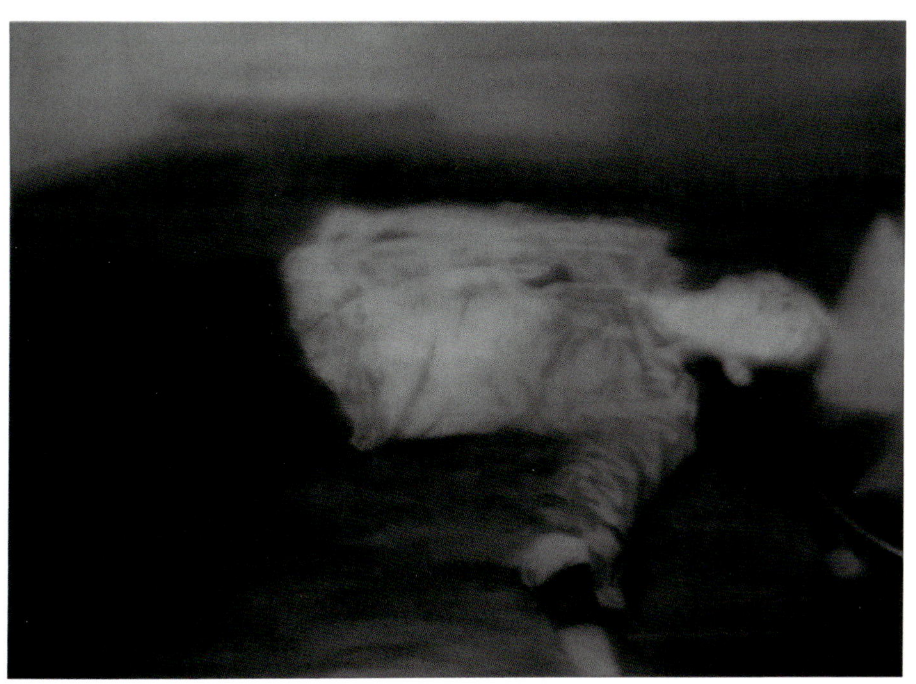

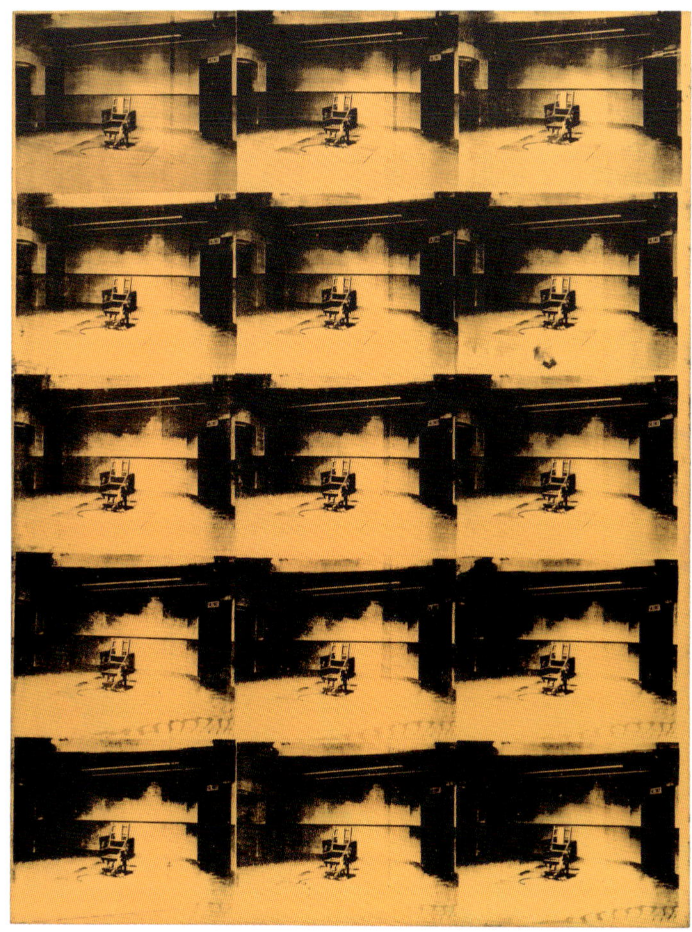

20. Gerhard Richter, *Erschossener 2* (*Man Shot Down 2*), 1988. Oil on canvas, 39 3/8 × 55 1/8 inches | 100 × 140 cm

21. Andy Warhol, *Orange Disaster #5*, 1963. Acrylic, silkscreen ink, and graphite on canvas, 106 × 81½ inches | 269.2 × 207 cm

hieroglyphs, coded in a way that is only half-understandable. Compare NASA's images of deep space, which are also deeply artificial, since most of the phenomena they're trying to show us occurs as radiation, at wavelengths that are invisible to the human eye, and so all the colors are applied afterward. And yet, somehow, they read as photos, which is to say, they're more profoundly deceptive.

The hurricane pictures, by contrast, are both more and less lifelike. They're half-real (from space, hurricanes do look something like that) and half charts in which colors are assigned apparently arbitrarily to windspeeds and rainfall patterns. And here they come, lifted out of their brief life on news shows and weather apps, and painted and hung on a wall. They are cartoons, half-imitative and half-playful, which doesn't mean they're comical, let alone trivial, but when they're turned into paintings they do have a slightly antic aspect to them, like a cartoon depicting the terrifying circular blades of a horror-movie buzzsaw.

Another advantage: precisely because their realism is so unreal, they tend to dissolve a bit, to detach themselves from the weather. One sees images within the images, like a Rorschach test, I suppose, and sometimes multiple images in sequence. I can spot a raccoon in one, a cyclops in another, a fetal ultrasound, an asshole, an acrobat juggling torches, a human eye, a page from an illustrated Koran, an underwater explosion radiating shock waves, another asshole, spermatozoa approaching an egg, another eye, this one with long lashes, and another that seems to belong to someone very hungover, a horseshoe crab, a galaxy, a cartoon ape, a brain scan, a nuclear atoll, and so on. They have their personalities, these rampaging storms flecked with bits of tranquility: it's no wonder we give them human names, as we don't with, say, forest fires or avalanches. The people experiencing them below probably have no interest in anthropomorphizing them; they are dealing with chaos, loss, and destruction on the ground. But from up here, at satellite distance and somewhat abstracted, each has its own style, its own way of moving, its own personality, like a wild animal loping across your back lawn at night.

And again, the hurricane paintings are measuring devices, of the landscape, yes, of rainfall, wind speed, direction, and the like; but also of clock time (a certain hour of a certain day), which turns into calendar time (the year in which the storm occurred), which turns into history, earth time, the gradual warming of the planet, and the plight that ensues. So they capture not just the past but the future. I don't know if they're meant to be prophetic in that way, still less if they're meant to be warnings of what's to come, but when we think of the end of the world, or the end of human life inhabiting it, hurricanes, along with droughts and fires, rank high among the signs that extinction is nigh. We do desire to name the things that hurt us, as much as we do the things we love.

I want to tell you that Lowman is among the most American of American artists. It's not just that the images are American, although they are, and it's significant that they are, when a picture of, say, Princess Diana's car crash would have done just as well. It's that no country, at least none that I know of, has its consciousness mediated by news as much

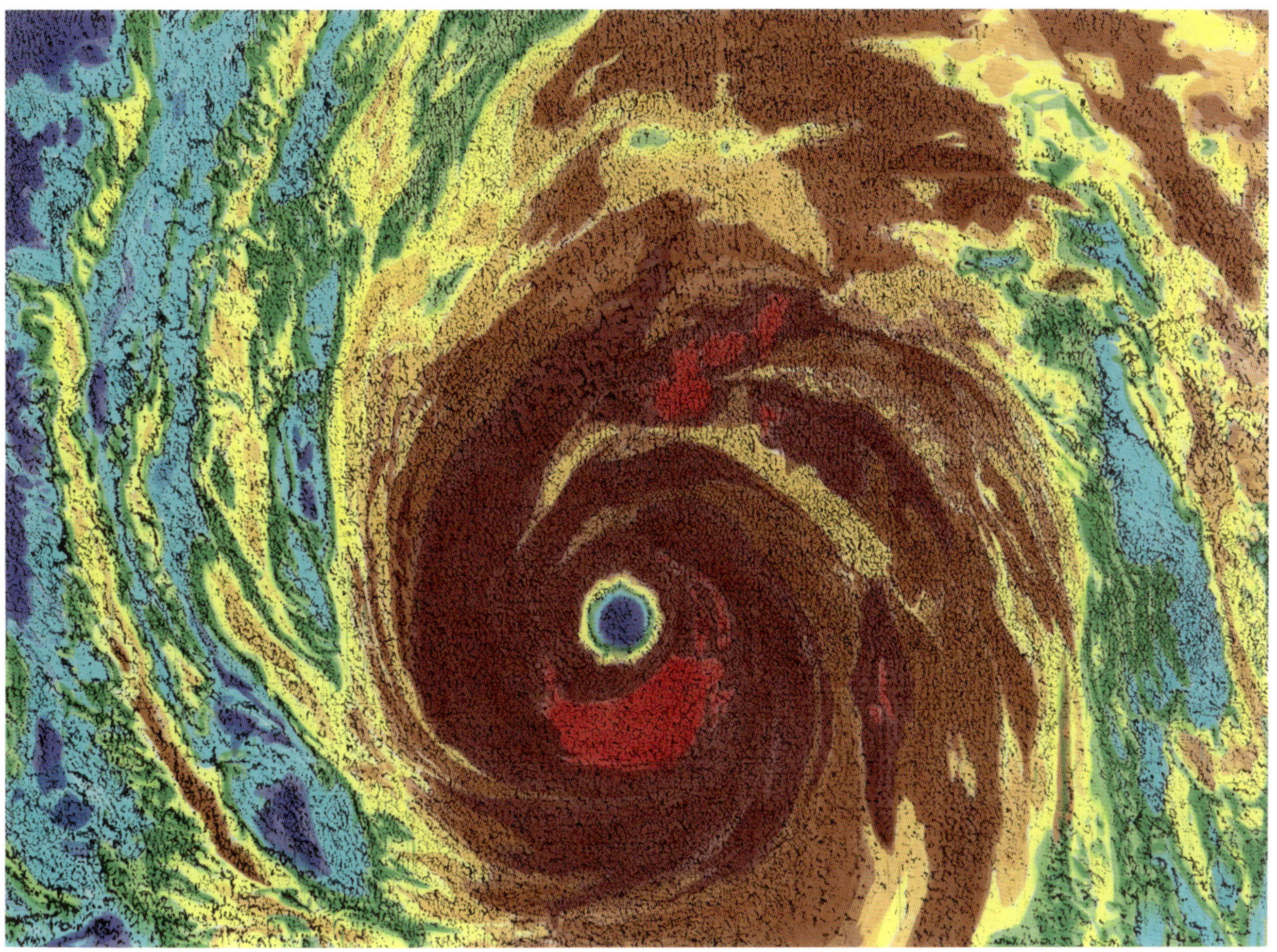

22. *Katrina*, 2020. Oil and alkyd on linen, 90⅛ × 126⅛ inches | 228.9 × 320.4 cm

as ours, nor is any more visual than ours, with our billboards and websites and magazines, our streaming services and dating apps, with entire picture industries—Hollywood, pornography, Instagram—that are predominantly American. According to one report I just read, Americans take, on average, about twenty photographs a day. Europeans take about five. I have no idea if this is entirely true, but it sounds plausible enough. Without taking a breath, I can name a dozen American disasters, including some that happened before I was born, that I remember only by remembering the photographs or stills of them: the *Hindenburg*, Kent State, Ruby shooting Oswald, the O. J. Simpson verdict, Elián González, mugshots and riots and wildfires. It's not just that I wasn't there to see them myself: almost none of us were. It's that there are no memorial poems, no stories passed down, few myths and legends. Which do you remember more: James Agee's prose or Walker Evans's photos? John Steinbeck's *The Grapes of Wrath* or Henry Fonda in the movie? Not since fifteenth-century Florence has a culture told its own history so predominantly through pictures.

And yet, it's not the pictures' multiplicity that drives Lowman: we've seen enough of that sort of art. It's a more oblique process, a matter of choosing one or six or twelve images from the trillions that are out there and fixating on them, worrying them until they're half-wiped-away, husbanding them, sometimes mocking them, or mocking what's been made of them, remaking them, and repeating them over and over again in various sizes and shapes and formats, the way someone, the way any of us, have ten thousand photos on our hard drive but only a few that we return to, over and over, not because they show something more significant than all the others but just because they're home base.

For some time now, Lowman has been making paintings that balance on a very thin wire: they are documents of our times, or a very small portion thereof, but first and foremost they're works of art. They resonate at strange harmonies. They're impersonal, in the sense that they ask nothing of you, their audience, not pity or horror, or even understanding; but they clearly mean something to Lowman, or else how would he choose among the millions of images that pass before us every day? They're simultaneously public and private, casual and obsessive, spectral and familiar, respectful and profane. It's an unending challenge, collecting this flotsam and making it stick, the project of a lifetime that has now moved forward by a considerable measure. You'll find it all, in its latest incarnation, here.

23. *Sandy Poppy*, 2022. Oil and alkyd on canvas on wood panel, 59 ½ × 61 ¾ inches | 151.1 × 156.8 cm

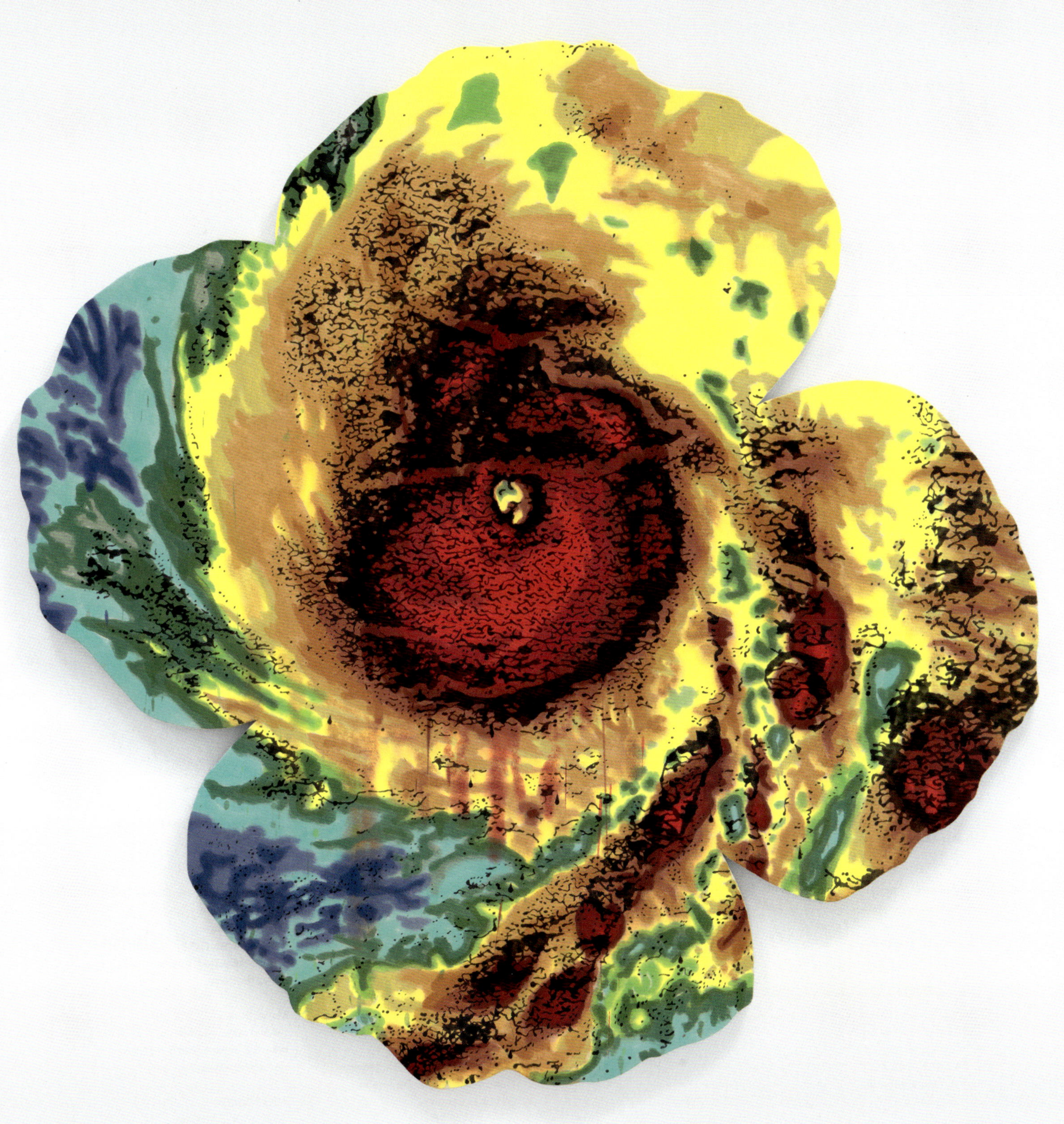

List of Works

Andrew, 2020
Oil and alkyd on linen
90 × 126 ¼ inches | 228.6 × 320.7 cm
Private collection
pp. 124–125

Andrew, 2022
Oil and alkyd on linen
90 × 126 inches | 228.6 × 320 cm
pp. 145, 146–147 (detail)

Andrew Paper, 2022
Oil on paper
22 ½ × 30 inches | 57.1 × 76.2 cm
Brian Morfitt and Lauren Anderson Morfitt
p. 148 (bottom)

Before During After (Caffi), 2021
Oil and alkyd on linen
66 ⅛ × 42 ⅛ inches | 168 × 107 cm
p. 101

Big Stash, 2020
Oil on linen
77 ⅛ × 117 inches | 195.9 × 297.2 cm
pp. 94 (detail), 95

Bikini Atoll March 1, 1954, 2021
Oil and alkyd on linen
48 × 84 inches | 121.9 × 213.4 cm
Private collection
pp. 86–87

Burning Farm, 2022
Oil and alkyd on linen
37 × 95 inches | 94 × 241.3 cm
p. 109

Carpel/Void (Pink No. 2), 2021
Oil and alkyd on linen on wood panel
56 ¾ × 47 ½ inches | 144.1 × 120.7 cm
Javier & Monica Mora Collection, Miami
p. 68

Ciao Venezia (Ippolito Caffi), 2021
Oil and alkyd on linen
137 × 92 inches | 348 × 233.7 cm
AMA Collection
pp. 102, 103 (detail)

Cobble Hustle Weave, 2022
Oil, acrylic, alkyd, latex, dirt, and nylon thread on canvas on wood panel
48 ¾ × 77 ¼ inches | 123.8 × 196.2 cm
Private collection
pp. 104 (detail), 107

Collection, 2018
Oil, alkyd, and dirt on linen
60 × 62 inches | 152.4 × 157.5 cm
Berezdivin Collection, San Juan, Puerto Rico
p. 78

Don't Forget to Howl at the Moon, 2021
Oil, alkyd, and gesso on linen
50 ¼ × 24 ⅝ inches | 127.6 × 62.5 cm
Collection of Brian Ip
p. 99

Drone, 2021
Oil and alkyd on linen
36 × 63 inches | 91.4 × 160 cm
p. 108

Dropcloth Scribble Drone, 2021
Oil and alkyd on linen
24 ⅝ × 50 ⅝ inches | 62.5 × 128.6 cm
p. 92

Escalade, 2005
Silkscreen ink on canvas on wood panel
59 × 62 inches | 149.9 × 157.5 cm
Private collection
p. 58

Fire (Temecula), 2011
Alkyd on canvas
42 × 63 inches | 106.7 × 160 cm
The Dicke Collection
pp. 74 (detail), 75

Florence, 2021
Oil and alkyd on linen
90 × 126 inches | 228.6 × 320 cm
p. 142

Florence, 2022
Oil and alkyd on linen
90 × 126 inches | 228.6 × 320 cm
Collection of Lara and William McLanahan
pp. 129, 130–131 (detail), 154

Florence Paper, 2022
Oil on paper
22 ½ × 30 inches | 57.1 × 76.2 cm
Collection of Diplo
p. 149 (top)

Florence Paper, 2022
Oil on paper
22 ½ × 30 inches | 57.1 × 76.2 cm
Private collection
p. 151 (bottom)

Harvey, 2017
Oil and alkyd on canvas
90 × 126 inches | 228.6 × 320 cm
Private collection
p. 119

Ida, 2022
Oil and alkyd on linen
90 × 126 inches | 228.6 × 320 cm
Private collection
p. 143

Irene, 2021
Oil and alkyd on linen
90 × 126 inches | 228.6 × 320 cm
pp. 136–137, 152 (right)

Irene Paper, 2022
Oil on paper
22 ½ × 30 inches | 57.1 × 76.2 cm
Collection of Andrew Menachem
p. 151 (top)

Irma, 2017
Oil and alkyd on linen
90 × 126 inches | 228.6 × 320 cm
Private collection
pp. 116 (detail), 117

Irma, 2021
Oil and alkyd on linen
90 × 126 inches | 228.6 × 320 cm
Private collection
pp. 135, 152 (left)

Irma, 2022
Oil and alkyd on linen
90 × 126 inches | 228.6 × 320 cm
Collection of Aïshti Foundation, Beirut, Lebanon
pp. 139, 153 (left)

Irma Paper, 2022
Oil on paper
22 ½ × 30 inches | 57.1 × 76.2 cm
Javier & Monica Mora Collection, Miami
p. 148 (top)

Irma Paper, 2022
Oil on paper
22 ½ × 30 inches | 57.1 × 76.2 cm
Private collection
p. 149 (bottom)

Katrina, 2020
Oil and alkyd on linen
90 ⅛ × 126 ⅛ inches | 228.9 × 320.4 cm
Collection of David Simkins
p. 163

Katrina, 2022
Oil and alkyd on linen
90 × 126 inches | 228.6 × 320 cm
Private collection
pp. 1–8 (details), 126–127

Keep the Faith, 2005
Alkyd and bumper stickers on canvas
60 × 60 inches | 152.4 × 152.4 cm
Private collection
p. 57

Kill the Pain No. 2, 2021
Oil and alkyd on linen
58 ⅛ × 41 ⅝ inches | 147.6 × 105.7 cm
Collection of Lewis Henkind and Donna Isaacson
p. 63

Last Day of Hurricane Season 2021 (NYT/V.A.), 2022
Oil on newspaper
22 × 24 inches | 55.9 × 61 cm
Private collection, Miami
p. 150 (bottom)

Maria, 2017
Oil and alkyd on linen
90 × 126 inches | 228.6 × 320 cm
pp. 120, 121 (detail)

Maria, 2018
Oil and alkyd on linen
84 × 120 inches | 213.4 × 304.8 cm
AMA Collection
pp. 122–123

Maria, 2022
Oil and alkyd on linen
90 × 126 inches | 228.6 × 320 cm
The Labora/Hartland & Mackie Family Collection
p. 140

Maria Paper, 2022
Oil on paper
22 ½ × 30 inches | 57.1 × 76.2 cm
Private collection
p. 150 (top)

Merapi/Cutouts, 2021
Oil on canvas on wood panel in two parts
Overall: 63 ¾ × 60 inches | 161.9 × 152.4 cm
Part 1: 15 ¾ × 60 inches | 40 × 152.4 cm
Part 2: 48 × 40 ¾ inches | 121.9 × 103.5 cm
p. 83

Night Watch, 2021
Oil and alkyd on linen
86 ⅛ × 39 ⅛ inches | 218.8 × 99.4 cm
Collection of Rosa and Carlos de la Cruz, Key Biscayne, Florida
pp. 96 (detail), 97

Picture 1, 2019
Oil and alkyd on linen
85 ⅛ × 64 inches | 216.2 × 162.6 cm
Private collection
pp. 19, 49

Picture 2, 2019
Oil and alkyd on linen
66 ⅛ × 96 inches | 168 × 243.8 cm
Collection of Maurice and Paul Marciano
pp. 15, 169–176 (details)

Picture 3, 2019
Oil and alkyd on linen
43 ¼ × 64 ½ inches | 109.9 × 163.8 cm
pp. 20 (detail), 21

Picture 4, 2018
Oil and alkyd on linen
87 × 60 inches | 221 × 152.4 cm
Collection of Rosa and Carlos de la Cruz, Key Biscayne, Florida
pp. 17, 50

Picture 6, 2019
Oil and alkyd on linen
87 × 132 inches | 221 × 335.3 cm
Private collection
pp. 29, 30–31 (detail), 52

Picture 9, 2019
Oil and alkyd on linen
44 × 67 inches | 111.8 × 170.2 cm
Astrup Fearnley Collection, Oslo
pp. 32, 51

Picture 10, 2018
Oil and alkyd on linen
72 ⅛ × 108 inches | 183.2 × 274.3 cm
Courtesy of Carmel Barasch Family Collection
pp. 25, 26–27 (detail)

Picture 11, 2019
Oil and alkyd on linen
43 × 62 ⅝ inches | 109.2 × 159.1 cm
pp. 22, 23 (detail)

Picture 12, 2019
Oil and alkyd on linen
45 ⅛ × 69 ⅛ inches | 114.6 × 175.6 cm
p. 36

Picture 13, 2018
Oil and alkyd on linen
66 × 96 inches | 167.6 × 243.8 cm
Private collection, courtesy Start Museum, Shanghai
pp. 40, 41 (detail)

Picture 15, 2019
Oil and alkyd on linen
36 ⅛ × 55 inches | 91.8 × 139.7 cm
p. 60 (bottom)

Picture 18, 2019
Oil and alkyd on linen
48 × 72 inches | 121.9 × 182.9 cm
p. 39

Picture 19, 2019
Oil and alkyd on linen
47 ⅝ × 71 ⅝ inches | 121 × 181.9 cm
Collection of Billur and Atilla Tacir
pp. 34, 35 (detail), 53 (right)

Picture 20, 2019
Oil and alkyd on linen
47 ⅛ × 72 ⅛ inches | 119.7 × 183.2 cm
AMA Collection
pp. 33, 53 (left)

Picture 21, 2018
Oil and alkyd on linen
65 × 48 ⅝ inches | 165.1 × 123.5 cm
p. 42

Picture 23, 2019
Oil and alkyd on linen
48 ¼ × 73 inches | 122.6 × 185.4 cm
p. 37

Picture 25, 2019
Oil and alkyd on linen
47 ⅜ × 69 ⅛ inches | 120.3 × 175.6 cm
Private collection, courtesy Start Museum, Shanghai
p. 43

Picture 27, 2019
Oil and alkyd on linen
38 ¼ × 58 ¾ inches | 97.2 × 149.2 cm
pp. 54 (detail), 60 (top)

Picture 28, 2018
Oil and alkyd on linen
30 × 43 ½ inches | 76.2 × 110.5 cm
pp. 45, 46–47 (detail)

Post-Apocalypse Now, 2020
Oil on canvas on wood panel
36 ¼ × 21 ¾ inches | 92.1 × 55.3 cm
p. 89

Remote Control (Scribble), 2021
Oil and alkyd on linen
48 × 84 inches | 121.9 × 213.4 cm
p. 93

San Andreas Fault, 2021
Oil and alkyd on linen
79 × 53 inches | 200.7 × 134.6 cm
p. 91

Sandy, 2020
Oil and alkyd on linen
90 × 126 inches | 228.6 × 320 cm
Private collection
pp. 141, 153 (right)

Sandy Poppy, 2022
Oil and alkyd on canvas on wood panel
59 ½ × 61 ¾ inches | 151.1 × 156.8 cm
Circa 1881
pp. 156 (detail), 165

Stratovolcano (Merapi), 2021
Oil and alkyd on linen
84 × 120 inches | 213.4 × 304.8 cm
Collection of Sims Lansing
pp. 80–81

Traffic, 2011
Oil and alkyd on linen
60 × 56 inches | 152.4 × 142.2 cm
Shuman Family Collection
p. 77

Trash Landing Marilyn #4, 2011
Oil and alkyd on canvas
74 × 44 inches | 188 × 111.8 cm
Rubell Family Collection
p. 65

Volcano (Iceland), 2011
Oil and alkyd on linen
49 ½ × 108 ¾ inches | 125.7 × 276.2 cm
Private collection, Austria
pp. 72–73

The Wall, 2005–2012
Mixed media
Overall dimensions variable
The Brant Foundation, Greenwich, Connecticut
p. 56

We Are Seeing People We Didn't Know Exist, 2011
Oil and alkyd on linen
62 × 75 inches | 157.5 × 190.5 cm
Private collection, East Hampton, New York
p. 115

Yonkers Sept. 1, 2021, 2022
Oil and alkyd on linen
82 ⅝ × 147 inches | 209.9 × 373.4 cm
pp. 111 (detail), 132–133, 155

You Can't Win, 2021
Oil and alkyd on linen
62 ⅛ × 72 ⅛ inches | 157.8 × 183.2 cm
pp. 84 (detail), 85

You Live at Home with Your Mom, 2018
Oil and alkyd on linen
63 ½ × 96 inches | 161.3 × 243.8 cm
p. 79

Published by David Zwirner Books on the occasion of

Nate Lowman: October 1, 2017
David Zwirner, 24 Grafton Street, London
October 3–November 9, 2019

Nate Lowman: Let's Go
David Zwirner, 533 West 19th Street, New York
March 10–April 16, 2022

David Zwirner Books
520 West 20th Street
New York, New York 10011
+1 212 727 2070
davidzwirnerbooks.com

Editor: Anne Wehr
Editorial coordinator: Jessica Palinski
Proofreader: Chris Peterson

Design: McCall Associates, New York
Photography coordination: Rebecca Ashby-Colón, Virginia Stroh
Production: Jules Thomson, Luke Chase
Color separations: VeronaLibri, Verona
Printer: VeronaLibri, Verona

Typeface: Post Grotesk
Paper: Périgord, 170 gsm

ISBN 978-1-64423-102-9

Library of Congress Control Number: 2023901118

Printed in Italy

Photography
Cover, pp. 116, 117, 119, 120, 121: Photos by Pierre Le Hors; pp. 1, 2–3, 4–5, 6–7, 8, 83, 111, 126–127, 129, 130–131, 132–133, 149 (top and bottom), 150 (top and bottom), 151 (top and bottom), 156, 165: Photos by Stephen Arnold; pp. 15, 17, 19, 20, 21, 22, 23, 25, 26–27, 29, 30–31, 32, 33, 34, 35, 36, 37, 39, 40, 41, 42, 43, 45, 46–47, 54, 58, 60 (top and bottom), 63, 68, 80–81, 84, 85, 86–87, 89, 91, 92, 93, 94, 95, 96, 97, 99, 104, 107, 109, 124–125, 135, 136–137, 139, 140, 141, 142, 143, 145, 146–147, 148 (top and bottom), 163, 169, 170–171, 172–173, 174–175, 176, back cover: Photos by Kerry McFate; pp. 49, 50–51, 52–53: Photos by Anna Arca; pp. 56, 59, 65, 66, 72–73, 74, 75, 77, 115: Photos by Jeffrey Sturges; pp. 57, 78, 152–153, 154–155: Photos by Maris Hutchinson; p. 79: Photo by Alessandro Zambianchi; p. 101: Photo by Claire Dorn; pp. 102, 103: Photos by Sebastian Bach; pp. 122–123: Photo by Dario Lasagni; p. 108: Photo courtesy David Nolan Gallery; p. 158 (left): Photo courtesy Erich Lessing/Art Resource, NY; p. 158 (right): Hirshhorn Museum and Sculpture Garden, Smithsonian Institution, Washington, DC. Gift of Joseph H. Hirshhorn, 1966. Photo by Lee Stalsworth, Hirshhorn Museum and Sculpture Garden. Artwork © 2023 Estate of Kenneth Noland/Licensed by VAGA at Artists Rights Society (ARS), New York; p. 159 (top left): Photo by George Steinmetz, courtesy Dia Art Foundation, New York. Artwork © 2023 Holt/Smithson Foundation and Dia Art Foundation/Licensed by VAGA at Artists Rights Society (ARS), NY; p. 159 (top right): Art Gallery of Ontario. Gift of Sandra Simpson, 1993. Photo © AGO. Artwork © Estate of Jack Goldstein; p. 159 (bottom left): Photo © RMN-Grand Palais/Art Resource, NY; p. 159 (bottom right): Henry Clay Frick Bequest. Photo © The Frick Collection; p. 161 (top): Artwork © Gerhard Richter 2023 (0029); p. 161 (bottom): Photo courtesy The Solomon R. Guggenheim Foundation/Art Resource, NY. Artwork © 2023 The Andy Warhol Foundation for the Visual Arts, Inc./Licensed by Artists Rights Society (ARS), New York

Cover: *Harvey*, 2017 (detail)
pp. 1–8: *Katrina*, 2022 (details)
pp. 169–176: *Picture 2*, 2019 (details)
Back cover: *Picture 19*, 2019 (detail)

Works on pages 15–37, 43, and 60 were included in *Nate Lowman: October 1, 2017*, David Zwirner, London, 2019
Works on pages 126–143, 148 (top), 149–151, and 165 were included in *Nate Lowman: Let's Go*, David Zwirner, New York, 2022

Nate Lowman would like to thank David Zwirner, Stephen Arnold, Rebecca Ashby-Colón, Aaron Aujla, Oscar Bedford, Camille Beinhorn, Spike Blake, Elizabeth Brannan-Williams, Maria Bresciani, Nick Brierley, Andrea Brignolo, Sergio Brunelli, Phong Bui, Susan Cernek, Sara Chan, Luke Chase, Angela Choon, Cristina Covucci, Andrew Crichton, Jun Deng, Fabio Ferrandini, Zeno Ferrandini, Joanna Fiorentino, Ruthie Fish, Kit Fretz, Emily Gachot, Roger Gaitan, Richard Gamble, Anne-Claire Giraudon, Doro Globus, Kayla Guthrie, Lily Harants, Shannon Hartofil, Amy Hordes, Rupert Hughes, Maris Hutchinson, Brandon Israels, Branwen Jones, Matthew Kenny, Vida Lercari, Jim Lewis, Julia Lukacher, Greg Lulay, Kieran Magzul, Colin McElroy, Kerry McFate, Davide Meneghello, Clive Murphy, Mark Nelson, Jessica Palinski, Mari Perina, Chris Peterson, Jared Preston, Keith Roberts, Bennet Schlesinger, Harper Scott, Janna Singer-Baefsky, Molly Stein, Virginia Stroh, Jayson Thompson, Jules Thomson, Lynne Tillman, Atticus Wakefield, Anne Wehr, Alexandra Whitney, Nick Wildermuth, Andrew Woolbright, Sam Yehros, Joey Young, Suzanna Zak, David Zaza, Rhys Ziemba, and Lucas Zwirner.

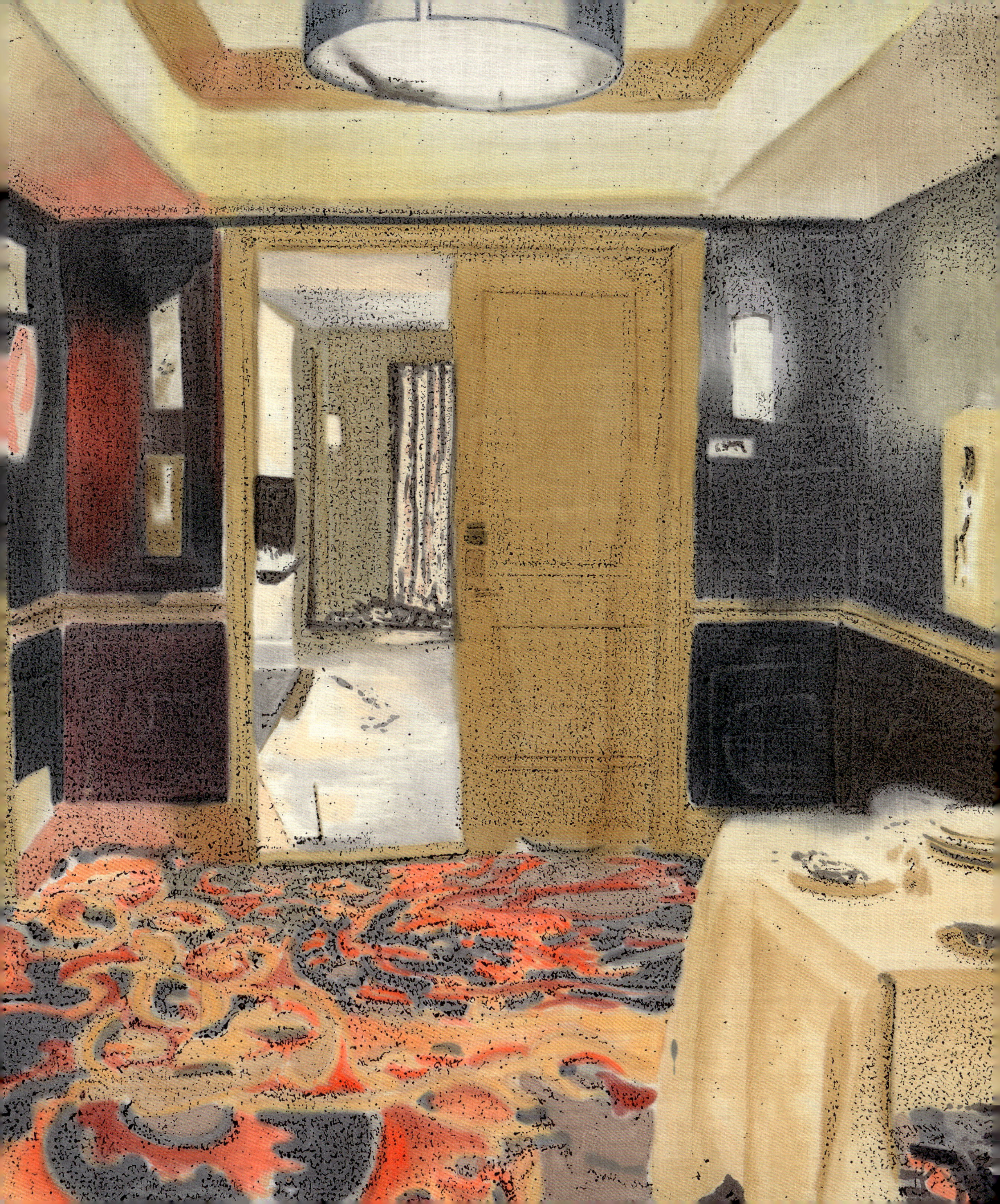

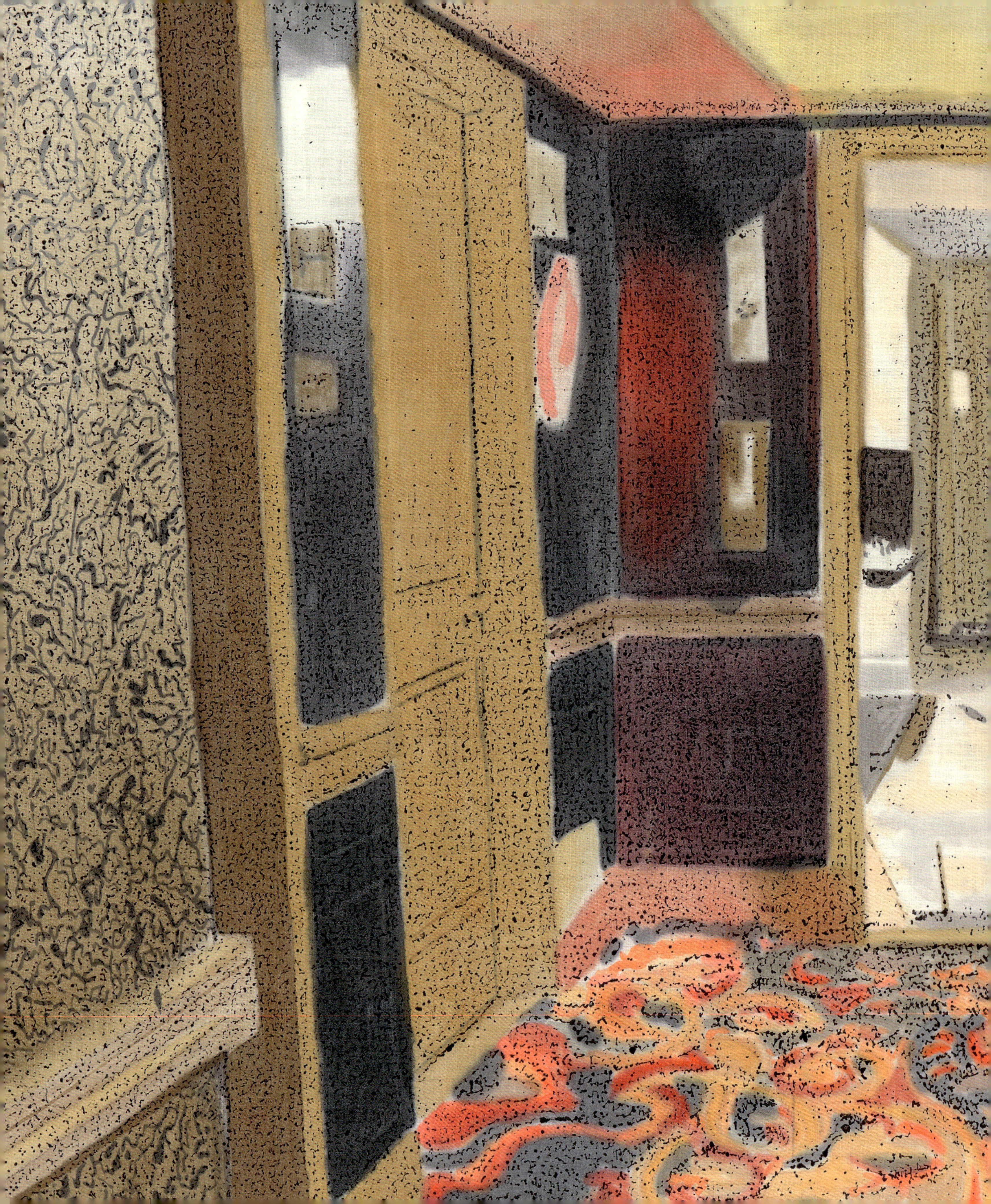

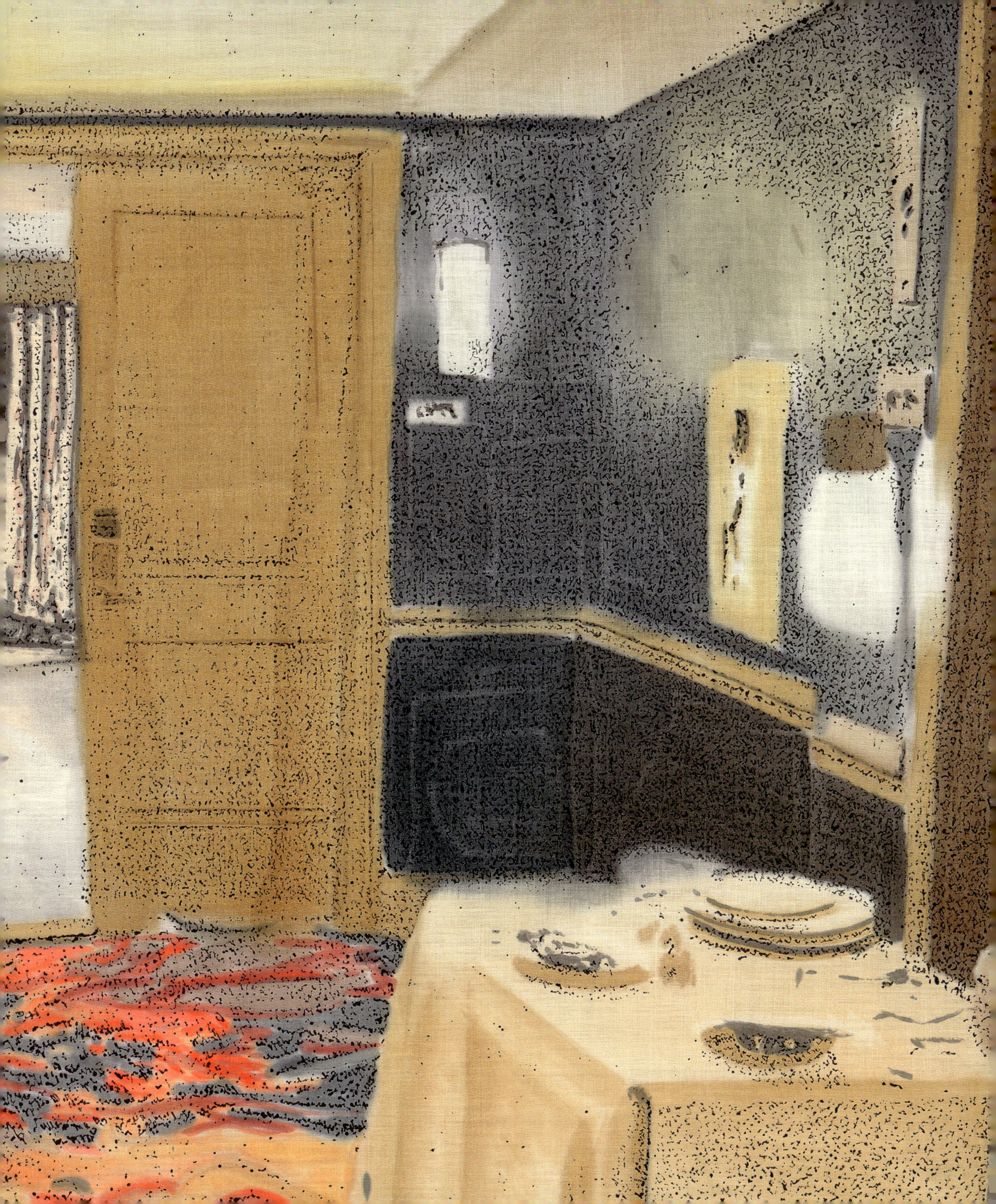

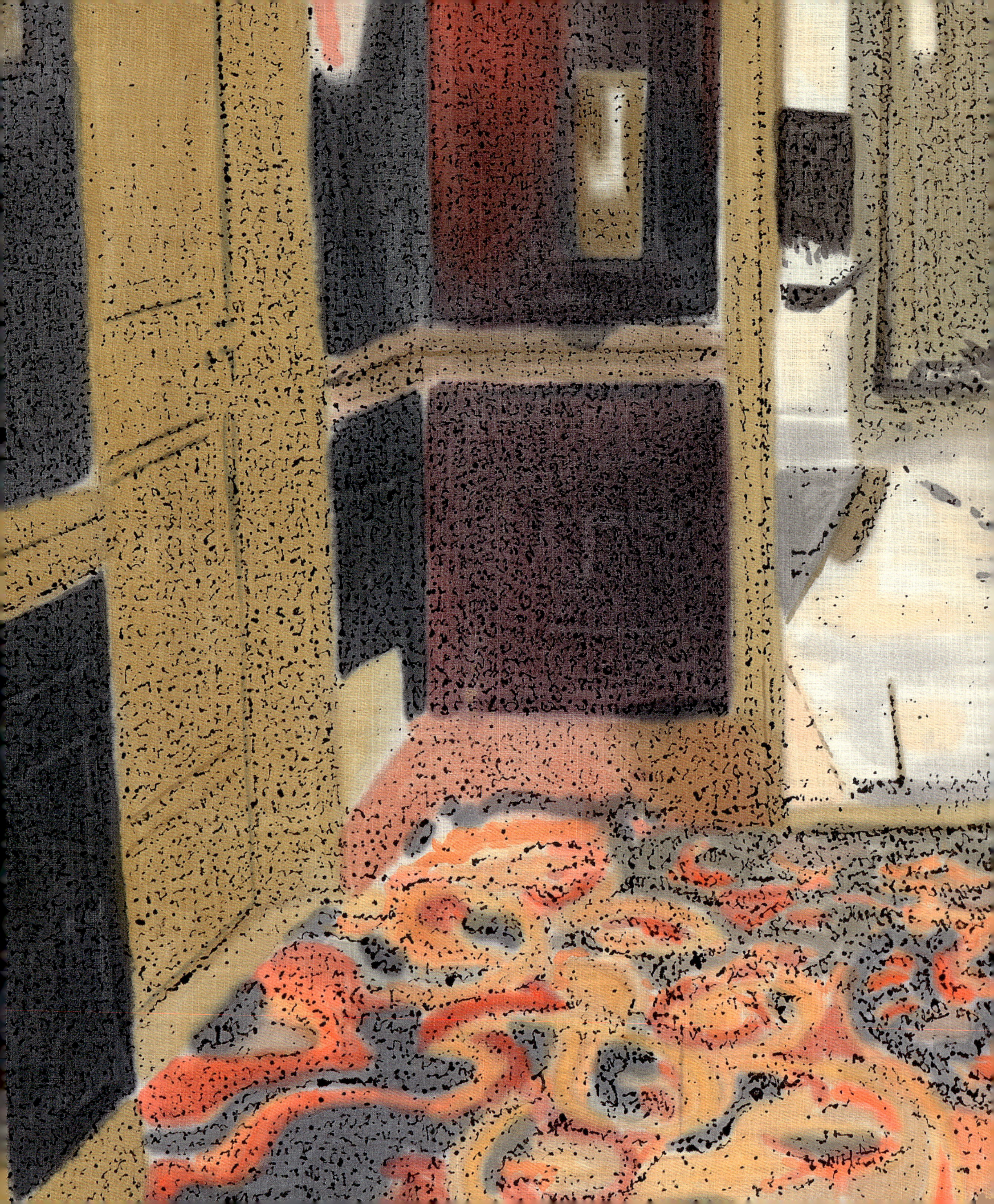

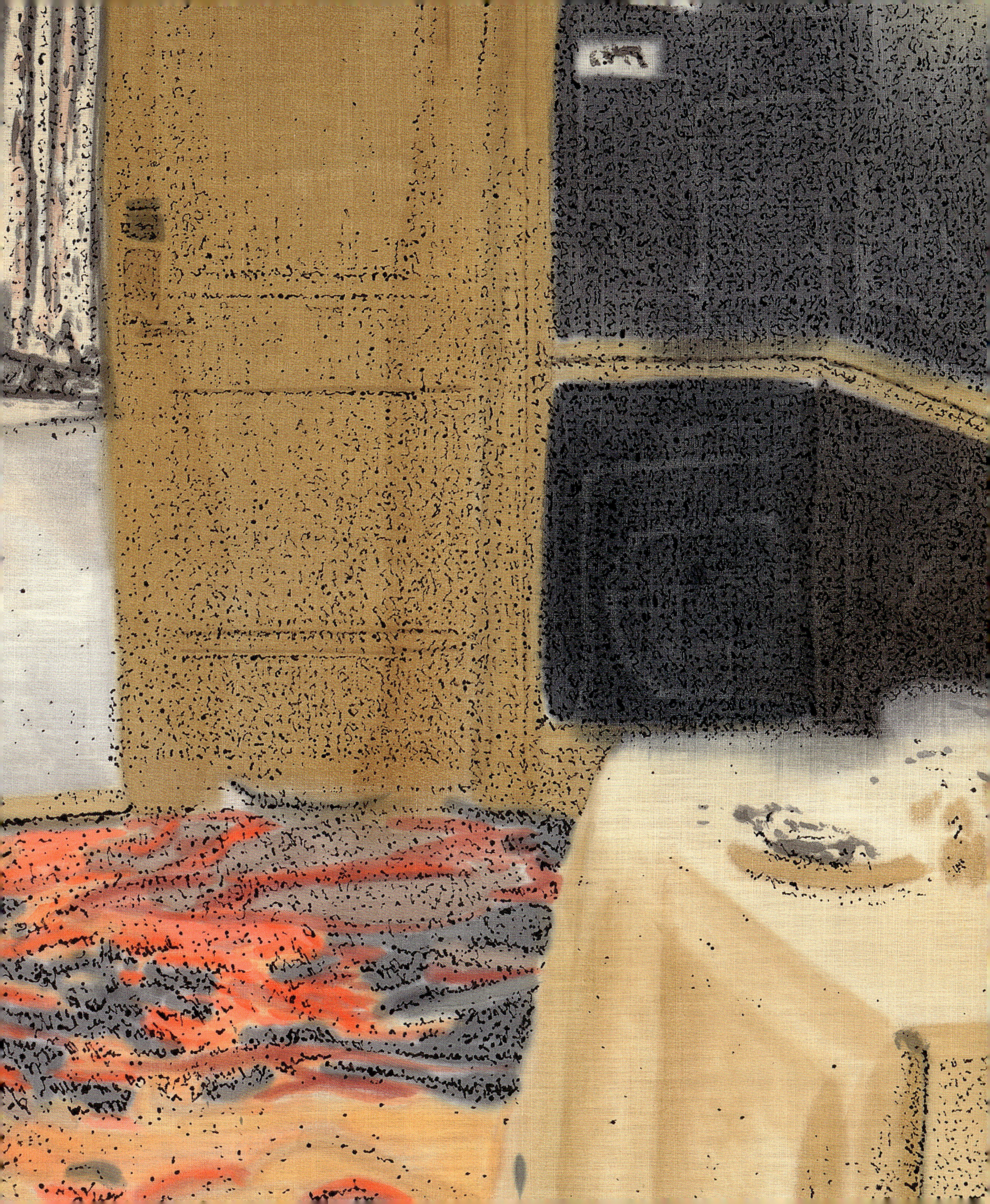

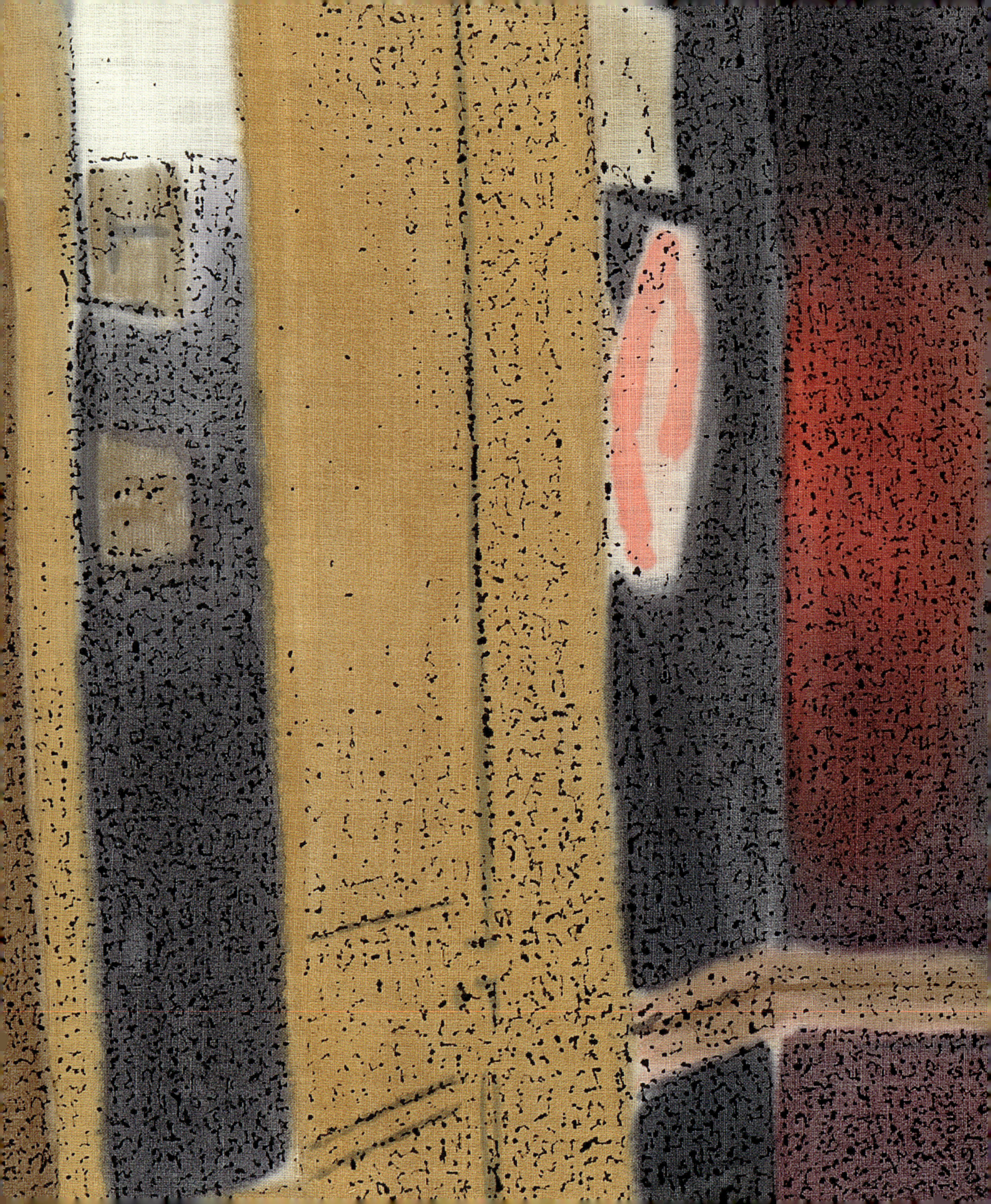

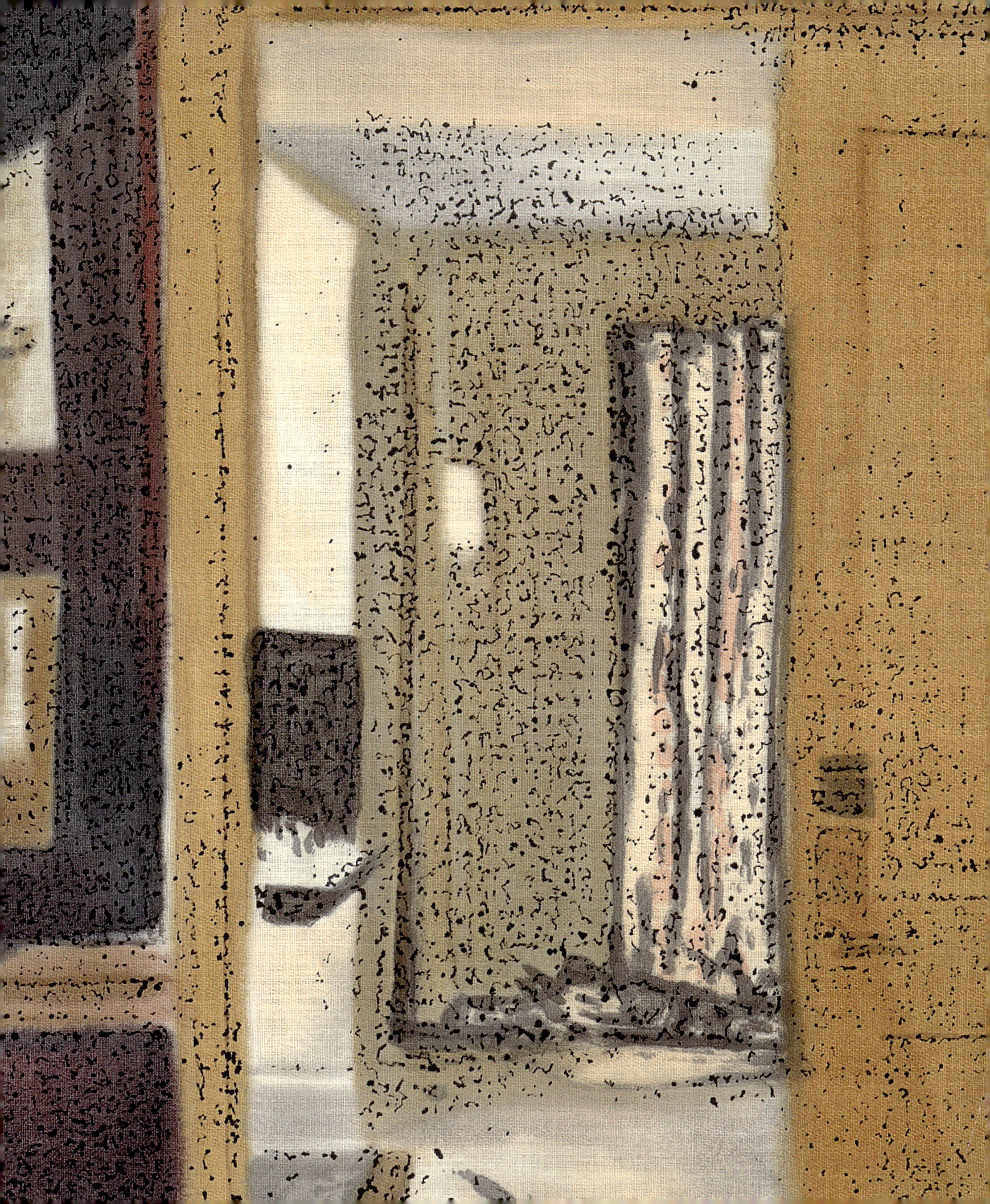

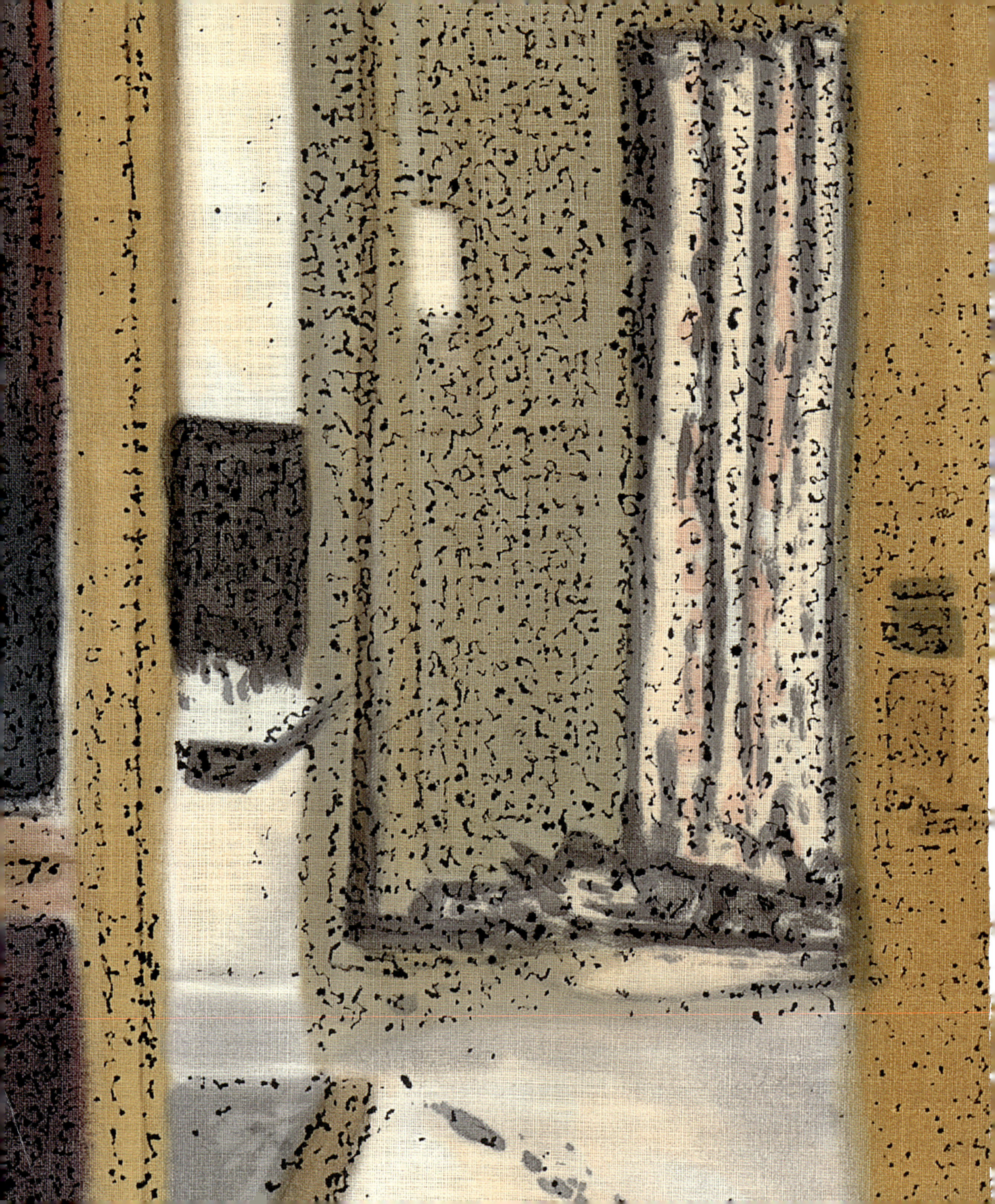